The Business 2.0

B2 UPPER INTERMEDIATE Student's Book

John Allison and Jeremy Townend with Paul Emmerson

MACMILLAN

The Business 2.0
B2 UPPER INTERMEDIATE

To the student

The objective of *The* **Business** 2.0 is to help you learn two things: how to do business in English and the language you need to do it. The new language and structures are presented in the Student's Book whilst the eWorkbook provides language practice and extension.

Here is a summary of what you will find in each.

Student's Book
The modules

The Student's Book contains 48 modules in eight units. Each unit deals with a key sector of activity in the business world. There are six different types of module:

1 About business

These modules contain information and language for the topic area of each unit. The focus is on understanding the topic and the general sense of the texts – don't worry too much about details such as new vocabulary.

2 Vocabulary

These modules build on the important words and phrases associated with the topic and provide thorough practice.

3 Grammar

These modules help you practise the grammar in a communicative and meaningful way, in business situations relating to the unit topic. Before you start, read the 'Refresh your memory' box to remind yourself of the key grammar points. Use the Grammar and practice section at the back of the book for consolidation.

4 Speaking

These modules develop understanding and speaking skills in typical business situations. In these modules, you build up a checklist of useful expressions to use in the speaking activities. The activities themselves allow you to practise these expressions and your speaking skills in realistic situations with other people.

5 Writing

These modules provide practice for the most important types of document you will need to write at work. You analyse a model text, focus on key language and use both as a basis for doing a writing output activity.

6 Case study

The case studies provide an opportunity to apply all the language, skills and ideas you have worked on in the unit. They present authentic problem-solving situations similar to those you will meet in business.

Internet research

Every module includes an Internet research task to encourage you to explore the topic in more detail. The tasks can be done before or after working on the module. Remember that to search for an exact phrase, you may get more accurate results if you put quotation marks around it.

Other features

In addition to the eight main units, the Student's Book contains the following:

Business fundamentals
This opening section introduces you to basic business principles and vocabulary. It provides a solid foundation for you to build on in the course and will help you get the most out of all components of *The* **Business** 2.0.

Reviews
These units can be used in three ways: to consolidate your work on the units, to catch up quickly if you have missed a lesson, and to revise before tests or exams.

Additional material
This section contains all the extra materials you need to do pair- or group-work activities.

Grammar and practice
This section gives a useful summary of grammar rules with clear examples, and also provides further practice of the essential grammar points in this level of the course.

Recordings
Full scripts of all the audio recordings are provided, allowing you to study the audio dialogues in detail. However, try not to rely on reading them to understand the listenings – very often you don't need to understand every word, just the main ideas.

Glossary
In each module, there is a short glossary of words you may not know. The definitions for these are in the Glossary at the back of the book. Words in red are high-frequency items, which you should try to learn and use. The others, in black, are words you just need to understand.

eWorkbook

The **Business** 2.0 eWorkbook provides everything you would find in a printed Workbook, as well as extra multimedia resources. It is mainly intended for self-study or home study and contains material to support and enhance the activities in the Student's Book.

Language practice
This section contains activities to consolidate the language presented in the Student's Book. You can practise grammar, vocabulary, listening, pronunciation, reading and writing.

Watch
This section contains a video clip and worksheet to accompany each unit in the Student's Book. The video clips are episodes of a mini-drama that illustrate the communication and people skills in each unit. The exercises allow you to practise the functional language in the video.

Tests
You can test yourself at any point in the course using the eWorkbook, by setting either the time or the number of questions. Your test scores are recorded for your reference.

Print and work
This section offers a pen-and-paper version of the activities in the Language practice section. You can also download the audio tracks required for these activities.

Grammar help
You can refer to this section for helpful grammar rules and examples.

Word lists
This section contains the key words and definitions from the Vocabulary modules in the Student's Book.

Dictionary
Use the Dictionary Tool to link to the *Macmillan Dictionary* online http://www.macmillandictionary.com.

Writing tips
This section provides explanations and exercises on aspects of writing, such as spelling, punctuation and paragraphing.

Listen
This section contains all the audio recordings from the Student's Book and eWorkbook, together with the audioscripts. You can download all the material in this section to a mobile device for listening on the move.

We sincerely hope you will enjoy working with *The* **Business** 2.0. Good luck!

John Allison   Jeremy Townend   Paul Emmerson

Contents

Business fundamentals	PAGES 6–9 Business organization Economic cycles Breakeven analysis CVs and recruitment		
	About business	**Vocabulary**	**Grammar**
1 Building a career PAGE 10	1.1 The education business Reading: *What price a degree?* Discussion: Your degree – who should pay?	1.2 Education and career Collocations relating to higher education and funding Action verbs for CVs Verbs relating to career stages	1.3 Tense review Past, present and future tenses Time markers
2 Information PAGE 22	2.1 IT solutions Reading: *The IT fallacy* Discussion: Attitudes to IT	2.2 Information systems and communication Comparisons Verbs relating to IT Expressions for giving information	2.3 Comparing solutions and getting help Comparatives and superlatives Polite requests and responses
Reviews 1 and 2	PAGES 34–35		
3 Quality PAGE 36	3.1 What quality means Reading: *Two kinds of quality* Discussion: 'Taken-for-granted' quality, 'enchanting' quality and planned obsolescence	3.2 Quality and standards Word-building Adjectives relating to quality Collocations relating to quality standards	3.3 Passive structures and *have something done* be + past participle (past, present and future tenses; modals) *have something done*
4 Feedback PAGE 48	4.1 The project team Reading: *Smells like team spirit* Discussion: Project management and team-building	4.2 Managing people and projects Character descriptions Adjectives for character types Colloquial expressions Project management collocations	4.3 Regrets, speculation and habits modals + *have* + past participle Third conditional *used to; be/get used to*
Reviews 3 and 4	PAGES 60–61		
5 Selling more PAGE 62	5.1 Social media marketing Reading: *Social marketing doesn't have to suck* Discussion: Attitudes to social media marketing	5.2 The marketing mix The four Ps, the four Cs, mix coherency and mix dynamics Marketing techniques Marketing collocations	5.3 Questions for persuading Question tags Negative questions
6 New business PAGE 74	6.1 Developing a business Reading: *Five simple rules for building a blockbuster brand* Discussion: Developing an idea for a new business	6.2 Funding a start-up Types of funding Vocabulary relating to funding Steps in a funding application Phrasal verbs	6.3 Future continuous and future perfect *will be doing* *will have done* *will have been doing*
Reviews 5 and 6	PAGES 86–87		
7 Financial control PAGE 88	7.1 Accountants Reading: *Why it's trendy to be a future accountant* Discussion: Accountancy as a career choice	7.2 Financial documents and regulation Vocabulary relating to financial documents Accounting terms Verbs for enabling and preventing	7.3 Cause and effect, ability, articles *owing to, stemmed from, led to, resulted in,* etc. *can, could, was/were able to, managed to, succeeded in,* etc.
8 Fair trade PAGE 100	8.1 Fair trade or free trade? Reading: *Why fair trade is a bad deal* Discussion: Fair trade vs. free trade	8.2 Contracts and corporate ethics Collocations with *contract* Expressions used in a contract Types of unethical behaviour	8.3 Obligation and permission, inversion *can, can't, must, mustn't, have to, don't have to, (not) be allowed to* Using inversion in legal documents
Reviews 7 and 8	PAGES 112–113		

Additional material PAGES 114–121   Grammar and practice PAGES 122–137   Recordings PAGES 138–147

Glossary PAGES 148–159

Speaking	Writing	Case study
1.4 Interviewing: giving reasons Expressions for giving reasons Roleplay: a job interview	**1.5 Cover letters** Analysis: paragraph function Language focus: dynamic sentences	**1.6 Mangalia Business School** Discussion, reading, listening and presentation relating to a Romanian business school
2.4 Telephoning Expressions for telephoning Roleplay: telephone situations	**2.5 Memos** Analysis: paragraph order Language focus: register	**2.6 Meteor Bank** Discussion, reading and listening relating to a Nigerian bank
3.4 Delivering presentations Expressions for signposting Presentation: presenting a product	**3.5 Emailing: quality problems** Analysis: level of formality Language focus: formal and informal expressions	**3.6 Zaluski Strawberries** Discussion, reading, listening and presentation relating to a Polish strawberry cooperative
4.4 Coaching Expressions for coaching Roleplay: an interview between a manager and an employee	**4.5 Reports** Analysis: paragraph function Language focus: linking words and expressions	**4.6 Trident Overseas** Discussion, reading, listening and roleplay relating to a British oil company operating in Africa
5.4 Dealing with objections Expressions for dealing with objections Negotiation: selling a study trip	**5.5 Mailshots and sales letters** Analysis: paragraph function and content Language focus: the tripling technique	**5.6 Backchat Communications** Discussion, reading, listening and negotiation relating to a South Korean mobile phone supplier
6.4 Presentations: taking questions Expressions for commenting on questions Presentation: a 60-second talk	**6.5 A company profile** Analysis: structure guidelines Language focus: impact collocations	**6.6 Angels or demons?** Discussion, reading, listening and presentation relating to pitching an idea to business angels
7.4 Communicating in meetings Expressions for communicating in meetings Roleplay: a meeting	**7.5 Minutes** Analysis: presentation and content Language focus: action verbs	**7.6 Car-Glazer** Discussion, reading and listening relating to a Czech glass replacement company
8.4 Negotiating a compromise Expressions for negotiating a compromise Negotiation: trading commodities	**8.5 Assertive writing** Analysis: adopting the correct tone Language focus: assertive expressions	**8.6 Green Hills Coffee** Discussion, reading, listening and negotiation relating to a coffee producer and a Guatemalan supplier

Business fundamentals

- industry groups and sectors
- types of business, business models and management structure

Business organization

Discussion

1 With a partner, decide which industry group and sector these companies belong to.

BASF   Boeing   Carrefour   China Life   GlaxoSmithKline   Google   Nestlé   Total

Industry group	Sector
Oil & Gas	Oil & Gas Producers, Oil Equipment & Distribution, Alternative Energy
Basic Materials	Chemicals, Forestry & Paper, Industrial Metals & Mining
Industrials	Construction, Aerospace & Defence, Packaging, Electronic & Electrical Equipment, Engineering, Transportation, Business Support Services
Consumer Goods	Automobiles, Food & Beverages, Personal & Household Goods, Tobacco
Health Care	Health Care Equipment and Services, Pharmaceuticals & Biotechnology
Consumer Services	Retail, Media, Travel & Leisure
Telecommunications	Fixed and Mobile Telecommunications
Utilities	Electricity, Gas, Water
Financials	Banks, Insurance, Real Estate, Equities
Technology	Software, Hardware, Computer Services

2 List five large companies in your country. Identify their industry group and sector.

Reading

3 Read the summaries and name companies or people you know for each category.

Type of business

Sole trader/Sole proprietorship The business is owned by one person who is responsible for any debts.
Partnership Two or more people run the business together. All partners share profits and losses.
Limited company/Limited liability company (Ltd/LLC) The company is responsible for any losses, not the owners. The company is private, i.e. shares cannot be sold to the public.
Public limited company/Corporation (plc/Corp/Inc) The company is owned by shareholders who receive dividends and who may gain or lose money if the share price goes up or down.

Business model

B2B (business to business) Companies sell to companies.
B2C (business to consumer) Companies sell to individuals.
C2C (consumer to consumer) Individuals sell to individuals.
B2B2C (business to business to consumer) Third-party vendors or consultants sell a company's products to consumers.

Management structure

The Board Chairman, CEO, CFO, Non-Executive Directors
The Management Committee/top management CEO, CFO, Directors of Marketing, HR, IT, etc.
Middle management Managers of divisions, departments, branches, etc.
Supervisory/first line management Supervisors, team leaders, etc.

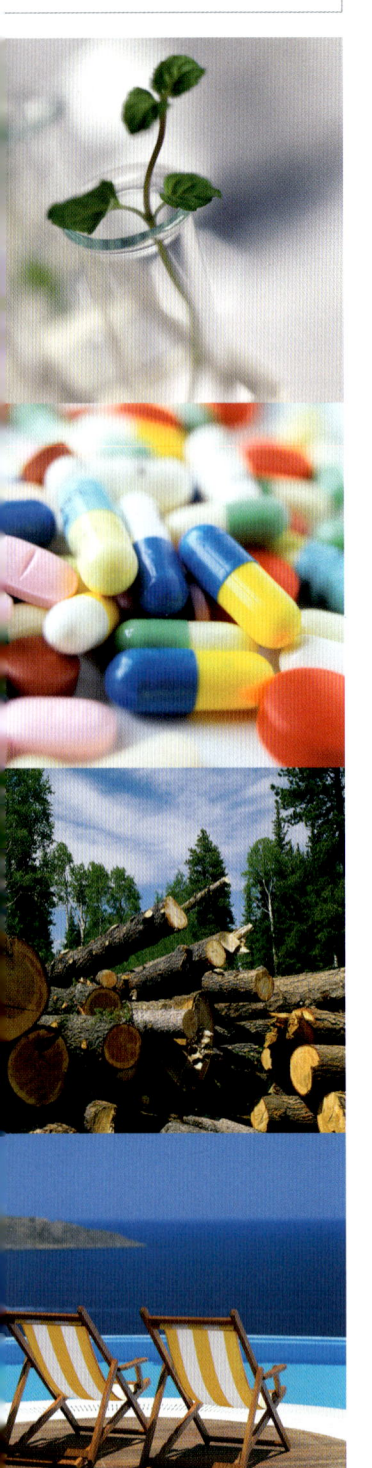

Glossary PAGE 148
beverage
dividend
equities
utility

Discussion

4 In groups, discuss the questions.

1. Which sectors and types of business would/wouldn't you like to work in? Why?
2. What level of management do you hope to reach in the short-term and in the long-term?

- the business cycle
- the investment cycle

Economic cycles

Reading

1 Read the article and choose the best alternative in bold.

The Business Cycle

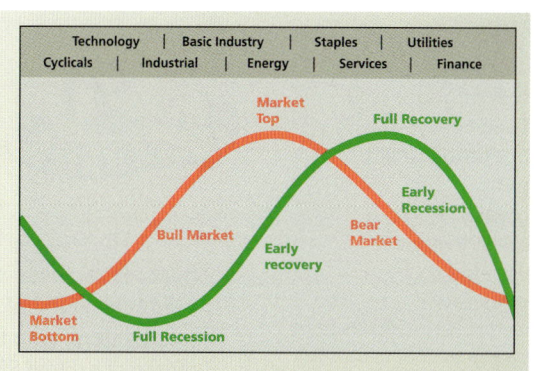

Economic growth usually follows a pattern of contraction and expansion punctuated by troughs and peaks.

When an economy is in recession, central
5 banks lower interest rates to encourage spending. After reaching market bottom, stock markets start to invest in the technology and industrial sectors. The bull market begins well before recovery is
10 visible in the economy.

The stock market reaches market top before full recovery in the economy, and investors move into staples and services. But as growth increases, so does inflation and central banks raise interest rates in order to control it.

The markets then expect a period of contraction and become bearish: investors prefer
15 to invest in utilities and bonds. Economic growth starts to slow, the economy moves into recession and the cycle continues.

Glossary PAGE 148

bear market
bond
bull market
euphoric
greater fool investor
staple
trough
value investor

1 Interest rates usually **rise / fall** in a period of recession.
2 When inflation increases, central banks **lower / raise** interest rates.
3 A bull market is **optimistic / pessimistic** about the economy.
4 A bear market begins **before / after** recession.
5 Bonds are a more popular investment than stocks in a **bull market / bear market**.

2 Read the article and mark statements 1–5 *T* (true) or *F* (false).

The Investment Cycle

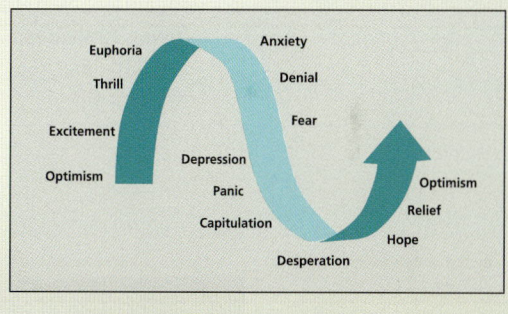

The first phase is accumulation. After the market has bottomed, innovators and early adopters begin to buy at attractive prices in a market which is still bearish.
5 In the mark-up phase, the fear of the majority of investors of losing money becomes weaker than the desire to make a profit and investors become first bullish, then excited and finally even euphoric.
10 In the distribution phase, value investors begin to sell. Prices can remain high for some time and greater fool investors continue to buy, hoping for further rises. Eventually, prices drop and sellers settle for a breakeven or a small loss.

Mark-down is the most painful phase. It is only when the market has plunged 50% or more that many investors first panic, then give in.

Adapted from http://www.investopedia.com

1 Early adopters are unwilling to take risks. ☐
2 Innovators buy when the market is bullish and sell when it is bearish. ☐
3 Most investors buy when prices are rising and sell when they are falling. ☐
4 During the distribution phase, value investors wait until prices begin to drop before selling. ☐
5 Greater fool investors prefer to make a small loss rather than accept a breakeven. ☐

Discussion

3 In groups, discuss the questions.

1 What stage of the business cycle is the economy in now? How long will it last?
2 What are the advantages and disadvantages for individuals, companies and countries when central banks **a)** raise or **b)** lower interest rates?

Business fundamentals

- completing income statements
- producing a breakeven analysis chart

Glossary PAGE 148
cost of goods sold
fixed cost
operating profit
plot
royalty
sales revenue
variable cost
wholesaler

Breakeven analysis

Reading

1 Read the article and complete figures a–d in income statements A and B.

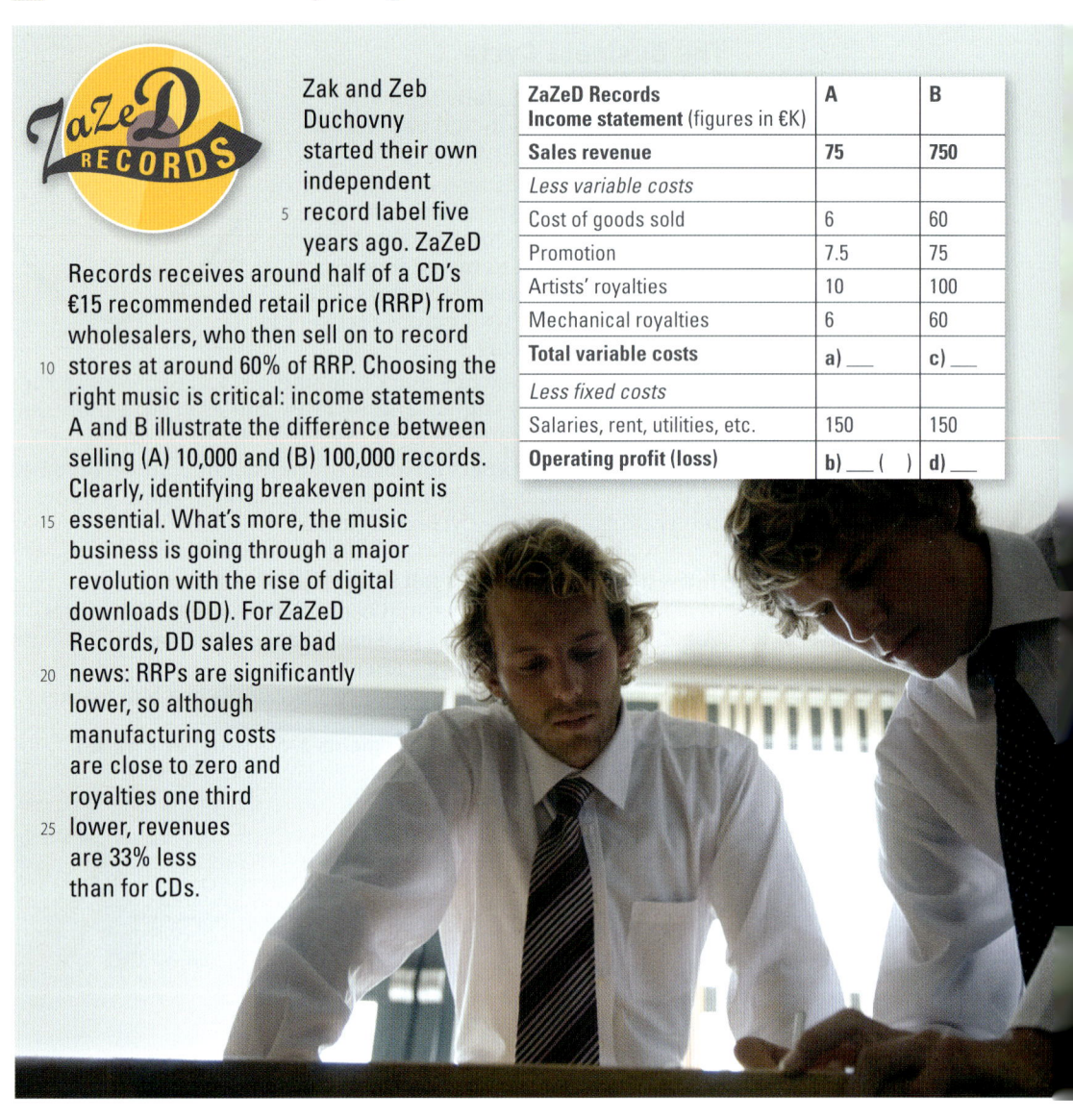

Zak and Zeb Duchovny started their own independent record label five years ago. ZaZeD Records receives around half of a CD's €15 recommended retail price (RRP) from wholesalers, who then sell on to record stores at around 60% of RRP. Choosing the right music is critical: income statements A and B illustrate the difference between selling (A) 10,000 and (B) 100,000 records. Clearly, identifying breakeven point is essential. What's more, the music business is going through a major revolution with the rise of digital downloads (DD). For ZaZeD Records, DD sales are bad news: RRPs are significantly lower, so although manufacturing costs are close to zero and royalties one third lower, revenues are 33% less than for CDs.

ZaZeD Records Income statement (figures in €K)	A	B
Sales revenue	75	750
Less variable costs		
Cost of goods sold	6	60
Promotion	7.5	75
Artists' royalties	10	100
Mechanical royalties	6	60
Total variable costs	a) ___	c) ___
Less fixed costs		
Salaries, rent, utilities, etc.	150	150
Operating profit (loss)	b) ___ ( )	d) ___

2 Draw a breakeven analysis chart with € on the vertical axis from 0 to 750, and sales on the horizontal axis from 10K to 100K. (See the example on page 119.) Enter the following information:

1. Draw a horizontal line representing ZaZeD Records' fixed costs.
2. Plot the sales revenues for turnover of **a)** 10,000 and **b)** 100,000 albums and draw a straight line connecting these two points.
3. Plot the total for fixed plus variable costs for turnover of **a)** 10,000 and **b)** 100,000 albums and draw a straight line connecting these two points.
4. With a partner, calculate the same revenues and costs for digital downloads rather than CDs. Using another colour, draw lines for DD revenues and total costs on the chart.
5. Draw vertical lines from the horizontal axis to the points where the revenue and total costs lines cross to identify the respective breakeven points.

Discussion

3 In small groups, discuss the questions.

1. What sort of questions does a breakeven analysis provide answers to?
2. What are the implications of the trend towards digital downloads for record labels, artists, composers and consumers?

- dynamic collocations for CVs
- writing your CV
- roleplaying a job interview

CVs and recruitment

Collocations

1 Using 'power verbs' to make dynamic collocations helps your CV have maximum impact. Connect the verbs in the boxes to as many nouns as possible.

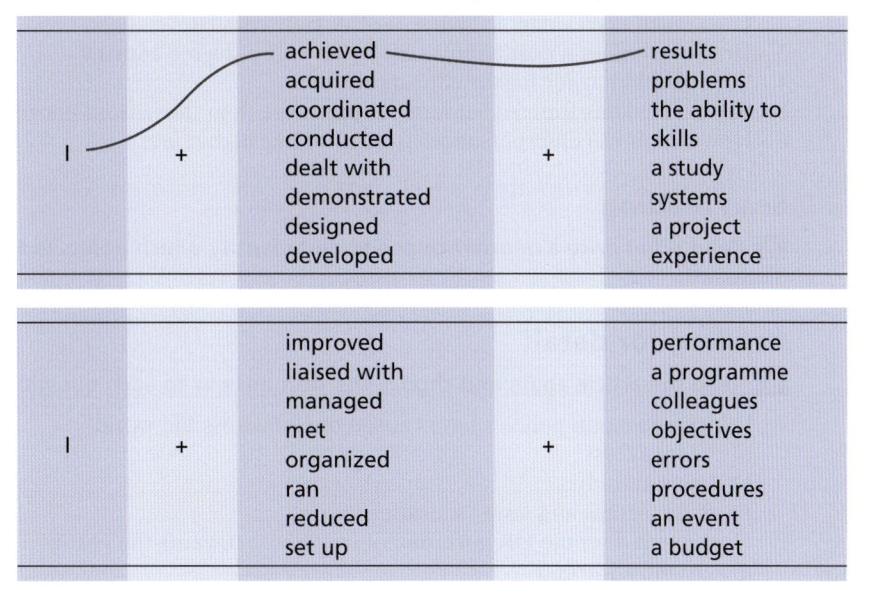

I +	achieved acquired coordinated conducted dealt with demonstrated designed developed	+	results problems the ability to skills a study systems a project experience

I +	improved liaised with managed met organized ran reduced set up	+	performance a programme colleagues objectives errors procedures an event a budget

2 With a partner, brainstorm more nouns that collocate with these 'power verbs'.

arrange   check   ensure   establish   follow   handle
increase   introduce   monitor   plan   research   update

Writing and roleplay

3 Imagine yourself ten years from now. Using the framework below, complete your CV with collocations from Exercises 1 and 2. Then exchange CVs with a partner and roleplay job interviews for positions you would like to obtain in ten years' time.

Glossary   PAGE 148

achieve
budget
deal with
handle
liaise
objective
reference
set up

Name ....
Date of birth ....
Nationality ....
Contact details ....
Career objective(s) ....
Major achievements ....
Professional experience ....
Education & training ....
Skills & abilities ....
Other ....
References ....

1 Building a career

- getting a degree: who should pay?
- higher education

1.1 About business The education business

Discussion

1 In small groups, discuss the questions below.

1. What difference does a degree make to your career and your earning potential?
2. How much does a degree course cost in your country?
3. How much does it cost a university to provide a degree course?
4. Who should pay for higher education?
5. Should students from richer families pay more than those from poorer ones?
6. How can universities persuade students to pay higher fees?

Scan reading

2 Read *What price a degree?* opposite and identify which points in Exercise 1 are discussed.

Reading for detail

3 Read the article again and choose the best answer to each question.

1. Which education policies have caused unrest across the world?
   a) wider access
   b) lower subsidies
   c) wider access and lower subsidies
2. How much does the UK government contribute towards the cost of a degree?
   a) around £100,000
   b) between £50,000 and £100,000
   c) less than £50,000
3. How do scholarships appear to favour students from wealthy families?
   a) they are better prepared
   b) they have equal opportunities
   c) they can pay for awards
4. What evidence suggests that the social benefits of education do not justify their cost?
   a) taxpayers have other resources
   b) taxpayers have other agendas
   c) taxpayers have other benefits
5. Why might universities show a preference for foreign students?
   a) they accept larger classes
   b) they exclude deserving locals
   c) they accept higher fees
6. Why don't private business schools need to increase class sizes or cut faculty pay?
   a) they can justify higher fees
   b) they have no subsidies
   c) they have resisted increases

Listening and discussion

4 🔊 1:01–1:04 Listen to four students reacting to the article. Match each speaker 1–4 with the correct summary a–d.

a) Education should be for all. ☐
b) Universities are obsolete. ☐
c) Let market forces decide. ☐
d) Reserve universities for the elite. ☐

5 Discuss your own reactions to the article and your opinions on elitism in education.

Internet research

Search for the keywords *world's best universities* and *best business schools*. Choose the institution you would most like to attend. Hold a class opinion poll to find the most popular choices.

What price a degree?

Take a random sample of views on higher education in almost any country in the world and you'll find that almost everyone believes that sending as many young people to university as possible is a good thing. What's more difficult to agree on is who should pay. The debate is a controversial one: cuts in higher education funding have sparked unrest in many countries across the world, including Austria, Germany, Chile, Colombia and the UK. Protests in the form of strikes, demonstrations and even riots prove that people are willing to go to great lengths to defend their right to higher education.

Widening access to a university education is an admirable political goal, but the uncomfortable truth is that governments simply do not have the resources to match their ambitions. Faced with this reality, many believe that universities should be paid for by those who get the most benefit from them: graduates. Certainly, a rough cost-benefit analysis suggests that students get good value for their money. A recent UK report estimates that the real cost of a degree is in the region of £100,000. Under the latest system, the average graduate will pay back no more than half of that, and only start to pay if and when their annual earnings are more than double the minimum wage.

However, others feel that this system favours students from well-off families, who can put the prospect of paying off such a sum into perspective. For bright but poorer teenagers from working-class families, taking on such enormous debt is a mountain to climb. Even the scholarships that are intended to offer equal opportunities are mostly awarded to students who have benefited from special coaching at expensive private schools.

If graduates themselves don't pay, then responsibility falls to the taxpayer. Thus, a majority of taxpayers, mostly earning significantly less than graduates, end up paying for a minority of students, many of whom will go on to become comfortably wealthy. Now, robbing the poor to pay the rich might be justified, as long as it can be proved that the overall benefits of education to society are greater than its cost. However, the trend towards cuts in education budgets across the world points unmistakeably to the fact that the ordinary taxpayer does not see the benefits to society, and would rather see public money spent elsewhere.

Unfortunately, the question of who should pay has been exacerbated by a dramatic rise in the cost of providing higher education. Despite a growing cross-border market for education, competition and new delivery models like e-learning have failed to cap universities' spiralling costs. Whether governments continue to provide subsidies or not, and in spite of massive hikes in student fees, university revenues remain significantly lower than their costs. This presents universities with new dilemmas. Should they try to cut costs by having larger classes and less experienced faculty? Should they increase fees further? And should they offer more places to higher-paying foreign students, at the risk of excluding deserving locals?

Intriguingly, private business schools do not meet the same resistance to price increases, and numbers of for-profit institutions have grown rapidly to meet the increasing demand for higher education. How is it that these businesses continue to be profitable when universities are unable to cope? The essential difference is that private business schools have been willing and able to invest money in improving quality and providing new and better facilities and services. These schools understand that they can only increase their perceived value to the customer by offering top-class conditions for learning and by serving their graduates well beyond their degree ceremonies. When private business schools offer a complete program of study, extracurricular activities, counselling, networking, placement and ongoing professional development services, their fees suddenly seem less excessive. Put simply, people will happily pay more if they can see they're getting better value for their money. Public universities, no longer sheltered by benevolent governments and taxpayers, now find themselves exposed to a potential extinction event. Adopting the business school model may prove the only alternative to going the way of the dinosaurs.

Glossary PAGE 149

cap
exacerbate
extracurricular
faculty
fee
hike
spark
subsidy

1 Building a career

- collocations relating to higher education
- action verbs for CVs
- verbs relating to career stages

1.2 Vocabulary   Education and career

Brainstorming

1 Think of as many good reasons as possible for studying business.

2 The letter below discusses reasons for attending business school. Choose one verb for each of 1–10 to complete the letter with the correct collocations.

Dear Sonia,

You asked my advice about going to business school. Well, don't miss out on a wonderful opportunity to (1) **gain / boost / make** knowledge and to (2) **make / acquire / do** skills which will serve you for a lifetime. As well as (3) **gaining / receiving / improving** your employability and (4) **having / boosting / making** your future earnings, you'll (5) **get / have / obtain** lots of fun (6) **going to / doing / getting** parties and (7) **doing / making / learning** friends. If you choose a good school, you'll (8) **enhance / receive / learn** tuition from experienced professors and (9) **obtain / do / make** practical experience that will really (10) **enhance / obtain / gain** your CV. In your shoes, I wouldn't hesitate for one moment!

3 Look again at the list you made in Exercise 1. Are any of the ideas in the letter to Sonia the same as yours? Which phrases would you add to your list?

4 With a partner, decide which collocations from Exercise 2 relate to professional rather than personal experience. Use them to write sentences about yourselves that you could use in a job interview.

Reading and vocabulary

5 Complete the extract about how to pay for studies with the verbs from the box.

| arrange   borrow   finance   obtain   subsidize   support   win |

If you're not lucky enough to be married to a millionaire or to have parents with very deep pockets, you may be wondering how to (1) _____ the next step in your education. Customs vary from country to country. One of the most popular solutions is to (2) _____ a student loan, sometimes interest-free or tax-deductible, that is only repayable when you are in full-time work. Many students who are unable to (3) _____ money from friends or family prefer to (4) _____ themselves by working part-time, and some are able to (5) _____ grants from local government or to (6) _____ scholarships from their universities. If you're already in work, try persuading your employer to (7) _____ your studies – in some countries, companies are bound by law to contribute towards further education.

Discussion

6 What are the advantages and disadvantages of the methods of financing your education mentioned in the article? Which ones would you use?

7 Work with a partner. You are going to ask questions and exchange information to complete a description of a businesswoman's education. Student A: turn to page 114. Student B: turn to page 116.

8 Talk about your education. Was it different from your parents' education? What sort of education would you like your own children to have?

Glossary   PAGE 149

boost
deep pockets
drop out
enhance
miss out
start over
working party

Vocabulary

9 Complete the CV with appropriate action verbs from the boxes. Then use them to write sentences for your own CV.

| contacted | exceeded | met | presented | recruited | trained |

2006–2008 Sales manager, Way2Go Travel, UK
(1) _____ corporate clients by phone and (2) _____ incentive travel programmes to Boards of Directors
(3) _____ and (4) _____ new sales reps
(5) _____ sales targets for every month and (6) _____ annual objectives by 20%

| chaired | designed | drew up | implemented | managed | motivated |

2008–2011 Sales and marketing manager, Hondo Holidays, Texas
(7) _____ sales materials and (8) _____ innovative advertising campaigns
(9) _____ and (10) _____ a team of 40 telesales operators
(11) _____ a working party and (12) _____ proposals for a new e-commerce division

Paraphrasing

10 Decide which verbs from the box can refer to people who:

to be dismissed	to be laid off	to be made redundant	to be on assignment
to be promoted	to be resting	to be suspended	to be transferred
to give in your notice	to join a company	to quit	to take a sabbatical

1 are currently enjoying having no work.
2 lost their jobs due to poor company performance.
3 are making positive career moves.
4 are leaving a job they were unhappy with.
5 are making a geographical change.
6 lost their job due to disciplinary problems.

Listening for gist

11 🔊 1:05–1:10 Listen to six speakers talking about career changes. Use expressions from Exercise 10 to describe each situation.

12 With a partner, discuss the situations below. What would you do if:
1 you were promoted to a job you knew was too difficult for you?
2 you were made redundant after 25 years' service?
3 you were unfairly dismissed for harassing an employee?
4 you gave in your notice the day before the firm announced a 33% salary increase?
5 you were transferred to Alaska?
6 you were on sabbatical for a year?

Internet research
Search for the keywords *action verbs for résumés/CVs*. Update your CV using dynamic action verbs and phrases.

Listening and discussion

13 🔊 1:11–1:13 Listen to three people talking about career choices. Make notes on the problems they face. Discuss what you would do and why. Then compare your answers with page 119.

1 Building a career

- past, present and future tenses
- time markers

1.3 Grammar — Tense review

Analysis

1 Decide which time markers in the box are usually associated with the present simple and which are associated with the present continuous.

> always   at present   at the moment   currently   often   usually

2 Decide which time markers in the box are usually associated with the past simple and which are associated with the present perfect.

> ago   already   ever   for   in   just   last   never   (not) yet   since   when

Refresh your memory

Past simple
She *worked* in Paris last year.
Past continuous
She *was working* on a presentation when her laptop crashed.
Past perfect
She *had* already *worked* in Paris as a student.
Present simple
She usually *works* in London.
Present continuous
She's *working* in Tokyo at the moment.
Present perfect simple
She *has worked* in three countries so far.
Present perfect continuous
She *has been working* for us since 2009.
Zero conditional
If she *works* hard, she *gets* a bonus.
First conditional
If she *works* too hard, she'*ll get* sick.
Second conditional
If she *worked* for the competition, we'*d lose* business.
Third conditional
If she'*d worked* on her interview skills, she *would have got* that job.
will
She'*ll* probably *work* for us for another year.
going to
She's *going to work* on her presentation tonight.
Present continuous for future
She's *working* in Kyoto next month.

▶ Grammar and practice pages 122–123

Glossary   PAGE 149
come along
fancy
put on weight

Discussion

3 With a partner, interview each other about the past, present and future. Ask and answer the questions below.

The past	The present	The future
When did you first …?	What do you usually …?	What are you doing on …?
What were you doing when …?	What do you do if you feel …?	How are you going to …?
Before you …, had you ever …?	At the moment, what are you …?	When do you think you'll …?
What would you have done if you hadn't …?	How many … have you …?	What will you do if …?
	How long have you been …?	If you were extremely rich, what would you …?

Listening

4 🔊 1:14 Every ten years, the Franklin School of Business organizes a reunion party. Listen to a conversation between two of its graduates, Fraser and Jess, and take notes to answer the questions.

a) What is Fraser doing at the moment?
b) Where did Fraser work before?
c) Why did Fraser leave that job?
d) What has Fraser been doing recently?
e) What did Jess do after leaving the business school?
f) What is Jess doing at the moment?
g) What is Jess doing soon?
h) What does Fraser discover about Jess?

5 Write out your answers to Exercise 4 as complete sentences, taking care to use the correct verb forms.

Internet research

Search for the keywords *how to write accomplishment statements*. Make a list of key points to remember when describing your accomplishments in a résumé or interview.

'We have a very low drop-out rate.'

Roleplay

6 Imagine you are attending a class reunion twenty years from now. First, complete the role card below.

Name: _____
Qualifications and year obtained: _____
Marital and family status: _____
Previous jobs and dates: _____
Current job and starting date: _____
Future plans or ambitions: _____
Personal achievements: _____
Current activities: _____
Other professional achievements: _____

7 You are now at the opening cocktail party. Circulate around the room and talk to as many of your former classmates as possible. Make polite conversation following the cues below.

What … do?
What … at the moment?
What … after leaving college?

How long … your most recent job?
What … recently?
What … next?

Balloon debate

8 Work in groups of three or four. You all work for the same private business school. Due to budget restrictions, there is not enough money to pay everybody's salary, so one person must be made redundant. Choose one of the positions below, then each present details of your past accomplishments, current projects and future objectives. The group must then decide who has made a good case for continuing and who has to drop out.

MARKETING MANAGER

Accomplishments
created positive image and brand name;
doubled student numbers
Projects
develop new markets and international contacts;
establish partnerships with major corporations
Objectives
become one of top ten schools in the world;
open a campus on every continent

PERSONNEL MANAGER

Accomplishments
fired boring professors, hired top consultants;
arranged seminars by famous entrepreneurs
Projects
implement performance-related incentives;
introduce student evaluations of teachers
Objectives
higher salaries and longer holidays for all staff;
paid sabbaticals for all teaching staff

HEAD OF ADMINISTRATION

Accomplishments
made school profitable after years of losses;
negotiated reduction of debt with banks
Projects
get corporate sponsorship and government funding;
offer scholarships for underprivileged students
Objectives
improve facilities and profitability;
introduce paperless administration

DIRECTOR OF STUDIES

Accomplishments
replaced old books with multimedia programs;
developed exchange programs all over the world
Projects
develop revolutionary methods of learning;
provide individual tutoring for every student
Objectives
100% success in exams with only 50% study time;
educate future Nobel prize-winners

1 Building a career

- interview questions and answers
- expressions for giving reasons
- roleplaying a job interview

1.4 Speaking Interviewing: giving reasons

Listening and discussion

1 🔊 1:15–1:20 Listen to six interview questions. Which are the most difficult to answer? How would you answer them?

Listening

2 🔊 1:21–1:22 Olivia is being interviewed for a job in marketing. Listen to two extracts from her interview and answer the questions.

1. What was the first question?
2. What does Olivia say about benchmarks and feedback?
3. Why does she discuss objectives with her family?
4. What was the second question?
5. What does Olivia say about people skills?
6. What ability has she demonstrated in her previous experience?

3 🔊 1:21–1:22 With a partner, find suitable words to complete the expressions in the checklist. Then listen again and check your answers.

Useful expressions: Giving reasons

Introducing a point

Firstly, …
As _____ measuring professional success, I think …
As _____ as my personal life is _____, I try …

Seeing both sides

On the whole …, however …
It's _____ that lots of people have similar qualifications …, but, on the other _____, not so many people have excellent people skills.

Combining reasons

It's important not _____ to understand what the company expects …, but _____ to listen very carefully to the feedback I get …
For one _____, working as a team … is essential in marketing, and for _____, real quality is only possible when …

Adding ideas

Besides, …
What's _____, they share the success when I achieve an objective.
I … get people to work together, and in _____, to share values like respect, honesty and hard work.

Language focus

4 With a partner, use expressions for **combining reasons** and **adding ideas** to complete these answers to interview questions. What were the questions?

1. Mainly for the variety. I _____ get out of the office a lot, _____ I meet a lot of different people. _____ the salary was much better than anything else I was offered!
2. Well, it's very close to what's known as the 'Plastics Valley'. _____ to lots of jobs, there are very good communications. _____, it's one of the most beautiful areas in the country.
3. Several reasons really. _____, it really relaxes me after a hard week, and _____, it keeps me fit. You can't beat badminton for a good workout; and _____, it's a great way to meet people.

16 *The* Business 2.0

Glossary PAGE 149

benchmark
feedback
personality clash

5 With a partner, use expressions for **introducing a point** and **seeing both sides** to explain the advantages and disadvantages of the following:

1 Living in your parents' home or moving away and sharing a flat with friends.
  Example:
  Firstly, living with your parents is not always easy. On the whole it's cheaper to stay at home, but the experience of living away from home is richer. As regards sharing with friends, it's true that sometimes there will be personality clashes, but, on the other hand, it's good to know that there's always a friend around when you need help.
2 Studying something you dislike but are good at, and which pays well, or something you love doing, are perhaps not so good at, and which is badly paid.
3 Having a part-time job or borrowing money from the bank to pay for your studies, or working for two or three years before going to university.
4 Taking an interesting but badly-paid job in a small company in order to get more responsibility, or a boring but well-paid job in a large company with few career prospects.
5 Changing companies, cities and countries regularly to increase your experience and salary, or working all your life in the same town for the same company.

Roleplay

6 Roleplay these job interviews, following instructions 1–4.
Student A: Interview Student B for a job as marketing assistant for the world's biggest nightclub in Ibiza.
Student B: Interview Student A for a job as marketing assistant for the world's most famous circus.

1 Meet in separate groups of As or Bs to decide what qualities (e.g. energy, loyalty, maturity); skills (e.g. communication, organizational, IT) and experience (e.g. promoting student events, market research, customer service) you will be looking for in the ideal candidate. Prepare questions to test the candidate in each area.
2 Agree on a time limit, and meet a partner to hold the interviews. Each candidate should give reasons why they are the best person for the job.
3 After the interviews, meet again in your groups of As or Bs to decide which candidate will get the job.
4 Meet in your pairs of A and B to announce the result and give your partner reasons why they did or didn't get the job.

Internet research

Search for the keywords *how to answer interview questions*. Make a list of your favourite questions and practise asking and answering them with a partner.

eWorkbook
Now watch the video for this unit.

The Business 2.0   17

1 Building a career

- paragraph function
- dynamic sentences for cover letters
- writing a cover letter

1.5 Writing Cover letters

Brainstorming

1 In small groups, divide the list below into *Dos* and *Don'ts* for writing dynamic cover letters. When you have finished, compare your ideas with the lists on page 121.

Dos and Don'ts

_____ start your letter 'Dear Sir or Madam'.

_____ write a formal introduction in the first paragraph.

_____ ask directly for an interview.

_____ write at least 400 words – the more information you give, the better.

_____ use sophisticated language to make a good impression.

_____ follow the AIDA model used in advertising – attention, interest, desire, action.

Model

2 Complete this cover letter with the action verbs from the box.

| broken | capture | developed | doubled | exceeded | modernized | obtained |
| optimize | present | trained |

EMAIL

Dear Mr Crouch,

Having (1) _____ objectives and (2) _____ sales records in all my previous positions, and recently (3) _____ my MBA in marketing at Warwick University, I feel I am an ideal candidate for the position of European Sales Manager at Starfield Nightclubs.

In my last job as senior sales representative for Roxy Entertainment, I (4) _____ new products for teenage customers, (5) _____ sales staff and (6) _____ the membership management system. Over a two-year period, I more than (7) _____ average revenues per venue.

Nightclubs are a highly competitive sector of the entertainment industry, and I am certain I have the skills to (8) _____ market share and (9) _____ Starfield's profitability.

I would be happy to (10) _____ my ideas in more detail at interview, and I will call you early next week to arrange a meeting. If you have any questions, please feel free to contact me before then. Thank you for your time and consideration.

Yours sincerely,

Kiara Pointer

Analysis

3 Decide the purpose of each paragraph in Exercise 2. Which paragraph is intended to:
- request action?
- give details of the applicant's accomplishments?
- get the reader's attention?
- relate the applicant to the company, showing why the company should hire her?

Glossary PAGE 150

accomplishment
brokering
lead
outgoing
tender
venue

Language focus

4 Match sentence beginnings 1–10 with endings a–j to make typical dynamic sentences for cover letters.

1. My outgoing personality makes me
2. I recently graduated
3. I served as
4. I attended school
5. I supported myself
6. Jobs such as bartending enhanced
7. I have the skills to embark on
8. I would like very much to
9. I will follow up this letter with
10. I can arrange a time

a) my formal education.
b) to meet with you.
c) a phone call.
d) a strong candidate.
e) a career in insurance brokering.
f) talk with you.
g) by working in radio advertising sales.
h) from the University of Oregon.
i) in Michigan, Arizona and Oregon.
j) president of the debating society.

Output

5 In small groups, read the two job ads. For each position, list at least two qualities and two skills that the ideal candidate should have.

DEVELOPMENT OFFICER FOR EXECUTIVE EDUCATION

Based in Paris, you will promote the specialist training services of a top international business school to companies throughout Europe. You will generate and follow up leads, handle client appointments and presentations, prepare tenders and secure client commitment before handover to account managers.

BRAND MANAGER, EMEA

Based in London, but with extensive travel, you will be responsible for maintaining and developing a household name in video games. Liaising with head office in Japan, you will design and implement marketing campaigns for Europe, the Middle East and Africa, and ensure that cost and profit objectives are met.

6 Divide into two teams, A and B. Team A will apply for the position of Development Officer for Executive Education, and Team B for the position of Brand Manager, EMEA. Follow the instructions below to write your cover letter.

1. With a partner from the same team, list examples of your experience, skills and accomplishments.
2. Plan the four paragraphs of your cover letter, using the examples you listed above.
3. Write your cover letter. Use action verbs whenever possible.

7 Exchange cover letters with the other team. Read the other team's letters and decide which candidates to call to interview. Announce your decision to the other team.

Internet research

Search for the keywords *what not to put on your résumé*. Compile a class list of the top ten errors.

1 Building a career

- identifying strengths and weaknesses
- making a five-year plan
- presenting proposals

Glossary	PAGE 150
campus	
draw up	
heritage	
metropolis	
procurement	
sit back	
tailor	

1.6 Case study Mangalia Business School

Discussion

1 Decide which of the following features are more advantageous for an international business school.

history: more than 100 years old *or* modern new school
funding: public *or* private
students: 80% local and 20% foreign *or* 20% local and 80% foreign
faculty: business leaders *or* researchers
location: international metropolis *or* small seaside town
site: campus *or* city centre

Reading

2 Read the information about Mangalia Business School and list its strengths and weaknesses in terms of its ability to compete in a global market.

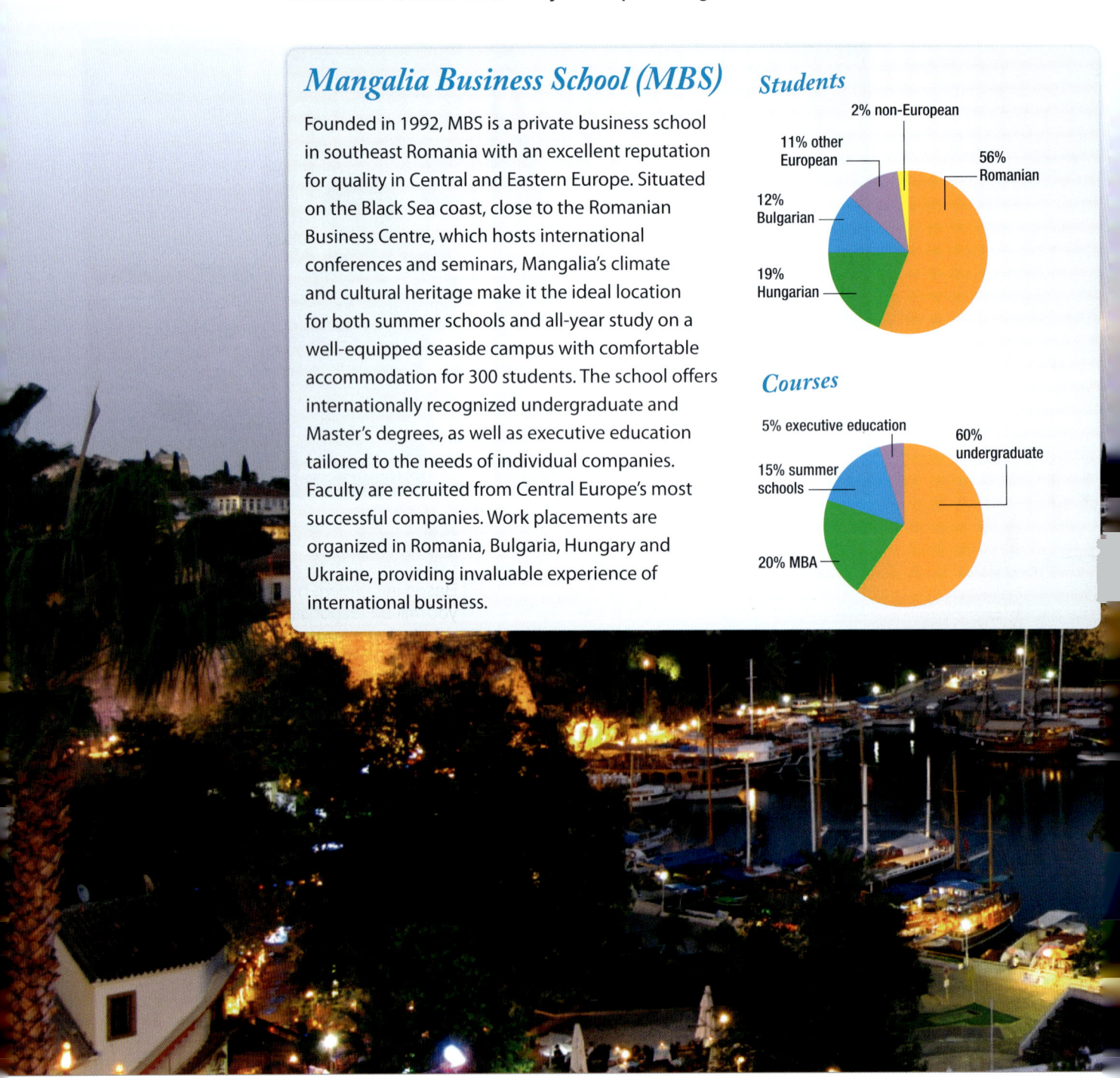

Mangalia Business School (MBS)

Founded in 1992, MBS is a private business school in southeast Romania with an excellent reputation for quality in Central and Eastern Europe. Situated on the Black Sea coast, close to the Romanian Business Centre, which hosts international conferences and seminars, Mangalia's climate and cultural heritage make it the ideal location for both summer schools and all-year study on a well-equipped seaside campus with comfortable accommodation for 300 students. The school offers internationally recognized undergraduate and Master's degrees, as well as executive education tailored to the needs of individual companies. Faculty are recruited from Central Europe's most successful companies. Work placements are organized in Romania, Bulgaria, Hungary and Ukraine, providing invaluable experience of international business.

Students

- 56% Romanian
- 19% Hungarian
- 12% Bulgarian
- 11% other European
- 2% non-European

Courses

- 60% undergraduate
- 20% MBA
- 15% summer schools
- 5% executive education

Internet research

Search for the keywords *how much is an MBA* to find out how much it would cost you to get an MBA. Draw up a budget including tuition fees, living expenses, travel, etc.

Listening

3 🔊 1:23 Listen to an extract from a presentation given by Radu Ionescu, the Dean of MBS, and answer the questions.

1. What alternatives is MBS facing due to globalization?
2. What does Radu Ionescu expect from his guests?
3. What has Ion Bumbescu offered, and what are his conditions?

Discussion

4 In small groups, hold a meeting to discuss the brief below and draw up proposals for MBS's five-year plan.

Mangalia Business School
Brief for international consultants

1 Sponsorship
Should MBS accept Bumbescu's offer to sponsor the school? (see point 3)

2 Tuition fees
Until now, fees have been average for business schools of this type. Should MBS maintain this policy, raise fees to a higher than average level, or reduce them to a lower than average level? (see point 3)

3 Development projects
MBS can afford to invest in the development projects below as follows:
At current (average) fee levels, one project only.
If Bumbescu's sponsorship is accepted, two projects.
If fees are increased, one additional project.
If fees are reduced, one project less.

The possible projects are as follows:
- strengthen faculty and increase research funding
- improve and extend facilities
- improve placement and career services
- develop international recruitment and exchange programmes
- your ideas …

4 Promotion
Please consider the following, as well as your own ideas:
Who should MBS target: undergraduates, future MBAs, corporate clients?
Where should MBS look for its future clients: Romania, Central Europe, Western Europe, the US, the Far East, worldwide?
How should MBS promote itself: materials, media, events, incentives?

Listening

5 🔊 1:24 Listen to a radio news report. How does this news affect your proposals?

Presentation

6 Present your proposals. The class should vote for the best presentation.

2 Information

- technology in the workplace
- attitudes to IT

2.1 About business | IT solutions

Internet research

Search for the keywords *smart dust* to learn about an emerging technology. Discuss possible applications, and how they might change our lives.

Discussion

1 Look at the pictures and answer the questions below.

1. How is the office of the 1950s different from today's workplace?
2. What do you imagine the office of the future will be like?
3. Do you expect technology to make your life easier or harder?

Summarizing

2 Read the article opposite. Decide which statement a–c best summarizes the writer's overall argument.

a) Technology helps people save time.
b) Technology makes people work harder.
c) Technology is a waste of money.

3 Read paragraphs 1–4. Choose the correct summary a–d for each paragraph.

a) How several factors have combined to make the workplace more pressurized.
b) Poorly planned IT systems generate more work, not less.
c) Managers see investment in information technologies as a productivity solution.
d) Working conditions have become uncomfortable in recent times.

4 Read paragraphs 5–7. Write a sentence to summarize each paragraph.

Listening

5 1:25–1:28 Listen to four people being interviewed about their attitudes to IT. Which are for and which are against IT?

6 1:25–1:28 Listen again and summarize each speaker's opinion. Do you agree with what they say? Why? Why not?

Discussion

7 To what extent do you agree with these statements?

1. The computer is the most important invention in the history of civilization.
2. A computer makes it possible to do tasks which were completely unnecessary before.
3. To make mistakes is human, but to really mess things up, you need a computer.

22 *The* Business 2.0

THE IT FALLACY

Glossary PAGE 150

cram
mad dash
mess up
oddly
overhaul
pressure cooker
slick
take a breather

1 In recent years, three forces – downsizing, globalization and the need for speed – have combined to change the work environment. What used to be a comfortably busy routine has become a non-stop workshop in which most people feel they can never stop to take a breather.

2 The result of downsizing is a mad dash to cram more work into fewer people. If six people are doing the work that ten used to do, and at the same time are expected to meet or exceed previous budget and productivity targets, something has to give. To this pressure-cooker environment, in which everyone is supposed to 'do more with less', we can add the globalization trend that has swept through corporate boardrooms. To the extent that global competitors have a lower cost structure – which many do because their labour costs are so much lower – US and European firms have yet another reason to keep budgets and headcounts lower. The final ingredient in this mix is fierce competition, which has resulted in the pressure to do everything faster.

3 One way corporate leaders justify the quest for efficiency and speed is to point to the multibillion-dollar investments that have been made in IT equipment and services. The new PCs and corporate networks are supposed to boost productivity and profits, and will, in fact, allow their companies to 'do more with less'.

4 This is true. But another truth has become buried under the technology sales pitches. Achieving those gains will happen only after a significant initial investment in training and 'system integration' to make sure that all the pieces connect well with each other. Pouring thousands of PCs and miles of cables into a corporation is a great way to waste money unless the systems and processes that technology is meant to automate are overhauled. Unfortunately, this has all become somewhat irrelevant. The expectation is that more technology means more speed and more output per employee – and when those results don't always magically occur, the only way to produce them is to require people to work longer hours.

5 Oddly, the same thing happens even when the technology delivers as promised. Consider the case of presentation software such as Microsoft® PowerPoint, which has become a standard office tool. Before PowerPoint, a graphics presentation would have to be created by a graphic artist. With PowerPoint and its software cousins, just about anyone can sit down at a PC and, without much training or practice, produce an on-screen presentation or a slick set of slides, handouts or transparencies that look fully professional.

6 On the one hand, this software is actually a productivity tool – it takes only hours to do what might have taken days previously, and the result is just as good, if not better. But it doesn't stop there. Now everyone sees how easy it is to use these programs, they are used more and more. Thus, a senior manager who wouldn't have considered asking an analyst to spend a couple of days working up a slide presentation using Stone Age technology, doesn't hesitate to direct the same analyst to prepare that presentation using the desktop PC and PowerPoint. The goal is for this analyst to save time by using the software; the likely outcome is that he or she spends more time on presentations and has less time available for other aspects of the job.

7 If you're starting to think that, instead of working on a plan to cope with pressure, tight deadlines and non-stop work, it's time to polish up your résumé and look elsewhere, I'm afraid I have some bad news. The grass really isn't much greener anywhere else – or at least, not a whole lot greener.

2 Information

- comparative phrases
- verbs relating to IT
- expressions for giving information

Glossary — PAGE 150
crash
in the loop
patch
plug-in
stretched

2.2 Vocabulary Information systems and communication

Discussion

1 'Information is too valuable to be left to IT departments. In today's business world, every manager should be a computer specialist.' To what extent do you agree?

Language focus

2 Decide whether these phrases indicate a small or a large difference.

> a bit more expensive   a whole lot more expensive   considerably more expensive
> far more expensive   marginally more expensive   infinitely more expensive
> slightly more expensive   somewhat more expensive

3 Use expressions from Exercise 2 and appropriate adjectives to compare:

1. two computers you have used.
2. two ways you communicate with your business contacts or your friends.
3. two software applications you have used.
4. two ways you use the Internet.
5. two printers you have used.
6. two electronic devices you would like to own.

4 Explain the difference between each pair of computing terms.

1. a server and a PC
2. a laptop and a tablet PC
3. a suite and an application
4. a patch and a plug-in
5. a virus and a bug
6. a crash and a hard-disk failure
7. the Internet and an intranet
8. a workgroup and a workstation

Reading and vocabulary

5 George Skopelitis is in charge of IT user support at First Northeast Bank. Choose the correct verbs to complete the email he sent to his boss.

> ✉ EMAIL
>
> Maurice,
>
> As you know, our IT resources are more and more stretched as we try to cope with an ageing system. We desperately need to (1) *advance / upgrade / promote* the operating system: software applications are (2) *crashing / collapsing / falling* more and more frequently, and the server (3) *fell down / went down / dropped down* three times last week. There have also been several cases where important documents have been (4) *rubbed out / blanked / deleted*. Of course, I have (5) *inserted / installed / placed* patches and (6) *uploaded / downloaded / unzipped* new drivers wherever possible, but we can't go on like this. What's more, there's no time for new projects like (7) *setting up / fixing up / pulling up* mobile Internet connections so that our sales teams can (8) *register / note / enter* data on the system when they're on the road. We really need investment now!

6 Complete these sentences with the correct verbs from Exercise 5.

1. Most PCs come complete with an office package, but sometimes you have to _____ it yourself.
2. On average, when a company's IT system _____, it takes ten days to fix everything.
3. IT users lack imagination. When asked to _____ a password, the most common choice is 'password'.
4. There are several programs which can rescue your data if you accidentally _____ files.
5. An incorrect memory address is the most common reason why PCs _____.
6. It only takes minutes to _____ a webmail account that you can access from anywhere in the world.
7. One of the few remaining advantages of desktops is that it's easier to _____ components.
8. Research suggests that people who _____ illegal mp3s are also big spenders on legal music sites.

24 *The* Business 2.0

Listening

7 1:29–1:36 Listen to eight messages on George's voicemail. Match speakers 1–8 with the problem they are experiencing a–h.

a) they can't install something
b) some computers need upgrading
c) they need to download a program
d) the whole system went down
e) they have to enter data quickly
f) their computer keeps crashing
g) a connection hasn't been set up
h) they deleted some files

8 1:29–1:36 Listen again and complete George's notes with the words from the box.

| an update | back | in | informed | know | ring | loop | touch |

1 give Ebony Brooks a _____ about backup
2 give Maurice _____ on appointments application
3 get in _____ with Martha re. laptops
4 get _____ to Lincoln Thigpen – presentation slides
5 keep Camilla Ramsey in the _____ on solutions to database problems
6 let Maurice _____ about Marketing's Internet connection
7 keep Marvin _____ about sound card driver
8 fill Cara Bickerson _____ on voice recognition software

Paraphrasing

9 Replace the expressions in bold with the expressions for giving information in Exercise 8.

1 Can I **give you an answer** later this morning? I'm in a meeting at the moment.
2 I'd appreciate it if you could **include me in the group of people you inform**.
3 We don't have a firm date for the meeting yet. We'll **tell you** as soon as we do.
4 While I'm away in the Far East, I'd like you to **give me regular progress reports** by email.
5 Before the meeting starts, can you just **give me some details** on what was said last time?
6 I just can't manage to **contact** her – I've tried everything: phone, fax, email, snail mail, even pigeon!
7 When you get back from your holiday, I'll **report** on what's been happening.
8 Could you **contact me by telephone**, please? My email server's down at the moment.

Discussion

10 With a partner, prioritize the tasks on George's to-do list for tomorrow.

> CEO wants Web meeting available in all departments asap – need half a day
>
> Sound card drivers for Marvin (President's nephew!) – simple – half an hour?
>
> Cara re. voice recognition – needs maybe an hour over lunch?
>
> CEO's assistant wants Wifi but she only works at her desk! – one hour or so
>
> Information from database vendors – a couple of hours, but probably no budget this year
>
> Abstract of presentation for New York conference – deadline is tomorrow – one hour
>
> 15 new laptops needed – HP's special offer ends tomorrow – an hour or two?
>
> Appointments application – two or three hours' work, but software update due in three weeks
>
> Ebony Brooks re. backup software – should take 30 minutes, but she's a slow learner
>
> Marketing's Internet connection is down again – at least an hour and a half

---

Internet research

Software, hardware, firmware, freeware, shareware, adware, spyware, malware, blogware … Use the define: function of your search engine to find definitions of these words (e.g. define: malware). How many more -ware words can you find?

2 Information

- comparatives
- superlatives
- polite requests and responses

2.3 Grammar Comparing solutions and getting help

Refresh your memory

Comparatives

half as	fast	
twice as	easy	as
ten times as	expensive	

a lot	faster	
far	easier	than
much	more expensive	

Superlatives

the fastest
the easiest
the most expensive

▶ Grammar and practice page 124

Language focus

1 Read the conversations comparing using the train with flying. Underline the comparative phrases.

A: Travelling by train is just as quick as flying.
B: Nonsense! Flying is much quicker.
A: Well, I prefer the train because it's less complicated.

A: The train isn't half as expensive as the plane.
B: As a matter of fact, the train is slightly more expensive these days.
A: Well, I still prefer the train because it's far more comfortable.

2 With a partner, have similar conversations using the adjectives in brackets to compare the following:

1. Taxis versus buses. (cheap, uncomfortable, …)
2. The car versus the bicycle. (healthy, dangerous, …)
3. Charter flights versus scheduled flights. (reliable, useful, …)
4. Motorways versus country roads. (safe, fast, …)
5. Bed and breakfast versus hotels. (comfortable, luxurious, …)
6. Campsites versus holiday clubs. (expensive, noisy, …)
7. Car ferries versus tunnels. (easy, quick, …)
8. Self-drive tours versus coach tours. (eco-friendly, boring, …)

3 What is special about the following? Use the adjectives in the box to help you.

| big expensive fast fast-growing large old profitable valuable |

1. The Bugatti Veyron Super Sport
2. The Izmailovo Hotel, Moscow
3. Exxon Mobil
4. Wal-Mart
5. The Nisiyama Onsen Keiunkan Hotel, Japan
6. Russia
7. Boeing 747
8. Groupon

Discussion and presentation

4 With a partner, choose a destination in the country you are studying in. In column 1, write four ways of reaching that destination (by bus, on foot, etc.). In columns 2–5, give each means of transport a score from 1 (= the worst) to 5 (= the best). Add up the total scores and present your conclusions to another pair.

	cost	time	comfort	carbon footprint	total

Expanding notes

5 Complete the article with a comparative phrase suggested by the prompts. The first two are done for you.

Since 1965, Moore's law has observed that computer chips become *twice as powerful* (powerful x 2) every 24 months. A similar formula, Kryder's law, says that hard disk space is only *half as expensive* (1/2 expensive) as it was two years ago. Gordon Moore says his law is (1) _____ (+ beautiful) he had first realized: contrary to Murphy's law—anything that can go wrong, will—Moore's law means everything gets (2) _____ (+ good + good). However, the picture is not (3) _____ (= positive) it once seemed. Yet another law, Wirth's law, states that software gets slower (4) _____ (+ rapidly) hardware gets faster! Moore's law also means that new products must be developed (5) _____ (+ quick + quick). Any product which is launched just two or three months late will be 10–15% (6) _____ (+ slow), (7) _____ (+ bulky) or (8) _____ (– generous) in storage capacity than the competition. Moreover, physical barriers like temperature make it almost impossible to run PCs at speeds (9) _____ (+ high) 5 GHz. It now makes sense to use more memory space to accelerate disk access, since space is becoming (10) _____ (– expensive) than computer processing speed.

6 Match the two halves of these quotations.

1 The nicer I am,
2 The more you chase money,
3 The more I want to get something done,
4 I'm a great believer in luck, and I find the harder I work,

a) the more I have of it. (Thomas Jefferson)
b) the less I call it work. (Richard Bach)
c) the more people think I'm lying. (Andy Warhol)
d) the harder it is to catch it. (Mike Tatum)

Glossary PAGE 151

bulky
carbon footprint

7 With a partner, complete these sentences to make your own quotations.

1 The older I get, the …
2 The more money you earn, the …
3 The harder you work, the …
4 The more I …, the …
5 The _____er the …, the …

Dealing with requests

8 Cross out the inappropriate response to these requests for help, as in the example.

1 Will you get me a cup of coffee, please?
 a) ~~No, I won't.~~
 b) Yes, if I can have one of your biscuits.
 c) Sorry, I've got too much to carry.
2 Can you tell me how to switch this projector on?
 a) Yes, I can.
 b) No idea, I'm afraid.
 c) I'm sorry, I never use it myself.
3 Could you possibly get me a sandwich when you go out to the post office?
 a) Yes, with pleasure.
 b) Sure, if you could answer the phone while I'm out.
 c) Yes, I could possibly.
4 I wonder if you could spare the time to make a few photocopies for me?
 a) Yes, I would.
 b) I don't see why not.
 c) I should think so.
5 Would you mind giving me a hand with this table? It's rather heavy.
 a) No problem.
 b) Yes.
 c) Not at all.

Internet research

Search for the keywords *Murphy's computer laws*. Hold a class opinion poll to find your three favourite laws.

Negotiating

9 Work with a partner to practise asking for help. Write a list of five things you need to do tomorrow. Then negotiate to delegate to your partner the ones you don't want to do.

2 Information

- listening for register and inference
- expressions for telephoning
- roleplaying telephone situations

Glossary PAGE 151

IP address
mustn't grumble
small talk
trivial

2.4 Speaking   Telephoning

Discussion

1 Decide how far you agree with these statements about telephoning. Write *I agree*, *It depends* or *I disagree*.

1 It's important to have a few moments of small talk before getting down to business.
2 You can never be too polite on the telephone.
3 It's much easier to say 'yes' than to say 'no'.
4 When you can't help someone, it's better to say 'no' directly than to make up excuses.
5 The caller decides when to end the call; the receiver should wait for the caller's signal.

2 Discuss your answers to Exercise 1 with a partner. Do you think it's different in other parts of the world?

Listening for register

3 1:37–1:40 Listen to four telephone conversations and answer the questions below.

1 Which one is polite, informal, impolite or too polite?
2 In which conversation are the speakers friends, acquaintances, colleagues from different departments or managers in a large company?

Listening for inference

4 1:37–1:40 Listen again and answer the questions for each conversation.

1 What guesses can you make about the speakers? Imagine how old they are, what they look like, what they do and what kind of lives they lead.
2 What is each speaker's opinion of the other at the end of the conversation?

5 1:37–1:40 With a partner, find suitable words to complete the expressions in the checklist. Then listen again and check your answers.

Useful expressions: Telephoning

Checking the other person can speak now

Have you got a _____ of minutes?

Requesting help

I _____ you to give me …
Do you _____ to know how to …?
I was wondering if I could ask you a _____.
Do you think you could _____ send me …?
Any _____ I could …?

Refusing help

I'd _____ to help you, but …
I _____ I could help you, but …
Normally I'd be _____ to help, but …
The _____ is, …

Ending the call

Anyway, I won't _____ you any longer.
I mustn't _____ any more of your time.
Anyway, I'd better _____.

Internet research

Search for the keywords *cellphone voicemail etiquette* to find tips for using new phone technologies. In small groups, decide on your top three tips.

6 Complete these dialogues with suitable expressions. Then practise them with a partner.

Alex: _____
Billie: Oh, hello, Alex. How's it going?
Alex: _____
Billie: No problem. I was just going to have a break anyway.
Alex: _____
Billie: Well, I'm sorry to disappoint you, but I don't know much about it actually.
Alex: _____
Billie: OK. But just let me know if there's anything I can do.
Alex: _____
Billie: OK, bye.

Chris: Hello, it's Chris here. I'm not disturbing you, am I?
Dee: _____
Chris: I'm just calling to ask if you'd mind doing me a favour, actually.
Dee: _____
Chris: Well, do you think I could possibly borrow your copy of Office 2010? I need to re-install it, and I can't find mine.
Dee: _____
Chris: Oh, I see. Well, never mind. I thought I'd ask, just in case. Anyway, I won't keep you from your work. Thanks.
Dee: _____

Erin: Hi. It's me. Sorry to bother you. You wouldn't happen to have the new IP address, would you?
Frankie: _____
Erin: Brilliant. Thanks a million.
Frankie: _____
Erin: OK, then. I'll let you get back to work. Thanks a lot. Bye.

Roleplay

7 With a partner, practise roleplaying different telephone situations. Use suitable formal/polite or direct/informal language, and include small talk, as appropriate.

Student A	Student B
Call 1 You are new in a small law firm where the managing partner also deals with all computer problems. Your PC has broken down, so you call her/him for help. Your partner will start.	**Call 1** You are the managing partner of a small law firm. You are also the firm's computer expert, but you are very busy and fed up with receiving calls about trivial computer problems. You receive a call from one of your new employees. You start by answering your phone.
Call 2 You receive a call from a colleague you like a lot. You start by answering your phone.	**Call 2** You have been having problems with your email. You think you have fixed it, but you need to test it. Call a colleague and ask them to send you a test mail to your new address. Your partner will start.

eWorkbook
Now watch the video for this unit.

For more telephone situations, Student A should look at page 114, and Student B should look at page 116.

2 Information

- memo style and register
- paragraph order
- writing a memo

2.5 Writing Memos

Discussion
1 First Northeast Bank has realized that many members of staff just ignore memos. Think of some reasons why memos often get ignored.

Model
2 Read the recommendations on memo style. Then answer the quiz that First Northeast sent to all their managers. Choose the option which best matches the style recommendations.

FIRST Northeast Bank
Recommendations – writing memos

1 Personalize your memos: use *I, you, we* to make people feel directly concerned.
2 Use active rather than passive verbs for a more conversational, reader-friendly style.
3 Use verbs in preference to nouns, and avoid jargon and technical terms; write sentences which 'your grandmother would understand'.
4 Make it clear and unambiguous what you want people to do and when.
5 Focus on the benefits to the reader, not on rigid rules or procedures.

Managers' quiz

1 A memo is **a document that you send to people inside the company** / **a method of documentary communication for internal use**.
2 The objective of a memo is **to solicit decisions and policy or behavioural changes** / **to get people to do something**.
3 In the past, we wrote memos on paper: now **we often send them by email** / **electronic transmission has been widely adopted**.
4 To write a good memo you need **careful forethought, layout and revision** / **to plan, organize and edit your ideas carefully**.
5 A good memo **tells you clearly what you have to do and when you have to do it** / **is one in which both the desired outcome and the target time frame are specified**.
6 The purpose of this quiz is **to ensure that the principal rules of memo-writing are respected** / **to help you write effective memos**.

Analysis
3 Read the suggested format for memos. The paragraphs in the memo below are not in the correct order. Number the paragraphs 1–4.

Format for memos
1 Define the problem.
2 Tell the reader why they should feel concerned.
3 Say what result you want to get.
4 Say what you want the reader to do and when.

VAN DER HEYDEN B.V.
Subject: Unauthorized software

☐ I would like us all to carry out this check by 15 September latest. Please examine your laptop carefully, and delete any unauthorized software. If you need help, I will be available every afternoon between 1 and 5pm Thank you for helping to protect our colleagues, our jobs and our company.

☐ If inspectors find unauthorized, copyright material on our systems, individual users, management and the company itself can face heavy fines and even criminal prosecution. It is in everybody's interest to avoid this risk.

☐ As you probably know, the European Commission is stepping up its fight against software piracy, and we expect to see systematic inspections of medium-sized companies like ours in the next six months.

☐ This is the reason why I'm asking every employee in the company to check that there is no unauthorized software on their computer. This could include unlicensed copies of business software, downloaded programmes and even mp3 music files.

Internet research

'Local High School Dropouts Cut in Half'
'Miners Refuse to Work after Death'
Visit the humor section of the US government's plain language site www.plainlanguage.gov/ examples to find the best examples of ambiguous language.

Language focus

4 Match the examples of officialese 1–10 with the reader-friendly versions a–j.

1 it is recognized
2 with a view to alleviating
3 adjacent to
4 it is imperative
5 it is inadequate
6 staff are reminded
7 area of concern
8 in the event of
9 forthwith
10 … is appreciated

a) difficulty
b) immediately
c) there's not enough
d) if there was
e) next to
f) please remember
g) we must
h) thank you for …
i) to solve
j) we realize

Writing a memo

5 With a partner, rewrite this memo in a reader-friendly style. Refer to Exercise 4 to help you.

To: All staff **From:** April Jenkins, site manager
Date: 10/8/12
Subject: Parking

It is recognized that on-site parking is currently inadequate and plans are currently being examined with a view to alleviating the problems.

One current area of concern is the area adjacent to the logistics warehouse. In the event of a fire, it would be very difficult for emergency vehicles to reach the fuel tanks behind the building. It is imperative that access to this and all buildings is kept clear.

Members of staff are therefore reminded that vehicles may only be parked in the official car parks. As from Monday 13 August any cars parked on access roads will be removed forthwith. The assistance of all motor vehicle users in this matter is very much appreciated.

Glossary PAGE 151

alleviate
fine
forethought
forthwith
officialese
time frame

Output

6 🔊 1:41 Listen to a voicemail message from your manager and write the memo he refers to.

7 Work with a partner. Your top management have asked you to make a proposal for the company's three-day international IT conference. Think about these questions.

1 Why is an IT conference important to an international company?
2 What objectives do you think management want to achieve?
3 What are the ingredients of a successful conference?

8 Write a memo proposing dates, a location and a programme for the IT conference. You will also need to get approval for your budget. (Last year's budget was $700 per person.)

9 Read all the memos and vote for the best proposal.

2 Information

- reasons for and consequences of staff turnover
- agreeing on a plan of action

2.6 Case study Meteor Bank

Discussion

1 When experienced staff leave a company, what are the consequences? Decide whether these results are *likely* or *unlikely*.

> better morale   better promotion prospects   higher salary costs
> higher training costs   improved customer service   increased productivity
> more mistakes   more overtime   younger, more dynamic teams

Reading

2 Read the newspaper clipping. What reasons can you think of to explain why experienced staff have been leaving Meteor's IT department?

Rising Star promises to make sparks fly

YOUNG Londoner Saul Finlay has been appointed IT Manager at Meteor Bank. Thanks to an aggressive commercial policy, the Nigerian bank is growing rapidly all over West Africa, especially through its subsidiaries in Ivory Coast, Ghana and Cameroon. Together with the rising demand for electronic banking services, rapid growth is putting increasing pressure on the bank's IT department in Lagos. In an interview yesterday, Finlay promised to 'drag the IT department kicking and screaming into the twenty-first century'. When asked if …

3 Read the memo and answer the questions.

Meteor Bank

To: Astrid Kuhn, Managing Director
From: Joseph Ikpeba, Operations Manager
Subject: IT policy

Our system down time problems are going from bad to worse (see attached figures) and we are beginning to lose corporate clients. The problem appears to be the result of exceptionally high staff turnover in the IT department. Half of our systems administrators are new graduates with less than one year's experience, and Saul Finlay is recruiting again for the third time in six months.

I'm afraid I have to remind you that both down time and staff turnover were very minor problems before Saul arrived in 2010. Saul's answer is that he needs investment in even more new hardware. However, I am not sure that this is the solution; I feel strongly that we should investigate further, not least because some staff have implied that the system failures might be deliberate.

Could I possibly ask you to speak to some of the people involved and to hold an executive committee meeting as soon as possible to decide how to deal with these problems?

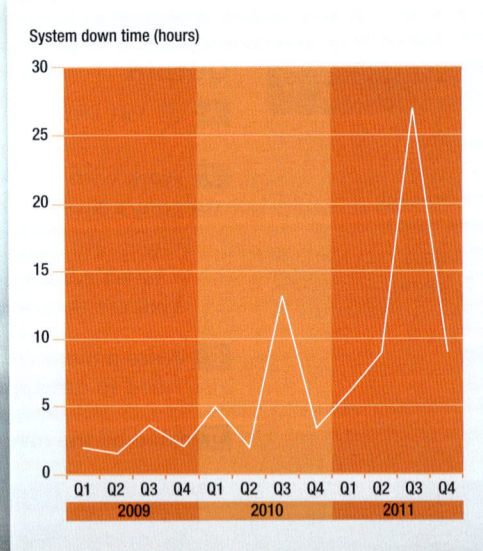

IT Turnover	2009	2010	2011
Total IT staff	64	68	78
New hires	7 (11%)	19 (28%)	31 (40%)
Retirements	4 (6.3%)	5 (7.3%)	6 (7.6%)
Departures	3 (4.7%)	10 (14.7%)	15 (19.2%)

1 Who wrote the memo and why?
2 What does he want?
3 What has changed at Meteor Bank since 2010?
4 What reasons can you suggest for the trends in the figures?

Listening and note-taking

4 🔊 1:42–1:45 Astrid Kuhn decided to investigate. Listen to the reactions she received when she spoke to four members of staff, and complete the notes.

Tonye Ameobi | Vincent Bonvalet | Kehinde Ojukwu | Joseph Ikpeba

Glossary   PAGE 151
down time
drag someone kicking and screaming
malicious
morale
outsource
recruit
subsidiary
turnover

	Tonye Ameobi, HR Manager, Lagos	Vincent Bonvalet, IT Manager, Ivory Coast	Kehinde Ojukwu, Senior Systems Administrator, IT department, Lagos	Joseph Ikpeba, Operations Manager
Opinion of Saul Finlay				
Mistakes				
Successes				
Recommended solutions				

Discussion

5 To what extent do you feel Saul Finlay is to blame for Meteor's problems?

6 Work in groups of three or four. Student A: turn to page 115. Student B: turn to page 117. Student C: turn to page 120. (If there is a fourth student, they should be the chairperson.) Discuss the agenda below and draw up an action plan for Astrid Kuhn.

Executive Committee Meeting
1. How can we reduce staff turnover?
2. How can we reduce system down time?
3. How should we react to accusations of malicious damage in the IT department?
4. Should we agree to Saul Finlay's request for investment in IT equipment in Lagos, or invest in improving our IT network in our foreign subsidiaries?
5. Should we consider outsourcing IT?
6. How should we evaluate Saul Finlay's performance, and what action is needed, if any?

Internet research
Search for the keywords *keeping good employees*. Compile a class list of the top ten ways to reduce staff turnover.

Review 1

Building a career

1 Complete the text about going to university. Definitions are given in brackets to help you.

How do you choose your university? Unless you are lucky enough to win a (1) s_____p, (money awarded to excellent students), you'll have to decide if you can pay the (2) f_____s (price of tuition). Perhaps you'll be impressed by the quality and reputation of the (3) f_____ty (all the teachers), or perhaps by the sports and social (4) f_____ies (rooms, equipment and services). You may also want to think about the choice of (5) e_____r (other than learning) activities and whether the university has a good (6) p_____t (helping students find a job) service.

2 Make expressions by matching the beginnings and endings of each phrase.

1 widening access to — a
2 the uncomfortable
3 the resources to match
4 students get good value
5 a mountain
6 to go to
7 robbing the poor
8 governments continue to provide
9 massive hikes in
10 willing and

a) a university education
b) their ambitions
c) to pay the rich
d) truth
e) great lengths
f) for their money
g) student fees
h) able to invest
i) to climb
j) subsidies

3 Complete the sentences using the words in the box.

assignment	chair	dismissed	draw up	exceed
laid off	implement	meet	present	recruit
sabbatical	train

1 After you _____ new sales reps you have to _____ them.
2 It's good if you can _____ your sales objectives, but it's even better if you can _____ them.
3 It's not enough just to _____ a few proposals on paper: you've actually got to _____ the plans.
4 When you become more experienced, you might have to _____ working parties and even _____ new programmes to the Board.
5 If you lost your job because of the company's problems, you were _____, but if *you* did something wrong, you were _____.
6 If you are working in another geographical place, you are on _____; if you are not working because you want to study or write, you are on _____.

4 In each sentence, put one verb in the past simple (*did*), one in the past continuous (*was/were doing*), and one in the past perfect (*had done*).

1 I _____ (find out) the other day that Pierre from the sales department has been dismissed. I _____ (wonder) why I _____ (not/see) him for a while.
2 I _____ (just/finish) working on the spreadsheet when the computer _____ (crash). I can't explain it – I _____ (not/do) anything unusual with the program.

5 Put each verb into the most likely form. You might need an auxiliary like *will* or *would*. Use contractions.

A: If I (1) _____ (see) Anita, I (2) _____ (tell) her about the job vacancy as well.
B: But Anita's on vacation. She's trekking in the Himalayas. If you (3) _____ (see) her, it (4) _____ (be) very surprising!
A: Anita? Trekking in the Himalayas? Now that really is surprising. If Anita (5) _____ (go) on vacation, she usually (6) _____ (go) to the beach.

6 Fill in the missing letters to complete these linking words.

Introducing a point
1 As re__ __ __ds / As __ __ __ as … is con__ __ __ed

Seeing both sides
2 On the wh__ __ __ …, how__ __ __ __ … / It's true that …, but __ __ the o__ __ __ __ h__ __ __ …

Combining reasons
3 Not o__ __ __ …, but a__ __ __ … / For o__ __ th__ __ __ …, and for an__ __ __ __ __ __ …

Adding ideas
4 Bes__ __ __ __ __, … / In add__ __ __ __ __ __, …

7 Use one expression from each of the categories in Exercise 6 to complete this text.

I've lived in the same town all my life. My family and friends are here, and it's calm and peaceful. (1) _____, there's a good sense of community and I'm happy. But I'm starting to wonder about my career. (2) _____ it's a small town and there aren't many interesting jobs, _____ I want to develop my language skills and work in an international environment. (3) _____ salary _____, that's not so important right now – experience is more important. So I don't know what to do. (4) _____ I think the best thing is just to wait and see what jobs are available locally – _____, if I see a really interesting job advertised in another area, I'll apply for it and see what happens.

8 Complete the sentences from cover letters with the action verbs in the box.

| broke | developed | doubled | enhanced | supported |

1 I _____ previous sales records.
2 I more than _____ average revenues per nightclub.
3 I _____ a range of new products for teenage customers.
4 I _____ myself financially by working in radio advertising sales.
5 These part-time jobs _____ my formal education.

Review 2

Information

1 Match each verb with a phrase a–f.

1 meet ☐   3 make ☐   5 waste ☐
2 keep ☐   4 boost ☐   6 take ☐

a) a multibillion-dollar investment in IT equipment and services
b) or exceed budget and productivity targets
c) only hours to do what might have taken days previously
d) productivity and profits
e) budgets and headcounts low because of global competitors
f) money by investing in IT without at the same time overhauling the business processes it is meant to automate

2 Complete the definitions by underlining the correct words in **bold**.

1 Another word for an iPad is a **laptop / tablet**.
2 A short set of commands to correct a bug in a computer program is called a **patch / plug-in**.
3 If you get a better or more recent version of some software (or hardware), you **promote / upgrade** it.
4 A collection of PCs and servers all connected together on a local area network is called a **workgroup / workstation**.
5 If a server stops working for a time, you say that it **went down / fell down**.
6 If you load and configure a new piece of software on your computer, you **insert / install** it.
7 To keep your computer programs up-to-date, you have to frequently **download / offload** patches and new versions.
8 If you make some new technology ready for use (for the first time), you **set it up / fix it up**.

3 Match the beginnings and endings of the phrases.

a) fill   in touch with someone
b) get   someone an update
c) get   someone in on something
d) give   someone know about something
e) give   back to someone about something
f) let   someone a ring (= call)

4 Match the expressions in Exercise 3 with the definitions below. Be careful – some are very similar.

1 Tell someone about things that have happened recently. ☐
2 Give someone the most recent information. ☐
3 Tell someone something. ☐
4 Speak or write to someone, especially after you have not spoken to them for a long time. ☐
5 Contact someone by telephone. ☐
6 Give someone an answer at a later time. ☐

5 Correct the mistake in each sentence.

1 X's software is far more expensive as Y's.
2 Y's software doesn't have nearly as many features than X's.
3 My Internet connection is lot faster than yours.
4 My Internet connection is only halve as fast as yours.
5 Big brands can be double as dear.
6 Ink jet printers cost a fracture of the price of laser printers.
7 Why buy a PC? They are a lot fewer reliable than Macs.
8 There's infinity more software for PCs.
9 I think Yahoo® is a more better search engine than Google.
10 Have you tried the Microsoft Live® search engine? It really is the most better.

6 Put the requests in order of politeness, from 1 (most informal and direct) to 6 (most polite and indirect).

1 ☐   2 ☐   3 ☐   4 ☐   5 ☐   6 ☐

a) Could you give me a hand?
b) Give me a hand!
c) Will you give me a hand, please?
d) Do you think you could give me a hand?
e) I wonder if you could just give me a hand for a moment?
f) Would you mind giving me a hand?

(Note: Answers may vary but should be similar. The order can also depend on how you say each sentence.)

7 Complete the expressions used in telephoning.

1 I was w_ _ _ _ _ing if I could a_ _ you a fa_ _ _r?
2 Anyway, I won't k_ _ _ you any l_ _ _ _ _r.
3 I'm not dist_ _ _ing you, am I?
4 Is t_ _ _ _ any ch_ _ _ _ I could …?
5 Do you ha_ _ _n to know if …?
6 Have you g_ _ a co_ _ _ _e of minutes?
7 I mustn't t_ _ _ up any m_ _ _ of y_ _ _ t_ _ _.
8 Is this a g_ _ _ t_ _ _ _ to c_ _ _?

8 Match the expressions in Exercise 7 with these uses.

a) checking the other person can speak now ☐☐☐
b) requesting help   ☐☐☐
c) ending the call   ☐☐

9 Rewrite the memo replacing the underlined phrases with the more user-friendly language in the box.

| if there was   issue   know   need   please |
| regularly   remember   thank you for |

As you (1) <u>are aware</u>, government regulations state that fire drills have to be carried out (2) <u>on a regular basis</u>. This is a particular (3) <u>area of concern</u> for us following the minor incident in the factory last month. Clearly, (4) <u>in the event of</u> another fire, we would have to pay significantly more for our insurance cover.

We are planning to have regular drills from now on. (5) <u>I would be grateful if you could</u> make sure that all staff in your section know exactly what procedures to follow when they hear the alarm. (6) <u>You are reminded</u> that these drills will be held at random times and without your previous knowledge.

If you (7) <u>require</u> any further information, please do not hesitate to contact me.

(8) <u>We appreciate</u> your cooperation.

3 Quality

- the Japanese approach to quality
- product quality

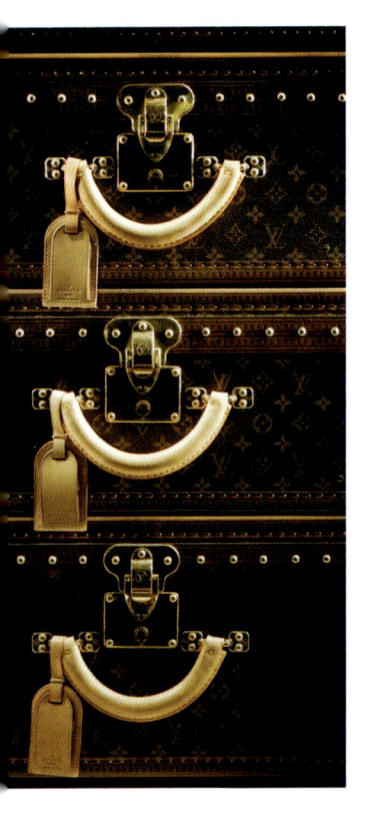

3.1 About business   What quality means

Discussion

1 The box below contains factors that influence decisions to buy. Number the factors 1–7, depending on how important they are to you. (1 = most important; 7 = least important).

> design   durability   environmental friendliness
> modernity   price   quality   value for money

2 Discuss how the order would change if you were buying:
- a car
- a washing machine
- an mp3 player
- a packet of breakfast cereal
- a leather bag
- a laptop

Scan reading

3 Read the article opposite. Match the headings a–h with paragraphs 1–7. There is one extra heading.

a) No survival without quality
b) Reliability is not enough
c) Quality and cost
d) Quality culture
e) Superficial quality
f) Quality in design
g) Closing the gap?
h) Quality for quality's sake

Reading for detail

4 Read the article again and mark these statements *T* (true) or *F* (false).

1 Western companies have caught up with the Japanese in terms of quality.
2 The Japanese expect things to work properly.
3 Producing reliable products guarantees a strong market position.
4 For a quality programme to succeed, senior management do not need to understand the key concepts.
5 Quality analysis is a sensible way to solve any performance problems.
6 The iPod is not the only Apple® product which has enchanting quality.

5 Find words or expressions in the text with the following meanings.

1 something which suddenly becomes very popular (paragraph 1)
2 try hard to do something difficult (paragraph 1)
3 expect something to be there as normal (paragraph 2)
4 a variety of objects or things (paragraph 3)
5 mistakes you should avoid (paragraph 4)
6 things which are fashionable for a short time (paragraph 4)
7 to make something unsuccessful or unpleasant (paragraph 5)
8 something surprising or impressive (paragraph 6)

Listening

6 🔊 1:46 Industry analyst, Warwick Fender, is speaking about quality in the household electrical goods sector. What products do you think he will talk about? Listen and check.

7 🔊 1:46 Listen again and complete the sentences.

1 The white goods industry has been accused of designing products to last _____.
2 Consumers today expect to _____ electrical goods more often.
3 Repairing products is expensive due to the cost of _____ and _____.
4 Ethical consumers are reassured that it is increasingly possible to _____ products.

Discussion

8 In groups look at the products in Exercise 2 and discuss the questions. Then present a summary of your group's ideas to the class.

1 Do the products have taken-for-granted quality, or enchanting quality, or both?
2 Are any of the products designed with planned obsolescence in mind?

Internet research

Search for the keywords *planned obsolescence* or *built-in obsolescence* to find examples of this practice and find out why manufacturers need to take it into account when designing new products. List the arguments for and against and report back to the class.

36   *The* Business 2.0

TWO KINDS OF QUALITY

As I write this, I'm travelling on a plane. The executive sitting next to me has carefully unpacked his Bose® headphones and iPod nano. Both these products have associations with quality, a concept which can be misunderstood but which is of great importance to success in business. The Japanese actually have two words for quality, and an understanding of each is necessary to compete today.

1

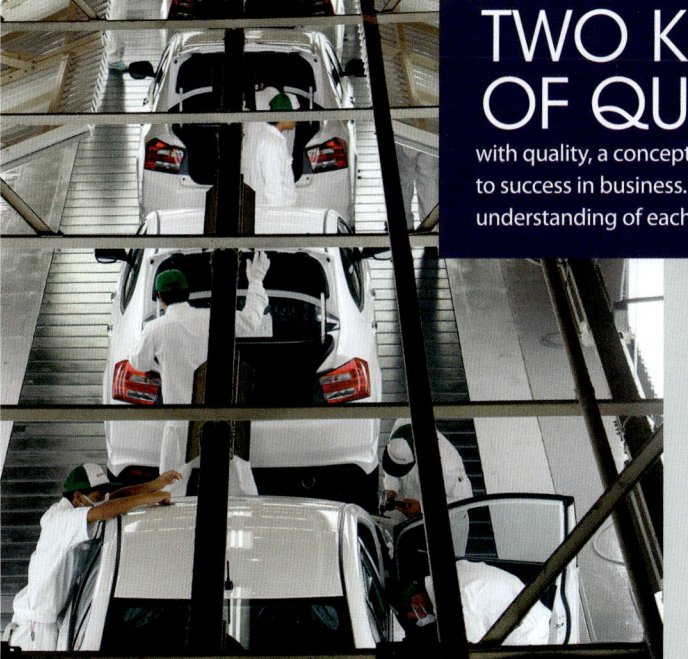

Quality remains an elusive target for many Western companies, even though the craze for quality has been around for some twenty years. Yes, progress has been made. In 1980, the average car produced by Ford™ had twice as many product flaws as the average Japanese car. By 1986, the Japanese auto industry lead over Ford had shrunk from 100% to about 20%, as Ford made quality its number one priority. But since that impressive burst of progress, many companies have struggled to keep up on quality, even as the Japanese began building more of their products in the West with local workers.

2

The truth is, the Japanese have an unfair advantage. Japanese culture intrinsically values quality and appreciates the small details. In fact, the Japanese expression for quality is *atarimae hinshitsu*, which can be roughly translated as 'taken-for-granted quality'. What do the Japanese take for granted when it comes to quality? They take for granted that things should work as they are supposed to, and they even see an elegance to things working properly, whether it's cars, subway schedules, traditional flower arranging or the famous tea ceremony.

3

Japanese manufacturers became so obsessed with taken-for-granted quality that they created a stream of innovations that built on the concepts of Ed Deming, the renowned quality management consultant. Their innovations included lean manufacturing, just-in-time industry and design for quality. In today's competitive markets, manufacturers need to make quick progress towards this kind of quality. If they don't, you can take for granted that they will go out of business. This is true even for small, entrepreneurial companies. The ability to create products and services that work is no longer a source of long-term competitive advantage. It has become just the price of admission to most markets. If the stuff your competitors make works better, your customers aren't going to be customers for long.

4

Though much improved, our quality record still isn't what it might be. Here are two traps I've seen a lot of companies fall into on the road to quality. One is faking a commitment. There's no way around it. Whether you're adopting total quality management (TQM), or other quality schemes, these techniques require everyone in a company to learn how to think and work differently. Too many senior executives adopt the latest fads as they come and go, without taking the time to learn what these processes are and how they work. They leave the detail of quality to the folks below them: a sure way to have a quality programme fail.

5

At the other extreme, some companies become so quality-process obsessed that quality management techniques cease to be a tool to improve the company's performance and instead become an end in themselves. Statistical analysis should be used for questions for which a company doesn't readily have an answer. Instead, organizations sometimes go through long analytical processes for problems that a little common sense could have solved. And nothing sours an organization on quality faster than meaningless work.

6

That brings us to the second of the two Japanese expressions for quality: *miryokuteki hinshitsu*, which means 'enchanting quality'. This kind of quality appeals not to customer expectations about reliability – that things should do what they're supposed to – but rather to a person's aesthetic sense of beauty and elegance. That's what I think Apple® got right with the iPod and its many offspring. The nano belonging to the man sitting next to me is a marvel, not just of miniaturization, but of rounded edges in a world of sharp corners.

7

And as I put on my own Bose headphones, I realize how much I appreciate being able to retreat to my Zen space amid the rumble of the aircraft engines, rattling serving carts and chattering passengers. If these products didn't work properly when you turned them on, nobody would buy them. They would lack *atarimae hinshitsu*. But with the hungry competitors in most markets today, taken-for-granted quality by itself may not get the job done.

Glossary PAGE 151

commitment
craze
end
fake
planned/built-in obsolescence
roughly
struggle
take for granted

3 Quality

- definitions of quality
- adjectives relating to quality
- collocations relating to quality standards

3.2 Vocabulary   Quality and standards

Discussion

1 In small groups, discuss which of these definitions best defines your idea of quality and why.

> Quality means delivering products or services to customers faster, better and cheaper.
> Quality is the correct application of procedures and standards.
> Quality means meeting the customer's needs and expectations.
> Quality means that goods are not defective or damaged.
> Quality is designing and producing reliable products that do what they're supposed to do.
> Quality is in the eye of the beholder.

Reading

2 Read the article which describes five stakeholders with different ideas of quality. Match each stakeholder with a definition above.

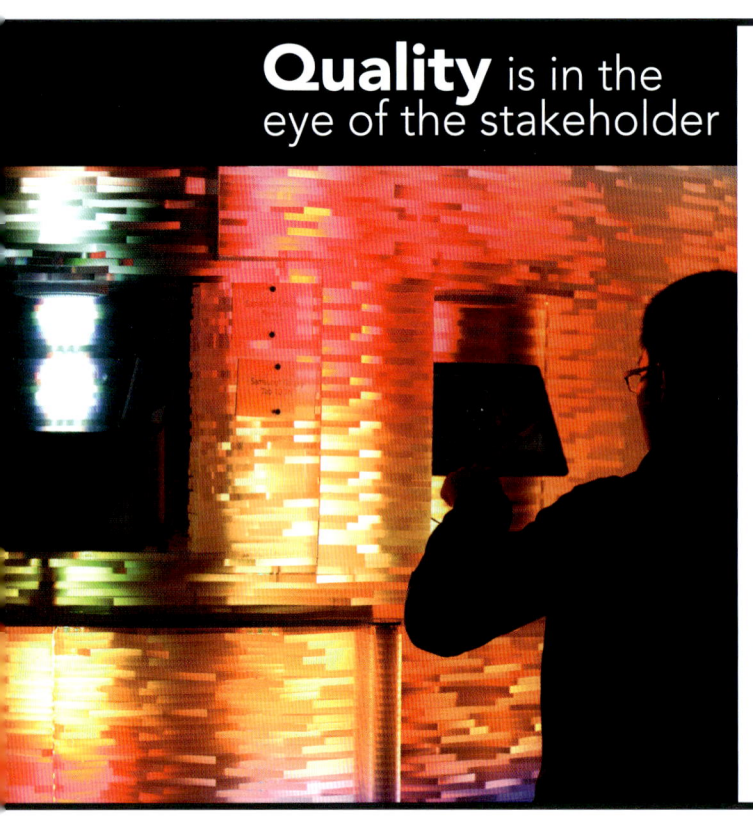

Quality is in the eye of the stakeholder

If a product or service lacks quality, most people would agree that it is substandard in some way. Perhaps the workmanship is shoddy, the packaging is flimsy or the service unreliable. But defining quality from a business perspective is less simple.

5 The **marketing manager**, who is responsible for evaluating consumer research, market conditions and competitor data, sees quality very much in terms of customer expectations and customer satisfaction.

To the **design engineer**, who designs products or components
10 to tight specifications and strict tolerances, quality has more to do with whether the design is fit for purpose and whether the product or part performs its intended function. Colour changes or deluxe models are secondary considerations.

The **process engineer** employs lean manufacturing
15 techniques to ensure that products are produced with the minimum waste of effort, money, time, space and materials. So quality involves what the Japanese call *kaizen* (continuous improvement), and doing things right first time (RFT).

Internal or external **quality auditors** verify compliance with
20 standards such as ISO 9001. Quality means that recorded procedures are in place, and are being applied and respected.

And finally, the **end user**. Whether they want something cheap, heavy-duty or disposable, they won't buy it in the first place if it is scratched, cracked or flawed in any way!

Listening

3 🔊 1:47–1:49 Listen to three people talking about quality. Decide which type of stakeholder each speaker represents.

Word-building

4 Complete the sentences with the correct form of the words in brackets. Check your answers in the article in Exercise 2.

1 Internal _____ carry out checks every year to ensure ISO standards are maintained. (audit)
2 Exacting technical _____ mean that this machine will give many years of service. (specify)
3 The components are machined to _____ of less than one millimetre. (tolerate)
4 Cheap copies of branded goods are often _____. (standard)
5 They changed their provider because the service was _____. (rely)
6 Adopting the RFT guidelines has led to an immediate _____ in product quality. (improve)
7 Our quality controllers make sure that we reach full _____ with ISO 9001. (comply)
8 Reports of strong customer _____ indicate that our production routines are effective. (satisfy)

Glossary   PAGE 152

cost-effective
fit for purpose
flawed
flimsy
in the eye of the beholder
machine
shoddy
stakeholder

Internet research

Search for the keywords *W Edwards Deming*. Who was he and what role did he play in the quality movement? Summarize your findings and report back to the class.

Speaking

5 Work with a partner. Decide whether these adjectives refer to quality positively (+), negatively (–) or both (+/–). Use a dictionary to help you decide.

| cracked | disposable | durable | flawed | flimsy | fragile |
| heavy-duty | poorly-designed | reliable | scratched | shoddy | tough |

6 Tell your partner about a product you bought that you are either pleased with or dissatisfied with. Use the adjectives in Exercise 5 to explain why.

Collocations

7 Match the words 1–10 with a–j to make common collocations relating to quality standards.

1 best
2 customer
3 statutory
4 design
5 continuous
6 resource
7 industry
8 quality
9 measurable
10 technical

a) requirements
b) expectations
c) fault
d) improvement
e) practice
f) objectives
g) assurance
h) specifications
i) management
j) standard

8 Match the collocations in Exercise 7 with the meanings below.

1 how the materials, investment or labour to produce a product or service are managed
2 a flaw in a product which is due to it being poorly designed
3 the qualities that the end user believes the product or service should have
4 what the Japanese call *kaizen*, constantly improving the product and process
5 the precise guidelines which establish how the product should be built
6 the accepted norm in a particular field of business
7 defined targets established to measure improvements in quality
8 compulsory rules imposed by the government
9 the most suitable or efficient way of doing something
10 the system put in place to ensure that quality targets are met

Discussion and presentation

9 Work in small groups. You are the product development team responsible for developing one of the following products: a disposable plate, a dishwasher, a supermarket bag, a mobile phone, a car tyre or your own idea. Choose a product and define what level of quality you want to achieve. Think about the following points.

- the quality of the final product for the end user
- the quality of the materials you will use
- how long you intend the product to last
- whether you want to have a high or low profit margin
- whether you intend it to be an upmarket or a cheap product

10 Take turns to present your product concept to the other groups. Be prepared to answer questions and explain your strategy. Vote for the best product concept.

3 Quality

- the passive
- have something done

3.3 Grammar   Passive structures and *have something done*

Refresh your memory

Passive
be + past participle
Will I *be met* at the airport?
They *could have been delayed*.
I've just *been sacked* (by the sales manager).
Passives can be less personal, perhaps to avoid blame.
Will the report *be finished* on time? instead of *Will you finish the report on time?*
have something done
Expresses an arrangement for a different person to do something for us.
I normally *have* my suit *dry-cleaned* every week.

▶ Grammar and practice pages 126–127

Passive structures; affirmatives, negatives and modals

1 Work with a partner.
Student A: You are a warehouse manager. The transport company you use has made some mistakes that you are angry about. Use active verbs to complain to Student B.
Student B: You are responsible for transport for the warehouse. Deal with Student A's complaints and use the passive to avoid taking the blame.

Student A
You've lost one of the cartons!

You delivered the goods two days late!
You damaged one of the machines!
Your trucks are very dirty!
You left one pallet in our loading bay!

Student B – sorry/carton/mislay
I'm very sorry to hear that one carton was mislaid …
admit/delivery/slightly/delay
it/should/be/pack/better
they/be/clean/at the moment
it/be/deliver/tomorrow

Now, change roles. Student B: You are a warehouse manager. The security company you use has made some mistakes that you are angry about. Use active verbs to complain to Student A.
Student A: You are responsible for security at the warehouse. Deal with Student B's complaints and use the passive to avoid taking the blame.

Student B
The alarm went off six times last night!
Your security guards don't follow procedures!
They damaged my Mercedes yesterday!
The new cameras don't work properly!

Student A
it/check/at the moment
they/be/train/next week
it/should not/be/park/in the loading bay
strange/they/service/yesterday

Passive questions and modals

2 In small groups, use the prompts to make passive questions about a security camera with a *yes/no* answer, as in the example. When you have finished, work with a partner. Close your books and try to ask and answer all the questions from memory.

camera/service/recently? Yes, it has./No, it hasn't.
Has the camera been serviced recently? Yes, it has./No, it hasn't.
1 **service/at the moment**? Yes, it is./No, it isn't.
2 **repair/last Tuesday**? Yes, it was./No, it wasn't.
3 **mend/soon**? Yes, it will./No, it won't.
4 **check/recently**? Yes, it has./No, it hasn't.
5 **clean/correctly**? Yes, it had./No, it hadn't.
6 **fix/by Friday**? Yes, it will (have)./No, it won't (have).
7 **use/in the meantime**? Yes, it can./No, it can't.
8 **change/if it can't be repaired**? Yes, it could./No, it couldn't.

Glossary   PAGE 152

faded
fitting
heap
night shift
round-the-clock
skip
stack
take the blame

have something done

3 Work with a partner. Your warehouse is in a mess and you have some new customers coming to visit it early tomorrow morning. Read the list of what needs doing and how much it will cost. You have a budget of €300. Decide together what you'll have done and what you'll do yourselves to give your visitors a good impression of the company.

> forklift has a flat tyre – repair €35
> skip is overflowing with rubbish – pick-up and emptying €80
> pallet truck is dirty – cleaning €25
> floor markings are faded – repainting €120
> pallets are in a heap – stacking €30
> boxes are all over the place – clearing up €50
> racks are unstable – fixing €180
> patch of oil is on the floor – cleaning €20

Listening for detail

4 🔊 1:50 Fuelflo manufactures fuel systems for civil and military aircraft. Recently, a customer, Airbridge, complained of a problem with fuel pumps. Listen and match the company departments with the problems.

| Logistics | Production | Sales | Stock |

1 _____ put the wrong fitting on the pumps.
2 _____ didn't give Production enough warning.
3 _____ sent two different parts together at the last minute.
4 _____ didn't spot the difference.
5 _____ decided to reduce stock movements.
6 _____ sent a delivery late.

5 Rewrite the notes in Exercise 4 using the passive to make the comments sound less personal and less aggressive.

1 *The wrong fitting was put on the pumps.*

6 At the end of the meeting, Fuelflo made plans to solve the problem. Rewrite sentences 1–6 using the prompts and the passive or *have something done*.

1 In future, we will arrange for the parts to be delivered separately.
   In future, we will have _____.
2 We will ask Airbridge for earlier warnings of any changes.
   Airbridge will _____.
3 Birgit will get someone to check the parts.
   Birgit will have _____.
4 Somebody must brief the Stock Department.
   The Stock Department _____.
5 We will give Airbridge a discount on their next order.
   Airbridge _____.
6 An independent auditor will check the procedures.
   We will have _____.

Roleplay

7 Work with a partner. You both work for a company producing bottled mineral water. Recently, some consumers have complained of a strange taste in a small number of bottles and some have had to be recalled. It is summertime and your bottling plant is working round-the-clock to meet demand.
Student A: You are an internal quality auditor. Your job is to identify and solve the problem by asking tactful questions. Turn to page 115.
Student B: You are the night shift supervisor. Try to avoid taking the blame, using the passive where necessary. Turn to page 117.

8 When you have identified the probable cause of contamination, in small groups, define what corrective action should be taken. Compare your solution with another group.

Internet research

Search for the keywords *bottle contamination recall* to discover how some real contamination cases happened and the consequences for the companies involved. Report back to the class.

3 Quality

- identifying problems and solutions in presentations
- expressions for signposting
- presenting a product

3.4 Speaking Delivering presentations

Discussion

1 Work with a partner. Which factors can make or break a presentation? List three 'make' factors and three 'break' factors, using the ideas in the box to help you.

> body language   clear structure
> delivery   knowledge of the subject
> length   use of technical jargon
> visual aids

Listening

2 1:51–1:54 Listen to four extracts from presentations. Identify the main problem with each speaker's presentation. Compare your answers with a partner.

a) Speed: too fast
b) Inappropriate pauses
c) Excessive jargon and acronyms
d) Long sentences
e) Incorrect vocabulary
f) No checking to see if listeners are following
g) Lack of signposting

3 Match the problems in Exercise 2 with solutions 1–7 below.

1 Using the correct word is important. Remember to use collocations and other common word combinations.
2 Keep sentences short. Your talk will be easier to follow and carry more impact.
3 Take time to check that your audience is following what you say.
4 Slow down. Pause. Give the audience time to think about what you are saying.
5 Learn and use key expressions to signal to your audience where you are in the talk.
6 Think about your listeners. Explain any jargon or acronyms they may not know.
7 Pauses in speech … are like punctuation in writing. Use them … to give more impact … to what you are saying.

Predicting and listening

4 Work with a partner. Quality assurance engineer Marc Pinto is presenting the graph below. What do you think it represents? What do you expect he will say about it?

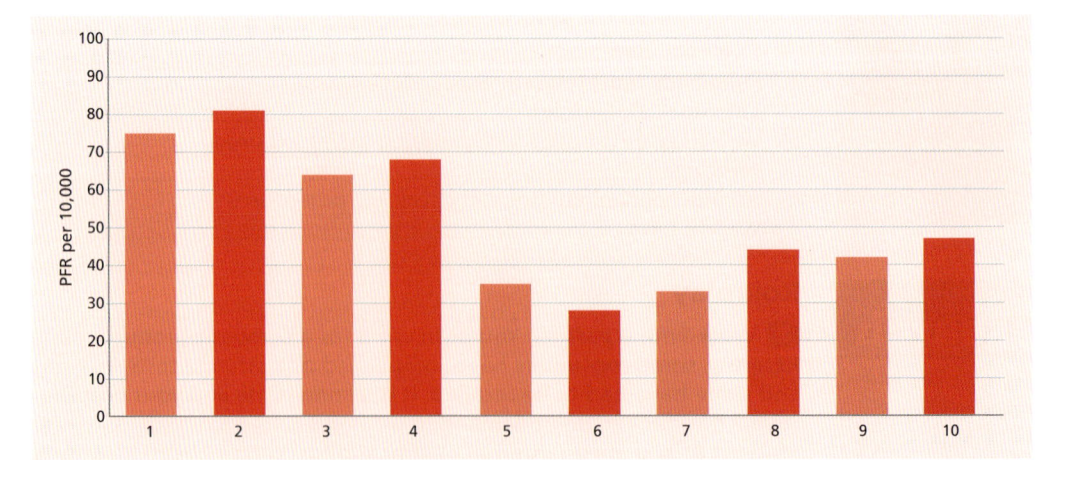

5 1:55 Listen to Marc's presentation and check your predictions.

6 1:55 Listen again and decide how well Marc presents his information. Use the ideas in Exercises 2 and 3 to help you.

Signposting

7 🔊 1:55 With a partner, find suitable words to complete the useful expressions for signposting presentations in the checklist. Then listen again and check your answers.

Useful expressions: Signposting

Referring to graphics	Checking understanding
This graph _____ the … _____ you can see, …	Is that _____ so far? Does that make sense?
Digressing	**Ending one point**
Just to digress a moment … By the _____ …	I think that _____ … That's all I want to say about …
Restating/reformulating	**Moving on**
In other _____, … What I mean is …	So, now let's turn to … Now, I'd like to _____ at … Anyway, …
Emphasizing	
And _____, that's why … I must emphasize that …	

Glossary — PAGE 152

acronym
digress
jargon
make or break
signposting

Presentation

8 You are committee members of your company's sports and social club. You have a budget of £450 to spend on one of the products below. Work in three groups, A, B and C, to prepare a short presentation of your product to persuade the committee to buy it. Use the presentation outline to help you, and prepare one or two slides to illustrate your talk.

Presentation outline
Technical facts and figures
Advantages (and disadvantages?)
Why the product is a better choice than the other two
Conclusion

eWorkbook
Now watch the video for this unit.

9 Take turns to present your product. After each talk, give feedback on clarity and impact using the table on page 121. As a committee, decide which product to buy.

Internet research
Search for the keywords *presentation signposting* and see how many other expressions you can find. List your five favourites and share them with the class.

A Dishwasher

Water consumption	16 l/load
Energy rating	A
Energy consumption	1.1 kWh
Capacity	12 place settings
Noise rating	45 dB
Price	£334

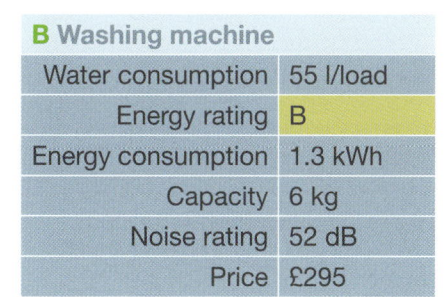

B Washing machine

Water consumption	55 l/load
Energy rating	B
Energy consumption	1.3 kWh
Capacity	6 kg
Noise rating	52 dB
Price	£295

C Espresso coffee machine

Water consumption	0.4 l/4 cups
Energy rating	A
Energy consumption	1.25 kWh
Capacity	4 cups/minute
Noise rating	n/a
Price	£423

3 Quality

- level of formality
- formal and informal expressions
- writing emails

3.5 Writing Emailing: quality problems

Discussion

1 In small groups, look at the quality problems below and answer these questions.

1. How could each problem impact on operations in a company?
2. What would you ask a supplier to do to solve the problem?

- A rented photocopier is out of order for the third time in a week
- A new lab-ware washing machine has a major design flaw
- Pallets of goods are often damaged in transit
- A subcontractor has just delivered 5,000 faulty sensors to the car production line

Model

2 Read the three emails on the left and match them with the replies on the right.

1

> **EMAIL**
>
> Dear Ms Luce,
>
> Due to unacceptable scratch marks, our QA Department has had to quarantine 45 of the batch of 100 dashboard modules delivered to the FX8 production line this morning.
>
> As you are aware, if we are forced to stop the production line, the normal penalty clauses will take immediate effect. So, in our mutual interest, I would be grateful if you could give this matter your immediate attention.
>
> Please could you keep me informed of what action you intend to take?
>
> Yours sincerely,
> Abdel Bakkar

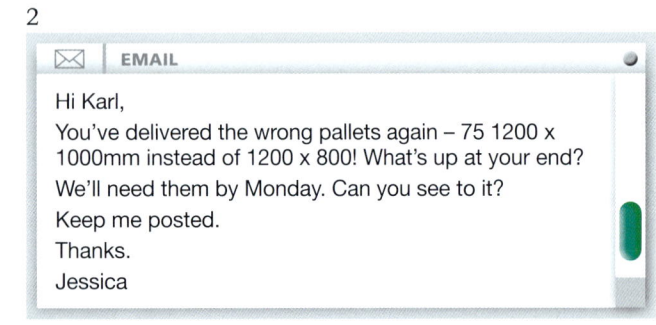

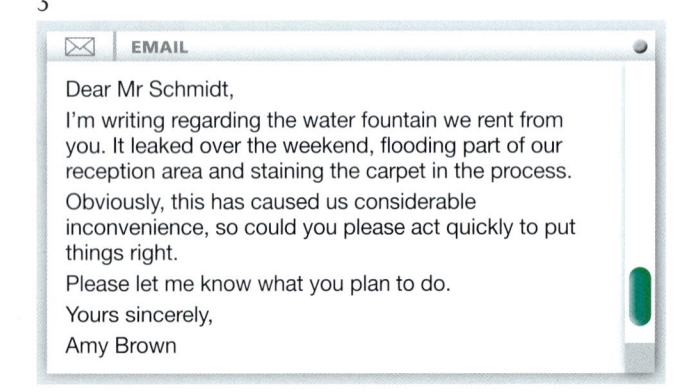

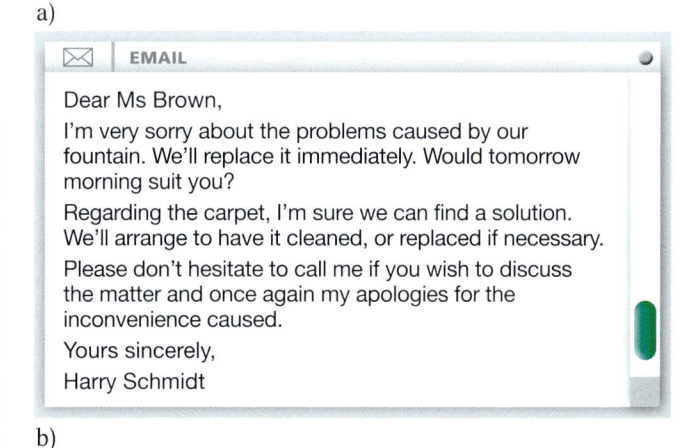

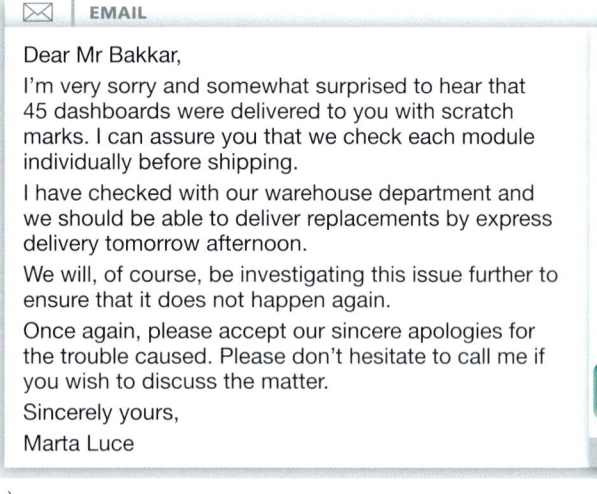

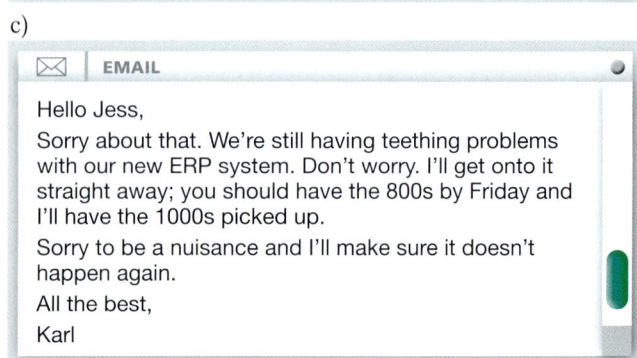

2

> **EMAIL**
>
> Hi Karl,
>
> You've delivered the wrong pallets again – 75 1200 x 1000mm instead of 1200 x 800! What's up at your end?
> We'll need them by Monday. Can you see to it?
> Keep me posted.
> Thanks.
> Jessica

3

> **EMAIL**
>
> Dear Mr Schmidt,
>
> I'm writing regarding the water fountain we rent from you. It leaked over the weekend, flooding part of our reception area and staining the carpet in the process.
>
> Obviously, this has caused us considerable inconvenience, so could you please act quickly to put things right.
>
> Please let me know what you plan to do.
>
> Yours sincerely,
> Amy Brown

a)

> **EMAIL**
>
> Dear Ms Brown,
>
> I'm very sorry about the problems caused by our fountain. We'll replace it immediately. Would tomorrow morning suit you?
>
> Regarding the carpet, I'm sure we can find a solution. We'll arrange to have it cleaned, or replaced if necessary.
>
> Please don't hesitate to call me if you wish to discuss the matter and once again my apologies for the inconvenience caused.
>
> Yours sincerely,
> Harry Schmidt

b)

> **EMAIL**
>
> Dear Mr Bakkar,
>
> I'm very sorry and somewhat surprised to hear that 45 dashboards were delivered to you with scratch marks. I can assure you that we check each module individually before shipping.
>
> I have checked with our warehouse department and we should be able to deliver replacements by express delivery tomorrow afternoon.
>
> We will, of course, be investigating this issue further to ensure that it does not happen again.
>
> Once again, please accept our sincere apologies for the trouble caused. Please don't hesitate to call me if you wish to discuss the matter.
>
> Sincerely yours,
> Marta Luce

c)

> **EMAIL**
>
> Hello Jess,
>
> Sorry about that. We're still having teething problems with our new ERP system. Don't worry. I'll get onto it straight away; you should have the 800s by Friday and I'll have the 1000s picked up.
>
> Sorry to be a nuisance and I'll make sure it doesn't happen again.
>
> All the best,
> Karl

Analysis

3 Work with a partner. Put the emails in Exercise 2 on the scale below, according to their level of formality. Does the potential impact on business affect the level of formality used?

informal ◄─────────────── neutral ───────────────► formal

Glossary	PAGE 152
batch	
dashboard	
ERP	
flaw	
pallet	
stain	
teething problems	
vial	

Language focus

4 Find more informal and more formal expressions in the emails in Exercise 2 to complete the table. Compare your answers with a partner.

	More informal	Neutral	More formal
Asking for action		Could you please act quickly to …?	
Promising action		We'll replace it … We'll arrange to …	
Reassuring		I'm sure we can find a solution.	
Asking to be contacted/updated		Please let me know what you plan to do.	
Apologizing		I'm very sorry about … My apologies for …	

Output

5 Work in groups of three. Decide who is A, B and C. Together, read the notes below and decide if the situation requires an informal, neutral or formal email. Then, write an email to your supplier to explain the quality problem and request action. Send your emails: A to B, B to C and C to A. Write an appropriate reply to the email you receive.

Internet research

Search for the keywords *email phrase bank* to find some more key expressions you can use in emails. Choose the five most useful and report back to the class.

A
We can't use the latest batch of vials (10,000) delivered last week as some of them are slightly bigger than normal and get stuck in the filling machine. We have enough stock for this week but need replacements by next Monday.
Contact: George Ramos

B
The forklift truck we bought from a new supplier last month has broken down again – this is the third time in the last two weeks. The technician sent to repair it has changed several parts but can't find the real cause. We need a vehicle we can rely on!
Contact: Ciara Leone

C
Our cleaning company has forgotten to put bin liners in the recycling bins. It's not a major issue but we need to send them a quick reminder to do it before the weekend.
Contact: Amanda Simmons

3 Quality

- quality control
- presenting recommendations for improving quality

3.6 Case study — Zaluski Strawberries

Discussion

1 With a partner, decide whether the following facts about strawberries are *T* (true) or *F* (false).

STRAWBERRY FACTS

1. Strawberries are rich in Vitamin D and low in fibre.
2. They contain no fat, cholesterol or salt.
3. Spain is the biggest producer of strawberries in the world.
4. The Romans cultivated strawberries as early as 200 BC.
5. Strawberries are members of the rose family.
6. They are unique, being the only fruit with seeds on the outside.
7. In medieval times, strawberries were regarded as an aphrodisiac. A soup made of strawberries and sour cream was traditionally served to newlyweds.
8. The word 'strawberry' comes from laying straw under the plants to protect the fruit.
9. Unlike many fruits, strawberries do not continue to ripen after harvest.

Reading

2 Read the internal email from a supermarket chain with outlets in the Netherlands and Belgium, and the extract from a strawberry cooperative's brochure. Answer the questions.

1. What expectations would consumers normally have about the quality of strawberries?
2. Why has the quality of incoming strawberries become an issue?
3. Why do you think Schuurman and Zaluski may have different views on quality?
4. What will Suzanne's next course of action be?

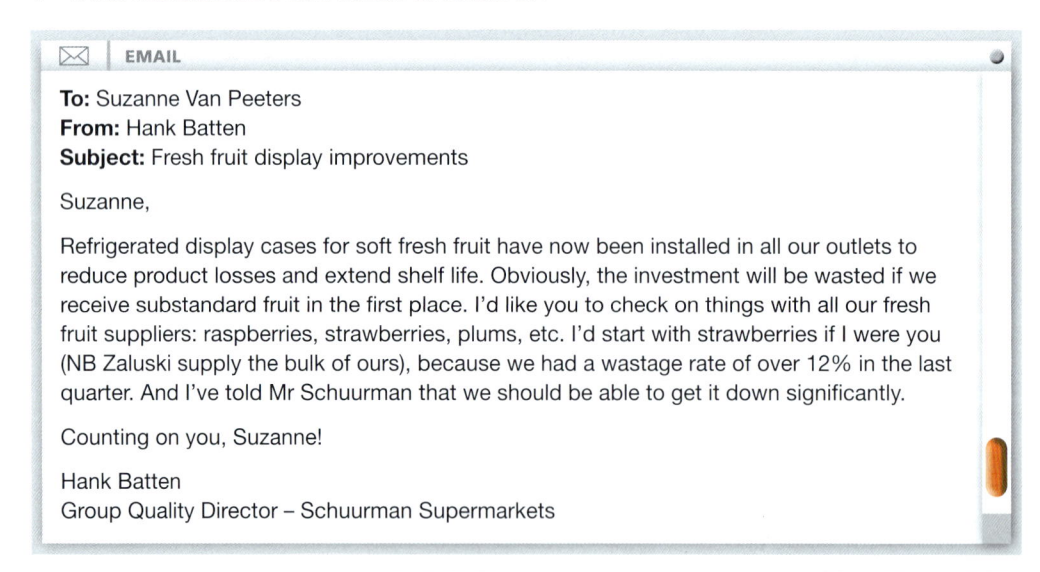

EMAIL

To: Suzanne Van Peeters
From: Hank Batten
Subject: Fresh fruit display improvements

Suzanne,

Refrigerated display cases for soft fresh fruit have now been installed in all our outlets to reduce product losses and extend shelf life. Obviously, the investment will be wasted if we receive substandard fruit in the first place. I'd like you to check on things with all our fresh fruit suppliers: raspberries, strawberries, plums, etc. I'd start with strawberries if I were you (NB Zaluski supply the bulk of ours), because we had a wastage rate of over 12% in the last quarter. And I've told Mr Schuurman that we should be able to get it down significantly.

Counting on you, Suzanne!

Hank Batten
Group Quality Director – Schuurman Supermarkets

… **THE ZALUSKI COOPERATIVE**, which represents nearly 50 small producers in the Pakość area, has been packing and distributing strawberries for more than 40 years. Traditional farming techniques, allied with the careful selection of appropriate strawberry varieties, ensure that we produce Polish strawberries of unrivalled quality.

Internet research

Search for the keywords *strawberry quality* to discover more about the main factors influencing the quality of strawberries you buy in the shops.

Listening for gist

3 🔊 1:56 Listen to the telephone conversation between Suzanne Van Peeters, Schuurman's Quality Manager, and Piotr Sieberski, Managing Director of Zaluski Strawberries. What is the purpose of Suzanne's call?

Reading for detail

4 Read the information below. Underline the main points Suzanne will need to raise during her audit meeting.

Key factors affecting strawberry quality and recommended best practice

TEMPERATURE
Less than a one-hour delay between harvest and the cooling of berries in the cooler is recommended. This means regular collection of picked fruit and frequent trips to the cooler.

Upon arrival at the cooler, fruit should be cooled to 0–1°C before being placed in the
5 storage room to await packing. Cold storage air temperatures should be monitored and records maintained.

When shipping by road, trucks should be cooled to near 0°C before loading. The refrigeration system must be checked on each load.

The golden rule is *Don't break the cold chain*. Once strawberries have been cooled after
10 picking, they should be kept cold until 30 minutes before eating.

PACKING
Care should be taken to pack only sound fruit from harvesting trays to punnets. Decaying, damaged or shrivelled fruit should be removed.

HANDLING
Strawberries are very fragile and bruise easily. Careful handling and sorting during harvest is needed.
15 Training and supervision of harvesting teams is critical. Harvesters should be given an incentive to pick with care. Crew supervisors should monitor harvested trays to ensure that only sound fruit are being placed in them. Shallow trays should be used to prevent squashing (no more than 5cm in depth).

RIPENESS
Strawberries do not continue to ripen after harvest and will not increase in sugar
20 content. Riper fruit tends to have a high sugar content and better flavour quality. Pick only ripe fruit, generally pink or red in colour.

CULTIVATION
The use of heavy nitrogen fertilization has been associated with softer fruit and less flavour.

Listening for detail

5 🔊 1:57 Listen to Suzanne's audit meeting with Piotr Sieberski and Klara Solak, the packing shed supervisor. Complete Suzanne's notes below.

Audit meeting – points to raise

Harvesting procedures
No (1) _____ paid for quality fruit.
Pickers receive little (2) _____ .

Transport
Strawberries are placed in trays (3) _____ deep.
Transport to cooler takes (4) _____ hours.

Cooling process
Berries are cooled to (5) _____ .
They keep no (6) _____ of storage shed temperatures.

Packing procedures
Packers receive little (7) _____ .
No (8) _____ is paid for good packing.

Shipping
The (9) _____ on each truck is not always checked.

Cultivation
The use of nitrogen fertilizers will stop in (10) _____ years.

Glossary PAGE 153
bruise
bulk
harvest
shallow
shelf life
sound
tray
wastage

Presentation

6 Work in small groups. You are quality consultants to Schuurman Supermarkets. Prepare a presentation of your recommendations for improvements to Zaluski's procedures to ensure top quality strawberries. Make your presentations and hold a class vote for the best one.

4 Feedback

- team-building strategies
- project management

4.1 About business The project team

Discussion

1 With a partner, discuss the meaning of these statements. Choose the two that you think are closest to the truth. Explain your choice to another pair.

Project management and team-building quotes
Nothing is impossible for the person who doesn't have to do it.
If you're six months late on a milestone due next week but still believe you can make it, you're a project manager.
There is no 'I' in teamwork.
If you don't know where you're going, any road will take you there.
Getting good players is easy. What's difficult is getting them to play together.

Listening

2 1:58 Listen to part of a project review meeting. What is being built? Which two stages of the project caused the delays? Choose from the list.

a) Land purchase
b) Project approval
c) Feasibility study
d) Geological survey
e) Excavation for foundations
f) Dam construction
g) Resettlement
h) River diversion

3 1:58 The Gantt chart relates to the updated schedule. Listen again and complete the stages in the chart.

Project schedule																																																
	Year 1											Year 2												Year 3												Year 4											
	J	F	M	A	M	J	J	A	S	O	N	D	J	F	M	A	M	J	J	A	S	O	N	D	J	F	M	A	M	J	J	A	S	O	N	D	J	F	M	A	M	J	J	A	S	O	N	D
Logistics	Feasibility study											Project approval						(2) _____																	Resettlement												
Engineering	(1) _____																															(3) _____					Excavation								(4) _____	

Reading

4 Read the first three paragraphs of the article opposite. Answer these questions.

1 What examples of 'ineffective team-building activities' does the author mention?
2 Why do companies continue to run them?

5 Read the rest of the article. Match the advice a–d with gaps 1–4 in the article.

a) Create an open and honest atmosphere.
b) Learn from the best leaders.
c) Have a common plan.
d) Focus on a clear objective.

6 Which essential team-building characteristic is missing in each situation 1–4?

1 We're going round in circles. It's like a ship without a captain!
2 The project scope is too wide and unclear.
3 I think we all know where we're going, but we have different views on how to get there.
4 We all get on OK, but everyone's too politically correct.

Internet research
Search for the keywords *Gantt charts* to discover more about them. How many different types of chart exist and how are they used in project management? Report back to the class.

Discussion

7 In small groups, discuss the questions.

1 Have you ever played volleyball? What are the principles of the game?
2 Volleyball has often been called the ultimate team sport. Why is this, and what lessons can be applied to project management?
3 What lessons can be learned from other team sports or group activities (e.g. playing in a band)?

SMELLS LIKE TEAM SPIRIT

Weekend retreats and touchy-feely exercises may do more to create bad feeling than build teams. Instead, take some lessons from a winning volleyball coach.

It's time someone finally said it: most of what passes for team-building these days doesn't really build teams. So why do companies spend millions of dollars annually to make their employees go through ineffective team-building activities: walking around in blindfolds, navigating rope courses, and sitting cross-legged on the floor with paper and crayons, illustrating their 'life paths'?

There are three reasons. While it's generally recognized that a great team will beat a mediocre team 99 times out of 100, little hard thinking goes on at most companies about how effective teams are actually built. Employees usually don't complain about silly team-building efforts, whether out of apathy or for fear of being labelled 'anti-team'. And thirdly, most team-building practitioners are well-meaning, sincere people whom no one wants to offend.

So if conventional team-building activities are largely ineffective, how do you build a great team? In 1978, I played a supporting role on a volleyball team that won the first National Championship in our university's history. That team was made up of people who weren't the most physically-gifted athletes in the world. But they merged into a force that was far greater than the sum of the players' individual abilities.

Nearly 30 years later, what I learned that season remains one of the most important lessons of my life. Great teams – whether composed of athletes, businesspeople, fire-fighters, military commandos, or what have you – teach us four key lessons:

1 _____. One of the most memorable features of my 1978 team was the level of intensity which the players brought to every practice and game. The atmosphere was charged with an emotional commitment that caused members of the team to constantly push each other to give everything in service of the goal.

Far too often, a company thinks it has a team-building problem when what it really has is a goal problem. If you want to build a great team, make sure its members share a determined passion to accomplish something. How do you get that kind of commitment? By involving everyone in the development of the goal.

2 _____. It's not enough to get a bunch of people together who care deeply about reaching a goal. They need to have a strategy for achieving it. The best team-building tool ever is a good strategy that everyone buys into. If you want to increase teamwork, don't focus on the team, focus the team on the task.

My team coach had a detailed strategy for winning that the players bought into completely. A part of the strategy was to overcome our physical shortcomings with a commitment to superior conditioning and training. So, for two months the team endured a schedule so demanding that it was the talk of the campus.

3 _____. Yes, trust and respect are key. But ironically, often the best way to increase levels of trust and respect on a team is to get them focused on the goal and the strategy. This gets people saying what they really think. When people say what they really think and are held accountable, trust and respect usually follow. Don't impose an atmosphere of false politeness.

There was plenty of conflict on the team and people sometimes lost their tempers. But on the court an atmosphere of respect always prevailed. All great business teams share that same quality.

4 _____. There's no getting around it: great teams usually have great managers. My old team coach still coaches volleyball at that same university today. He has an unrivalled 426–162 win-loss record and has also coached a US team to a World Championship and an Olympic gold medal.

So, learn how to be a great coach. Aspiring business leaders would be a lot better off if they spent less time reading management literature and more time around people like my old coach. The great college coaches may know more about team-building than anyone else in the world. After all, their leadership and team-building skills are measured in real time, in front of real crowds. And they start from scratch with a new team every year.

Glossary	PAGE 153

accomplish
aspiring
bunch
buy into
milestone
offend
scope
start from scratch

4 Feedback

- character descriptions
- adjectives to describe character
- collocations relating to project management

4.2 Vocabulary Managing people and projects

Discussion

1 With a partner, match the character types in the box with the descriptions a–e. Which type would be the most difficult to manage, and why? Which type are you?

> the bully   the leader   the maverick   the team player   the workaholic

a) This character does things their own way. They may be effective, but they're difficult to control.
b) This person has a natural ability to encourage others and take a project through to success.
c) This person doesn't know when to stop, and they often believe the office would collapse without them.
d) This person imposes their personality on others, making other people feel bad in the workplace.
e) This person has a natural ability to fit in. They make positive contributions and build good relationships.

2 Which character types in Exercise 1 do you associate with the adjectives in the box?

> aggressive   anxious   charismatic   confident   cooperative   decisive   easy-going
> friendly   helpful   impatient   independent   individual   motivating   obsessive
> over-critical   single-minded   stressed   unpredictable

Listening

3 🔊 1:59 Listen to an HR manager and a line manager talking about three members of their team. Decide which of the character types in Exercise 1 describes each person.

Anna _____   Bjorn _____   Katia _____

4 🔊 1:59 Listen again. Which adjectives do you hear that confirm your answers in Exercise 3?

Expressions

5 The expressions in bold were all in the recording. Match expressions 1–8 with the replies a–h. Use a dictionary to help you if necessary.

1 Marion is in danger of **burning out**.
2 How are you **settling in**?
3 If we want to succeed, we must **pull together**.
4 He's always **passing the buck**!
5 She **gets on well with** everyone.
6 Don't **let me down**, will you?
7 Dave isn't **pulling his weight**!
8 You should learn to **take it easy**.

a) Except Rob, but he doesn't like anyone!
b) I wish I could, but things are just too hectic.
c) I know. He asked me to do his report for him!
d) No, you can rely on me.
e) Perhaps we should run a team-building course?
f) Yes. She's a workaholic. It's affecting her health.
g) You're right, and that means more work for us!
h) Fine, thanks, though I still don't know everyone.

Internet research

Search for the keywords *project management tips* and decide whether you would make a good or bad project manager. Prepare a one-minute talk to the class to explain your decision.

Defining words

6 Match the people involved in a project in 1–5 with the definitions a–e.

1 Sponsor
2 Project manager
3 Project team members
4 End users
5 Key stakeholders

a) The people who will benefit from the end results of the project on a day-to-day basis.
b) The person or group of people who decided the project was needed in the first place.
c) Anybody who might be affected by the project, whether positively or negatively.
d) The person responsible for running the project and delivering on time and within budget.
e) Staff chosen for the skills they can bring to the project, often from different departments.

7 Read the list of people or groups involved in or affected by a motorway construction project. Match them with the key players 1–5 in Exercise 6.

a) truck and car drivers
b) the Ministry of Transport
c) a senior engineer in a major civil engineering company
d) a plant hire company, an environmental protection group and villagers living near the proposed route
e) a civil engineer, a surveyor, an environmental engineer and a transport consultant

Collocations

8 Complete the sentences with the correct form of the verbs in the box. In some sentences, more than one verb is possible.

| achieve | establish | fix | meet | miss | reach | set | stick to |

1 Unless the team really pulls together, we'll never _____ **the deadline** on the Malaysian order.
2 The project has been difficult so far. However, once we _____ **the next milestone**, everything should get easier.
3 To make sense of our tasks, we need to _____ **a timeframe** within which we can all work.
4 Frank is such an unreasonable boss: he always _____ **our targets** for overseas sales too high.
5 Congratulations! We've _____ **our targets** for quality this year due to all your hard work.
6 We've been vague about the schedule for too long. It's time we _____ **a date** for definite and moved on.
7 In the end, I _____ **my deadline** for my accountancy project, but it didn't matter: everybody else was late too.
8 Sam's excellent at getting things done on time, but she finds it impossible to _____ **her budget**.

Glossary PAGE 153

appraisal interview
bully
hectic
loner
maverick
milestone
pass the buck
pull your weight

Discussion

9 In small groups, take turns to describe your personality, your strengths and weaknesses, and what you would be good or bad at doing in a project.

4 Feedback

- modals + *have* + past participle
- third conditional
- *used to*; *be/get used to*

4.3 Grammar Regrets, speculation and habits

Past modals

1 Work with a partner. Speculate about what happened in the photo and where it was taken. Then change partners and exchange your ideas.

There might have been a tornado.
The photo could have been taken in the USA.

Refresh your memory

Past modals
Use modal + *have* + past participle.
We *would have hired* him but he moved abroad.
For past regrets, use *should/ought to/could* + *have* + past participle.
I *could have studied* another language at school, but I wasn't interested then.
For past speculation, use *may/might/could/must* + *have* + past participle.
You *must have left* the door unlocked when you went out.

Third conditional
Use *If* + past perfect in the condition. Use *would have* + past participle in the result.
If we *had spent* more on marketing, we *would have sold* more units.

Past state or habit
used to + infinitive
We *used to work* in a smaller office.

Familiarity with a strange or difficult situation
be/get used to + verb + *-ing*/noun/pronoun
We're *getting used to* the new management team.

▶ Grammar and practice pages 128–129

Regrets and third conditionals

2 With a partner, read the Fukushima Facts below. Say how the Fukushima nuclear accident, which resulted from a tsunami, could have been avoided or its impact reduced. Take turns to suggest what they *should/ought to/could have done* (A) and react using the third conditional (B), as in the example.

A: *They shouldn't have built the power plant on the coast.*
B: *Yes, if they'd built it inland, it **wouldn't/might not have been damaged**.*

Fukushima Facts

- ☢ The Fukushima power plant was built on the coast.
- ☢ It was built in a seismic area.
- ☢ The tsunami wave was 14 metres high.
- ☢ The plant was designed to resist a wave of 5.7 metres high.
- ☢ 80,000 people living in a 20 km radius of the plant were evacuated.
- ☢ TEPCO, the plant's operator, ignored the findings of a tsunami study in 2008.
- ☢ The plant's electricity supply was completely cut off as emergency generators were destroyed by the tsunami.
- ☢ Without electricity, it was impossible to pump cooling water to cool the reactors.

Used to, *be used to* and *get used to*

3 In small groups, brainstorm the situation before and after the Fukushima disaster. Think about:

- how things used to be
- how things are now
- what people are used to/are not used to
- what people have had to get used to.

Use the topics in the box to help you. When you've finished, report your ideas to the class.

| business | college | housing | jobs | production | school | staff | transport |

*I think many people **used to work** in businesses near the plant. A lot of businesses are probably still not up and running yet. I don't think these people **are used to** their new lives yet. They've probably **had to get used to** working elsewhere.*

Regrets

4 The photos show two people whose career paths have been very different. Which person regrets their decisions more?

Yeah, I remember Kim. I studied business administration at college with her. We had a great time. I took a job as a trainee accountant in London at the same firm as her. But I felt it just wasn't for me. I was earning good money, and they offered me a salary of £45,000 just to stay, but I said no. Instead, I downshifted. I left to become a dairy farmer. When I look at the people I used to work with, we're really different now. They live in nice houses and drive expensive cars. But overall, I think I made the right choice. I'm really happy on my farm. And I'm not at all stressed.

GRANT

I studied business administration at college, but I didn't really enjoy it. I always really wanted to be a vet, but I made the wrong study choices. In the end, I joined an accountancy firm. Now I'm a senior partner, which means I have a great salary. But I sometimes think there's something missing. My friend Grant, who joined the same time as me, left after a few years to start a farm. He asked me to help him set it up, but I said no. I think it was the wrong choice. He says his job's not at all stressful, but mine is constant pressure.

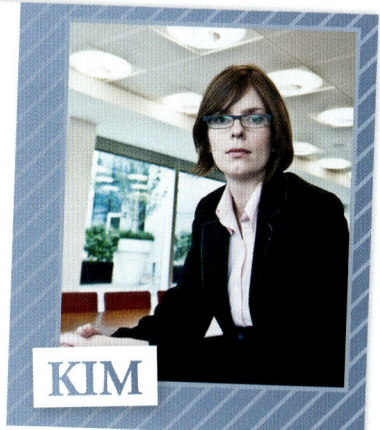

KIM

Glossary PAGE 153

downshift
evacuate
generator
impact
reactor
seismic
turn down

5 Complete the sentences with appropriate past modal forms of the verbs in brackets.
1. Grant _____ (have) a career as an accountant, but he left.
2. Grant _____ (earn) £45,000 or more, but he turned it down.
3. In the end, Grant doesn't think that he _____ (stay) at the accountancy firm.
4. Kim thinks she _____ (study) to become a vet, not an accountant.
5. Kim now thinks that she _____ (leave) the accountancy firm and started a business with Grant, but she said no.
6. Kim _____ (live) a less stressful life on a farm.

6 Complete the sentences with your own ideas, based on the stories about Grant and Kim.
1. If Grant had stayed at the accountancy firm, …
2. If Kim had studied to become a vet, …
3. If Grant hadn't become a farmer, …
4. If Kim had helped Grant start his farm, …

7 Look at the activities in the box. Which are part of Grant's past? Which are part of his life now?

earn a lot of money   have a slow pace of life   run my own business   work in London
work under pressure   work with animals

Internet research

Search for the keyword *downshifting* to discover more about this trend. Make notes on the different forms of downshifting and decide which you would adopt if you had the chance. Give a one-minute presentation of your idea to the class and vote for the best one.

8 Write sentences about Grant using the ideas in Exercise 7. Use *used to* or *be used to* and the correct form of the verb.

Discussion

9 Imagine you have recently quit a very well-paid business job to start a different life on a farm. Use the ideas in the box to imagine your life in the city and your life now.

food   holidays   home   how you spend your money   means of transport
social life   typical day

10 In groups, exchange memories of how you used to live. Say what you are finding it hard to get used to now.

4 Feedback

- procedures for coaching team members
- expressions for coaching
- roleplaying an interview

4.4 Speaking Coaching

Discussion

1 Decide how you would respond as a manager to each of these situations. Choose options from the list a–l.

1. A new employee has failed to complete an important project.
2. An experienced employee has failed to complete an important project.
3. A new employee has delighted customers with exceptional service.
4. An experienced employee has delighted customers with exceptional service.

a) fire the employee
b) supervise the employee more closely
c) scream and shout for twenty minutes
d) have a heart-to-heart talk to identify the causes
e) give them a final warning
f) do nothing
g) pay them a bonus
h) give them more autonomy
i) thank them for their hard work
j) give them a promotion
k) tell them not to overdo it
l) something else

Reading

2 Read the two procedures for coaching team members and explain why opinions a–f below are incorrect.

Recognizing merit

1. **Make contact**
   - Set the scene: describe the time, place and situation when the employee's performance was exceptional.
   - Refer to the work in question.
2. **Give praise**
   - Give a specific example of the facts or results you appreciate.
   - Point out the personal qualities which contributed to the employee's success.
3. **Conclusion**
   - Explain the positive consequences of the employee's behaviour for the company, the department and for you yourself.
   - Keep the interview short and avoid discussing other subjects: two or three minutes are usually enough.

Constructive criticism

1. **Make contact**
   - Set the scene: describe the time, place and situation when the problem occurred.
   - Describe the problem and the results.
   - State facts, not opinions.
2. **Diagnose the problem**
   - Elicit the causes of the problem (behaviour, method, equipment, organization, etc.).
   - Express your opinion.
   - Explain the consequences for the organization.
3. **Commit to action**
   - Offer suggestions which recognize the employee's good points but eliminate the faults.
   - Invite the employee to make comments.
4. **Conclusion**
   - Set new objectives, stating the methods to be used and a deadline.

a) Just let your people know if you're happy with their work: you don't need to go into details.
b) People know when they've messed up: they don't need me to tell them. I just shout to let them know how I feel about it.
c) Never mention an employee's qualities, next thing you know, they'll want a pay rise.
d) Don't expect your assistant to understand what went wrong; if she knew, she'd be doing your job!
e) Congratulating someone on a job well done is a good opportunity to set them more ambitious objectives.
f) If it works for the army, it works in business. Tell them to work harder, and no talking back!

Internet research

Search for the keywords *how to manage difficult people*. Draw up a list of your top ten tips.

Listening

3 🔊 1:60–1:61 Listen to two interviews between Mrs Gómez, a store manager in the Philippines, and Rafael, a department supervisor. Answer the questions.

1 What did Rafael **a)** do right and **b)** do wrong?
2 How do you think Rafael feels at the end of each interview?

4 🔊 1:60–1:61 With a partner, find suitable words to complete the useful expressions for coaching in the checklist. Then listen again and check your answers.

Useful expressions: Coaching

Setting the scene

As you _____, the last three weeks have been really busy.
It _____ there was a problem with …

Giving praise

_____ to you, everything has gone really smoothly.
I want to say how much I _____ your …
I'm very _____ for the support you have _____ me personally.
These are qualities the company _____.

Diagnosing a problem

Can you tell me _____ what _____?
Do you have any ideas _____ why …?

Committing to action

What do you think we can do to _____ this doesn't happen again?
So if you need help, you will _____ to me, won't you?

Concluding

Let's just _____ what we have agreed.
_____ in a month's time to see how you're getting on.
_____, Rafael, and thank you!

5 When giving constructive criticism, asking questions rather than making statements helps to reduce tension and establish a dialogue. Translate Mrs Gómez's thoughts into the questions you heard her use by putting the words into the correct order.

1 *I want to see you in my office, now!*
   Could / a / have / I / word / just / ?
2 *You should know better than to be rude to a customer!*
   You / afford / basic / can / can't / care / customer / forget / skills, / to / you / your / ?
3 *You're not a beginner any more!*
   You've / for, / been / now / three / us / what, / with / years / ?
4 *If this happens again, you're out!*
   You / can / consequences, / do / don't / have / kind / problem / this / of / realize / serious / you / ?
5 *That's all, we've already wasted enough time on this!*
   Is / add / anything / like / else / there / to / you'd / ?
6 *I take it you understand that.*
   Are / comfortable / that / with / you / ?

eWorkbook
Now watch the video for this unit.

Glossary PAGE 154

elicit
mess up
overdo
praise

Roleplay

6 With a partner, take turns to be a manager and an employee. Decide what the employee has done right or wrong, and roleplay interviews recognizing merit or giving constructive criticism. Follow the procedures in Exercise 2.

4 Feedback

- paragraph function
- linking words and expressions
- writing a report

4.5 Writing Reports

Discussion

1 Read the reasons for performance appraisals in the box. Decide which benefit the employer most and which benefit the employee.

> discussing rewards   encouraging communication
> identifying strengths and weaknesses   planning training
> reviewing progress   setting achievable goals   stating career objectives

2 With a partner, number the sections of a report in a logical order from 1–7.

☐ Introduction   ☐ Conclusions   ☐ Recommendations   ☐ Title
☐ Procedure   ☐ Findings   ☐ Executive summary

Model

3 Read the report and number the paragraphs in the correct order 1–6.

Introduction of annual appraisal interviews

☐ Firstly, Webwide Consulting used a system of anonymous questionnaires to investigate employee attitudes. For instance, some questions related to company image and job satisfaction. In addition, **interviews were held** with all staff.

☐ The Management Committee decided to engage Webwide Consulting on 11 October to advise on the possible introduction of formal appraisal interviews. **This decision was taken** owing to dissatisfaction with the existing system. This report covers the method by which **information was gathered** and sets out a plan for adopting appraisal interviews.

☐ **A survey was carried out by external consultants** regarding the possible introduction of formal annual appraisal interviews. Their findings clearly show that most staff and managers are in favour. Consequently, it is recommended that a formal system be set up as soon as possible.

☐ Three main areas of concern were revealed by the individual interviews.
  - Management are seen to lack interest in staff development.
  - Employees get little feedback on whether hard work is recognized.
  - Employees get no guidance on how to improve poor performance.

☐ 1 We should put in place a system of annual appraisal interviews within the next two months.
  2 Each interview should be 45 minutes in length due to the tight schedule.

☐ In conclusion, the survey results clearly show that a more formal approach to appraisal interviews would reduce staff turnover, increase motivation and foster team spirit.

Analysis

4 Answer the questions about the report in Exercise 3.

1 Which headings from Exercise 2 match the paragraphs in the report?
2 What other methods can be used to organize information in a report?

Internet research

Search for the keywords *plain English report writing* and write a short report on the advice you find. Exchange reports and give each other feedback.

Language focus

5 With a partner, match the linking words and expressions from the box with the categories a–e. Find examples of similar expressions in the report in Exercise 3.

| due to | finally | for example | moreover | next | overall | therefore | to sum up |

a) Sequencing
b) Giving examples
c) Adding
d) Expressing cause and result
e) Summarizing

6 Complete the sentences with appropriate linking phrases.

1. We wanted the survey to be anonymous. _____, names did not appear on the questionnaire.
2. Firstly, staff completed questionnaires. _____, they were interviewed by consultants.
3. The questionnaire covered job satisfaction. _____, some questions touched on company image.
4. Interviews were limited to 30 minutes each _____ the very tight schedule.
5. _____, the results were positive but we agreed that there were lessons to learn.
6. Formal appraisal interviews will be introduced _____ dissatisfaction with the existing system.
7. There are several reasons for adopting appraisal interviews, _____, they can motivate staff.

Output

7 It is possible to write a report in an active or passive style. An active style is more direct. A passive style is more impersonal. Make the report in Exercise 3 more direct by changing the phrases in **bold** to active sentences.

8 Look at the email and the notes below. What does your boss want you to do?

✉ **EMAIL**

From: Lou Tyler

Subject: Annual appraisal review

Remember when we set up the appraisal scheme last year, we agreed on a review after one year? Well, the review is finished and I attended a meeting on it yesterday. I've left the notes I took on your desk. I don't have much time to do the report so could you do a first draft?

APPRAISAL SCHEME REVIEW
- Appraisal interviews: done in December by line managers.
- During interviews: we asked for their feedback on the scheme. Most positive. One or two objections: lack of time (interviews too short – just 45mins); and lack of 'objective measurement of performance'.
- Overall, positive. Increase the time allocated (one hour? trial next year).
- Fred Berger (HR) to develop more objective performance indicators (targets to reach, etc.). Will report in January.
- Final scheme to be approved by Board of Directors.

9 Write a short report for your boss using the company template to help you.

Title

Introduction – Explain the background to the report and why you are writing it.

Procedure – How was information gathered?

Findings – What information was gathered?

Conclusions – What conclusions can you draw?

Recommendations – What recommendations can you make?

4 Feedback

- business methods in other countries
- discussing problems and solutions
- roleplaying meetings to set objectives

4.6 Case study　Trident Overseas

Discussion

1 Imagine you are working on a different continent from your own in which the business culture is different. Answer the questions.

1. In your opinion, can the same business methods and ethical standards be applied all over the world? Should they be adapted to local culture?
2. What cultural differences might you find? Consider these categories.

> management style　personal development
> productivity　recruitment　time management

Reading for detail

2 Trident is a British-based oil company which operates in Africa. Read the magazine article and the email from a sales manager. Answer the questions.

1. What determines petrol prices?
2. Why is customer service important?
3. How do local managers often behave?
4. Who owns the stations?
5. Why has John Thorpe been out of the office?
6. What did he find out?

TRIDENT — PUT THE SERVICE BACK IN STATION

Drivers in Europe and America have become accustomed to buying petrol in deserted, fully automated petrol stations. In Africa, however, customers are greeted with a friendly
5　smile and a polite welcome as they are directed to the appropriate pump. They can then sit back and watch uniformed forecourt staff fill the tank, top up the oil and wash the windscreen.

With extreme driving conditions, few new cars
10　and little available income for engine repairs, oil sales are strategic and highly profitable. In many African countries, petrol prices are government-regulated, so quality of service is the crucial factor in attracting customers who will buy oil as well
15　as petrol. At Trident, staff training is a priority; management aim to ensure that customers keep coming back for friendly service and expert advice.

✉ EMAIL

From: John Thorpe

Thanks for your email. Sorry I've taken so long to answer. Remember I told you I wanted to get out of the office more? Well, here I am in Kenya! I've just started a new job as sales manager for the southern region – from Nairobi to the Indian Ocean, down to Mombasa near the border with Tanzania.

Business in Africa can be very hierarchical; there are some really good managers, but for a lot of them, their idea of getting things done is to keep shouting until they get what they want. That's going to change! I have three district managers, who each have a team of sales reps who travel around the district meeting dealers. Some of the dealers own their service stations, so we have to handle them with kid gloves, or they'll just go over to the competition. More and more, we have what we call Young Dealers – employees who we train up to run the company-owned stations. So directly or indirectly, there are three layers of management between me and the forecourt staff and mechanics – sometimes all shouting as loud as they can!

In fact, there's been a lot of shouting in the Lamu district, and I've just come back to Nairobi from a three-day fact-finding trip. Their development project is way behind schedule, so I went down to have a word with the people in the field. It turns out it's quite a mess, and I could do with some help to sort it out, actually.

3 Complete the organizational chart for Trident in East Africa.

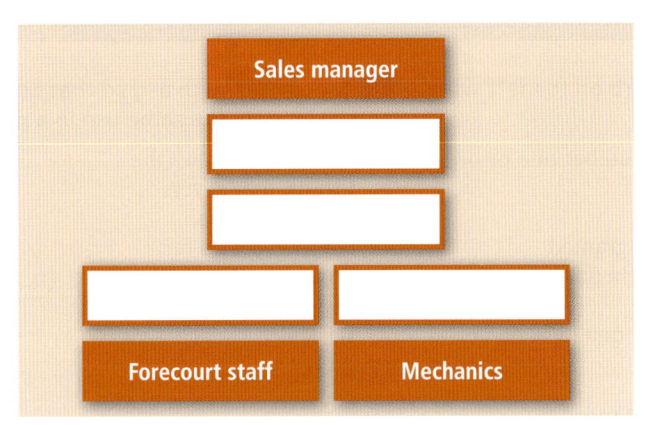

```
            [ Sales manager ]
                  |
            [              ]
                  |
            [              ]
               /     \
    [Forecourt staff] [Mechanics]
```

Glossary   PAGE 154

- could do with something
- dealer
- handle someone with kid gloves
- mess
- put up with
- sort out
- top up
- work your fingers to the bone

Listening

4 John Thorpe spoke to three Trident employees on his fact-finding trip. Before you listen, read the notes and add the four names mentioned to the organizational chart.

5 🔊 1:62–1:64 Listen to extracts from the interviews and complete the notes.

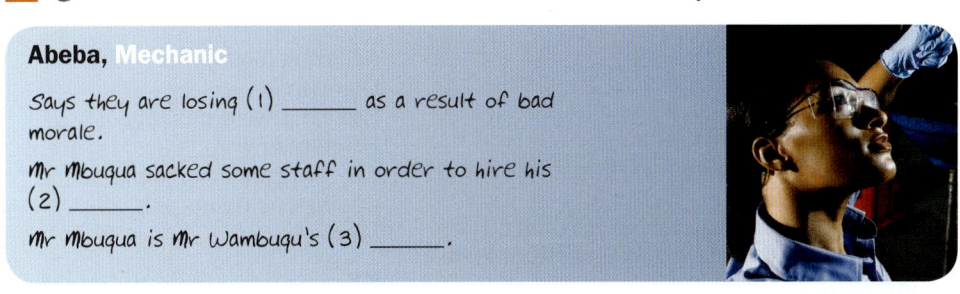

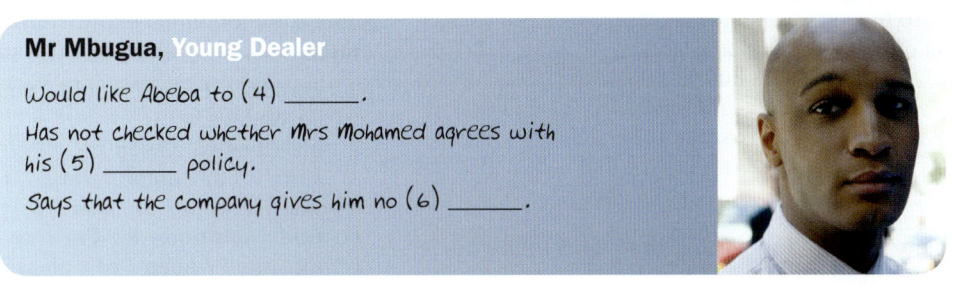

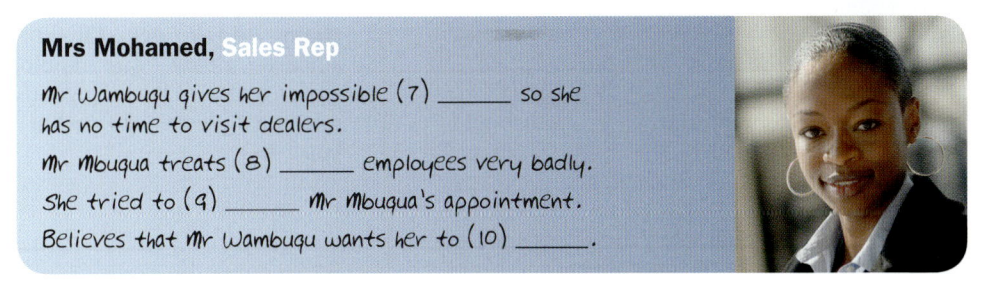

Abeba, Mechanic
Says they are losing (1) _____ as a result of bad morale.
Mr Mbugua sacked some staff in order to hire his (2) _____.
Mr Mbugua is Mr Wambugu's (3) _____.

Mr Mbugua, Young Dealer
Would like Abeba to (4) _____.
Has not checked whether Mrs Mohamed agrees with his (5) _____ policy.
Says that the company gives him no (6) _____.

Mrs Mohamed, Sales Rep
Mr Wambugu gives her impossible (7) _____ so she has no time to visit dealers.
Mr Mbugua treats (8) _____ employees very badly.
She tried to (9) _____ Mr Mbugua's appointment.
Believes that Mr Wambugu wants her to (10) _____.

Discussion and roleplay

6 John Thorpe has asked for your advice on handling the situation in the Lamu District. In small groups, discuss the problems and brainstorm possible solutions.

7 🔊 1:65 Listen to a voicemail message from Mr Wambugu. How does this affect your strategy?

8 With a partner from another group, roleplay meetings with Abeba, Mr Mbugua and Mr Wambugu to explain what action you have decided to take and, where appropriate, set new objectives.

Internet research

Search for the keywords *managing your manager* to find tips on how to develop a better working relationship with your boss. What advice would you give the Kenyan Trident employees on managing their respective bosses?

Review 3

Quality

1 Make expressions by matching a verb on the left with the words on the right.

1. struggle
2. take
3. make
4. fall into
5. become
6. appeal to
7. get
8. adopt

a) something a number one priority
b) an end in itself
c) to keep up
d) something for granted
e) a person's aesthetic sense
f) a trap
g) TQM or other quality schemes
h) the job done

2 Find an expression in Exercise 1 that means:

a) have difficulty in continuing to do something well ☐
b) expect something to always happen in a particular way, and not think about any possible problems ☐
c) develop into an activity you do for its own sake ☐

3 Fill in the missing letters to complete the text about different ideas of quality.

To the marketing manager, quality is about (1) m_ _ _ing the customer's needs and (2) ex_ _ _ _ _ _ions.
To the design engineer, who works with tight (3) spec_ _ _ _ations and strict (4) tol_ _ _ _ces, quality is about whether the design is (5) f_ _ for pur_ _ _e, and whether the product (6) perf_ _ms its intended functions. To the process engineer, quality is about using (7) l_ _n manufacturing to ensure that there is minimum (8) w_ _ _e (of effort, money, time and materials). To the quality auditor, quality means the correct application of (9) pro_ _ _ures, and (10) comp_ _ _ _ce with international (11) st_ _ _ _ _ds such as ISO 9001. To the end user, quality means that the goods are not (12) def_ _ _ive or (13) da_ _ged in any way. Any service that is provided has to be (14) rel_ _ _le.

4 Complete the sentences using the words in the box.

| faults | improvement | practice | requirements |
| specifications | standard |

1. If you have a system of continuous _____, you should be able to eliminate all design _____.
2. The process of 'benchmarking' is where best _____ is based on the industry _____.
3. Technical _____ in areas like safety are often based on statutory _____ imposed by the government.

5 Add one word to each sentence to make correct passive forms.

1. this machine serviced regularly?
2. Is the machine serviced at the moment?
3. Has the machine serviced recently?
4. the machine serviced last month?
5. Was the machine serviced during the lunch break yesterday, when production stopped for an hour?
6. Is the machine going to serviced next month?
7. The machine could been serviced last month.
8. The machine should have serviced last month.

6 Match 1–7 with a–g so that both expressions have approximately the same use in a presentation.

1. This graph shows the … ☐
2. I think that covers … ☐
3. In other words, … ☐
4. Is that clear so far? ☐
5. So, now let's turn to … ☐
6. Just to digress a moment, … ☐
7. Basically, … ☐

a) By the way, …
b) Does that make sense?
c) Now I'd like to look at …
d) What I mean is …
e) As you can see, …
f) That's all I want to say about …
g) I must emphasize that …

7 Write the pairs of expressions from Exercise 6 next to the most appropriate headings below.

Referring to graphics: _1 e_
Digressing: _____
Restating/Reformulating: _____
Emphasizing: _____
Checking understanding: _____
Ending one point: _____
Moving on: _____

8 Put the words in **bold** in the correct order to make some common email expressions. Mark the expressions *I* (informal), *N* (neutral) or *F* (formal).

1. **grateful / I / be / would / you / if / could** … reply by Wednesday. ☐
2. **me / posted / keep / .** ☐
3. **sorry / I'm / about / very** … the trouble caused. ☐
4. **see / can / it / to / you / ?** ☐
5. **find / solution / a / I'm / we / sure / can / .** ☐
6. **informed / keep / of / please / you / could / me** … developments. ☐
7. **worry. / don't / get / I'll / it / onto / .** ☐
8. **sincere / please / our / apologies / accept / .** ☐
9. **sure / make / I'll** … the goods reach you by Friday. ☐
10. **me / let / please / do / what / plan / know / you / to / .** ☐

60   *The* **Business** 2.0

Review 4

Feedback

1 Fill in the missing letters to complete the sentences about team-building.

1 A to__ __ __y-f__ __ly exercise is one where people express themselves honestly and physically.
2 If a lot of h__ __d thinking goes on, then the thinking involves much effort.
3 A well-known saying states that 'The whole is g__ __ __ __er than the s__ __ of its parts'.
4 If you have enthusiasm and the determination to work hard at something, then you show c__ __ __ __ __ment.
5 If you acc__ __ __ish a goal, it is the same as saying that you a__ __ __ __ve it (succeed in doing it).
6 If you believe in an idea or a strategy, then you b__ __ i__ __ __ __ it. (phrasal verb)
7 No one is perfect, but with effort we can ov__ __ __ __me our sh__ __ __ __ __mings.
8 If somebody is h__ __d acc__ __ __ __ __able for their thoughts and actions, then they have to explain them and be willing to be criticised.
9 Try to stay calm. Don't lose your t__ __ __ __r and get angry.
10 We have to go right back to the beginning and s__ __ __t from sc__ __ __ch.

2 Complete the descriptions using the two most appropriate adjectives from the box.

aggressive charismatic cooperative helpful impatient individual motivating obsessive stressed unpredictable

1 A bully is _____ and _____.
2 A team player is _____ and _____.
3 A leader is _____ and _____.
4 A workaholic is _____ and _____.
5 A maverick is _____ and _____.

3 Match expressions 1–8 with their meanings a–h.

1 burn out ☐
2 settle in ☐
3 pull together ☐
4 pass the buck ☐
5 get on/along well with ☐
6 let someone down ☐
7 pull your weight ☐
8 take it easy ☐

a) work with other people to achieve something
b) relax and not let things worry you
c) make someone else deal with something that you should take responsibility for
d) become familiar with a new job
e) have a friendly relationship with someone
f) do your share of the work
g) disappoint someone, because you didn't do what you promised
h) be unable to continue working because you have worked too hard

4 Match each verb with a noun. Several answers are possible, but the clues in brackets will guide you to one particular solution.

1 meet   a) a budget (= not change)
2 set   b) a date (= set/decide)
3 fix   c) a deadline (= finish at the right time)
4 miss   d) a deadline (= fail to reach)
5 achieve   e) a milestone (= arrive at)
6 stick to   f) a target (= decide/fix/establish)
7 establish   g) a target (= be successful after effort)
8 reach   h) a timeframe (= make it exist)

5 Complete the sentences using the correct form of the verbs in brackets. They are all past modals.

A: I regret what I did. I (1) _____ (should/do) things differently.
B: No, don't blame yourself. You (2) _____ (could/not/do) anything else. I (3) _____ (would/act) in exactly the same way if I'd been in your shoes.
A: You're wrong. Things (4) _____ (might/be) very different if I hadn't been so stupid. I (5) _____ (ought/not/pay) attention to that terrible advice in the astrology section of my magazine.

6 Cover Exercise 5 and complete the sentences below using third conditionals.

1 If I _____ (be) in your shoes, I _____ (act) in exactly the same way.
2 If I _____ (not/be) so stupid, things _____ (be) very different.

Before you check your answers, look at the modal verb you used in the second part of each sentence. Did you use *would* both times? What two other modals are both possible and common?

7 Reformulate the aggressive remarks as diplomatic questions. Use the words in brackets.

1 Come to my office right now! (can/word/you/my office)
   _____?
2 Why did it happen? (do/have/idea/why)
   _____?
3 It would have been a disaster! (do/realize/could/happened)
   _____?

8 Underline a word or expression in the memo below that is similar in meaning to: *consequently, due to, in conclusion, moreover*.

> Because of increased raw materials costs, it will be necessary to increase the price of all our products in the next quarter. Therefore, we need an urgent meeting to decide on the exact amount and timing of the increases. In addition, we need to discuss how to present this price rise to our customers. There might also be a case for reducing costs by outsourcing some of our production to a low-cost country. Overall, there is a lot to discuss, so please keep your schedules free for a full-day meeting on Monday 31 August.

Does using the new words in the instructions make the text more formal or more informal?

5 Selling more

- social media marketing strategies
- attitudes to social media marketing

5.1 About business Social media marketing

Discussion

1 Read the definition of social media marketing (SMM) below. Then, with a partner, discuss your reactions to the examples of SMM strategies as **a)** consumers and **b)** users of social networks.

Social media marketing (SMM) programs introduce products or companies to social networking services like Twitter, Facebook, Google+, YouTube and blogs. They encourage social media users to interact with the product or company, developing loyalty and spreading the message to other users. The promotional message then appears to come from a trusted, third-party source as word of mouth, rather than from the brand or company itself. Such programs are most effective when online marketing platforms are combined in a digital marketing mix.

Some examples of popular SMM strategies are:
- Monitoring brand image by tracking key words in blogs and discussion forums.
- Inviting customers to participate in games and competitions.
- Giving users points, badges or discounts for visiting stores or scanning products with their smartphones.
- Having employees represent the company on Twitter or in LinkedIn® and Facebook groups.

Listening for detail

2 2:01 Listen to a podcast interview with Michelle Hudson, a marketing blogger, and answer the questions.

1. What SMM practices does Michelle object to?
2. Why does Michelle feel these practices are damaging?

3 2:01 Choose the correct answers, then listen again and check.

1. Michelle says that *all / some / no* digital marketers are breaking the law.
2. The interviewer says that paying to place viral videos is *new / wrong / normal*.
3. According to Michelle, social media users are *trusting / honest / naive*.
4. Sponsors pay more for tweets with *a large following / expert knowledge / loyal friends*.
5. Selling friends on social media is *not detected / not forbidden / not allowed*.
6. To be paid to use Twitter you need *a fake account / a made-up name / a real account*.

Scan reading

4 Scan the text opposite to find out what these names refer to in the article.

1. Vegas   2. Revinate   3. TripAdvisor®   4. ScanBuzz™   5. Radian6

Reading for detail

5 Read the article carefully and mark these statements *T* (true) or *F* (false).

1. Good customer feedback encourages hotels to give good customer service. ☐
2. Revinate has many competitors that pick up on keywords in the hotel industry. ☐
3. Online travel agents and review sites represent a threat that hotels have no idea how to deal with. ☐
4. ScanBuzz helps pharmaceutical companies to know which physicians and institutions to lobby. ☐
5. Radian6 provides a control panel of key data in several different business sectors. ☐
6. Socially-reactive marketing uses social networks to respond to what customers are saying. ☐

Discussion

6 In small groups, discuss your reactions to what you have heard and read. What guidelines should marketers be given? Explain and justify your views.

Internet research

Search for the keywords *klout score*. How useful are measures of influence for individuals or brands? How can you increase your score?

Glossary   PAGE 154

dodgy
double-edged sword
endorse
gripe
lobby
stack up
sucks
thrive

Social marketing doesn't have to suck

Many people regret the way some marketers offer cash or other rewards in return for lying to one's friends, while other
5 dodgy companies sell bundles of 10,000 Twitter followers to help a particular brand look well loved. However, the ongoing collision of marketing and social networks
10 doesn't have to involve trickery or deception.

Picture this: you're sitting by the pool at a Vegas resort, when you decide to tweet a picture of
15 where you are to your friends at their fluorescent-lit offices. A few minutes later, a waiter shows up with an ice-cold beverage on the house, explaining, 'Thanks for
20 the tweet.' Guess what your next tweet will be about? Staying at the BEST HOTEL EVER!!

That's the scenario proposed by Marc Heyneker, co-founder
25 of Revinate, one of a new generation of Web-based tools that help companies monitor what people are saying about them. Similar tools are commonplace,
30 typically picking up on keywords on Twitter, Facebook, Yelp and so on, but Revinate is different in that it specializes in a single vertical market: the hotel industry.
35 Individual hotels and chains can see how they stack up to the competition and respond to isolated or repeated gripes and praise.

40 Heyneker says the hotel industry has been 'sitting on the sidelines': Their business has been disrupted by the double-edged sword of online travel agents and
45 review sites like TripAdvisor®, but hotels are often 'clueless' as to how to deal with the new landscape. Revinate typically pays for itself if it results in one extra
50 booking per month. In its first seven months, the service has signed up 491 hotels, including smaller individual hotels, Vegas resorts and popular hotel chains;
55 Heyneker plans to take on the restaurant business next.

Medimix's ScanBuzz™ applies a similar approach to help the medical industry listen in on what
60 people are saying about hundreds of pharmaceutical products and brands. A company looking to market a drug to fight a particular disease can monitor the social
65 web to research how many misdiagnoses are made and try to educate the relevant doctors and hospitals about the disease's symptoms. Meanwhile, Radian6
70 tackles the same job for consumer packaged goods, technology and other verticals, taking a more general approach than Revinate's hotel or Medimix's medical
75 industry dashboards.

Nowhere in these marketing schemes are people paid to lie to their friends: businesses use information in a purely reactive
80 way. All the data they access is on the open web, so any privacy concerns should be minimal. In the end, all that this socially-reactive marketing does is make
85 businesses more responsive to what their customers are saying about them, and it's hard to see how that could be a bad thing. By reacting quickly and
90 appropriately to conversations on the public web, businesses have a better chance of thriving in the unforgiving and increasingly powerful court of public opinion.

Adapted from http://www.wired.com

5 Selling more

- the four Ps and the four Cs
- marketing techniques
- collocations relating to marketing

5.2 Vocabulary The marketing mix

Discussion

1 Explain what you think is meant by these quotations. Do you agree with them?

'Marketing is what you do when your product is no good.' Edwin Land, Inventor of Polaroid photography
'Business has only two functions – marketing and innovation.' Milan Kundera, Czech writer

2 Read the text below and find the answers to these questions.

1 What are the four Ps?
2 What are the four Cs?
3 What is mix coherency?
4 What are mix dynamics?

The marketing mix

The most common variables used in constructing a marketing mix are *price*, *promotion*, *product* and *placement*. These are sometimes referred to as the four Ps. Each of these ideas can also be seen from a consumer's perspective. So, *product* converts into *customer solution*, *price* into *cost*, *place* into *convenience* and *promotion* into *communication*. These are the four Cs.

The concept of mix coherency refers to how well the components of the mix are blended together. For example, a strategy of selling expensive luxury products in discount stores has poor mix coherency between product and placement. Mix dynamics refers to how the mix is adapted to a changing business environment, to changes in the organization's resources and to changes in the product life cycle.

3 Decide how successful the mix coherency and mix dynamics are in these examples. Use the four Ps or the four Cs to explain your answers.

1 An upmarket women's hairdressing franchise is opening salons in underground railway stations.
2 Accessories and spare parts for a popular portable cassette player are now only available by mail order or on the Internet.
3 A distributor of T-shirts decorated with ecological symbols and slogans is advertising in women's fashion magazines.
4 An executive training company is promoting courses in business letter writing on TV.
5 A video games company distributes discount coupons at football matches.

Listening

4 The marketing techniques below are part of the promotion strand of the marketing mix. Match the marketing techniques 1–6 with their descriptions a–f.

1 undercover marketing
2 e-marketing
3 direct marketing
4 product placement
5 viral marketing
6 advertising

a) using electronic media like email or SMS to promote products
b) promoting products to target customers, for example, through addressed mail
c) persuading people to buy a product or service by announcing it on TV, radio or in other media
d) marketing that spreads from consumer to consumer, often online
e) marketing in which customers do not realize they are being marketed to
f) putting products or references to products in media like films or video games

5 2:02–2:07 Listen to six examples of marketing techniques. Match them with the categories 1–6 in Exercise 4.

Collocations

6 Complete the marketing collocations in sentences 1–10 with words from the box.

> bring   declining   enter   flood   leader   niche
> research   segmentation   share   study

1. The same product may interest teenagers in Europe and professionals in Africa: determining market _____ is about adapting the marketing mix to these different customer subgroups.
2. Most companies are reluctant to invest in promoting a product if it faces a _____ market.
3. A custom-made product can be profitable if the company identifies and develops a small market segment or _____ market effectively.
4. Companies often try to capture market _____ by cutting prices or offering special deals.
5. Market _____ is needed in order to estimate the cost of doing business in a particular area.
6. The purpose of conducting a market _____ is to obtain information about customers' needs and how well they are met.
7. The company with the biggest sales in the sector is known as the market _____.
8. Manufacturers sometimes _____ the market with cheap products to 'buy' new customers.
9. Every great idea needs a manufacturer who is willing to invest in order to _____ it to market.
10. The quickest way for large retail chains to grow is to _____ new foreign markets.

Discussion

7 The following sales promotion techniques are often used to stimulate sales. Give examples of these techniques. Use the products in the box to help you.

> holidays   music   printer cartridges   soft drinks   software

1. BOGOF: buy one get one free
2. loss leaders: products sold at a low price to encourage sales of another product
3. tying: making sales of one product depend on the customer buying another
4. cashback: money returned after the customer has paid for something
5. bundling: selling several products together as one combined product

8 Discuss solutions to these case studies. Explain how you would improve the marketing mix, what techniques you would use and what sales promotion techniques would help.

Glossary PAGE 154
blend
coupon
marmalade
razor
SMS
spare
stealth
subliminal

Internet research
Search for the keywords *Maslow's marketing filter*. Apply this technique to the ideas you developed in Exercise 8.

Old Orchard
Old Orchard is a high quality apple juice made using organic fruit and traditional methods. It is sold at a premium price in restaurants and tea shops. Market share and profit margins are declining. How can Old Orchard update its image and diversify into new markets?

Crunchy Morning
Crunchy Morning make an exciting new range of breakfast cereals with unusual flavours, e.g. mint, grapefruit, strawberry and marmalade. How can Crunchy Morning capture market share in a saturated market?

That Touch Cosmetics
That Touch Cosmetics are well-known in Western Europe for their sensibly-priced skin care and beauty products for women. New management have ambitious objectives for growth. How can That Touch grow in what seems to be a mature market?

5 Selling more

- question tags
- negative questions

5.3 Grammar Questions for persuading

Question tags for encouraging and persuading

1 With a partner, persuade each other that your sales skills are really not so bad, as in the examples.

1 **A:** (bad/cold calling) *I'm really bad at cold calling!*
   B: (good/meeting) *But you're good at meeting clients, aren't you?*
2 **B:** (not good/English) *I'm not very good at speaking English!*
   A: (can/Spanish) *But you can speak Spanish well, can't you?*
3 **A:** (terrible/remember faces)
   B: (never/forget names)
4 **B:** (afraid/upset customers)
   A: (never/a complaint yet)
5 **A:** (worried/forget something in my quotation)
   B: (everything last time)
6 **B:** (concerned/give too many discounts)
   A: (not give/next time)
7 **A:** (terrible/closing the sale)
   B: (can't sell/every customer)
8 **B:** (not good/answer objections)
   A: (have to/very patient)
9 **A:** (bad/asking for orders)
   B: (not get/if not ask)
10 **B:** (pessimistic/exceed my objectives)
   A: (like/get a bonus)

Refresh your memory

Question tags
Positive statement + negative tag
You're a frequent flyer, *aren't you?*

Negative statement + positive tag
You don't want to arrive exhausted, *do you?*

Use the same auxiliary or modal in the tag
You can't afford failure, *can you?*

If there's no modal, use *do*.
You need First Class service, *don't you?*

Negative questions
In contractions, put *n't* with the auxiliary
Don't you agree?

In the uncontracted, formal form, put *not* after the subject
Do your sales team *not* deserve the best?

▶ Grammar and practice pages 130–131

Negative questions

2 With a partner, take turns to make and answer customer objections using the negative questions in the box.

> aren't you worried   don't you ever   don't you think
> wouldn't it be better   wouldn't you agree

1 **A:** I don't really need a new car because … *I like my old one.*
   B: I understand. But … *aren't you worried that your old car will be expensive to maintain?*
2 **B:** I'm uncomfortable about investing in the stock market because …
   A: I see your point. But …
3 **A:** I'm not interested in tablet PCs because …
   B: I know what you mean. But …
4 **B:** I don't think buying a flat is a good idea because …
   A: I agree. But …
5 **A**: We haven't budgeted for new software because …
   B: I see. But …
6 **B:** I'm not ready to book a holiday now because …
   A: Point taken. But …
7 **A:** I prefer to keep my old phone because …
   B: I see what you mean. But …
8 **B:** We're unwilling to change supplier because …
   A: I take your point. But …

Internet research

Search for the keywords *How to close a sale*. Compile a class list of your top five tips for closing a sale.

Pronunciation

3 🔊 2:08–2:09 Listen to the two questions below. Pay close attention to the intonation at the end. Which one asks for information? Which one suggests someone will agree?

a) You don't happen to know how many you ordered last year, do you?
b) You don't really want to run out of components, do you?

4 🔊 2:10 Questions with falling intonation are useful for persuading. Listen to eight questions from a training seminar about closing the sale. Decide whether each question is for getting information (*I*) or persuading (*P*).

1 _____   3 _____   5 _____   7 _____
2 _____   4 _____   6 _____   8 _____

5 Here are more questions from the sales seminar. Add suitable tags.

1 Just a question. You couldn't possibly give me a discount, _____?
2 It's out of the question. We couldn't possibly sell at a loss, _____?
3 So we agree that you'll try to get approval for the budget, _____?
4 You don't happen to know the date of the next finance meeting, _____?
5 You didn't by any chance send me an email yesterday, _____?
6 Still no news from your purchasing department; we started to discuss delivery dates, _____?
7 It's already week five, so clearly, there's no way we could deliver before March, _____?
8 I don't suppose you could agree to postpone delivery until May, _____?

6 With a partner, practise saying the questions in Exercise 5 with appropriate intonation. Invent suitable responses.

Listening and speaking

7 🔊 2:11 Listen to attendees at the sales training seminar playing a game, and complete the rules.

> One person is the customer. The sellers have to persuade the customer to buy something by _____. The customer mustn't _____.

8 In small groups, play the game yourselves.

Glossary PAGE 155

cold calling
luncheon voucher
on the clock
tax-deductible

9 Make these sales arguments more persuasive by changing them to negative questions, as in the example.

After a hard morning's work, your employees need a good, healthy lunch.
After a hard morning's work, don't your employees need a good, healthy lunch?

1 They deserve more than grabbing a hamburger or eating a sandwich at their desks.
2 They've earned the right to sit down to a proper meal in a restaurant.
3 There's a better way to keep them satisfied and motivated all afternoon.
4 You know that not being able to eat properly is one of the main reasons staff quit their jobs.
5 Your staff would appreciate receiving luncheon vouchers as part of their compensation.
6 You'd like to actually save money because luncheon vouchers are tax-deductible.
7 It will be nice to do something positive for every employee.

10 Using question tags and negative questions, persuade a partner to buy one of the following.

- a 1975 Volvo with 650,000 km on the clock
- a collection of records of pre-war opera singers
- a small 1960s house 50 metres from an oil refinery
- a 4 x 3 metre painting of a tiger in the jungle
- a 33-year-old racehorse
- a camping holiday in Scotland in November

5 Selling more

- identifying sales techniques
- expressions for dealing with objections
- selling a study trip

5.4 Speaking Dealing with objections

Discussion

1 Decide to what extent you agree with each statement. Choose from *I agree/ It depends/I disagree*. Then compare your answers with a partner.

1. Customers will pay more to buy from people they like.
2. Customers make objections because they want to be persuaded.
3. Selling ideas to friends or family is no different from selling products to customers.
4. The customer is always right.

2 Imagine you're selling these products and services. What objections will the customer probably make, and how would you answer them?

1. A health club subscription
2. A private swimming pool
3. A custom-designed software package

Listening

3 2:12–2:14 Listen to three exchanges between sales representatives and their customers. What mistakes do the salespeople make?

4 2:15–2:17 Listen to three improved versions of the exchanges in Exercise 3. Decide which of the common sales techniques below each salesperson is using.

> **A** Welcome objections and try to establish agreement: listen to the customer's objections and use persuasive questions to show understanding.
>
> **B** Use the 'Feel, Felt, Found' formula: tell the customer you know how they feel, but give an example of other customers who felt the same way but found they were wrong.
>
> **C** Redirect the objection to obtain more information: use objections as an opportunity to find out what the customer's position really is.

Persuading

5 2:15–2:17 With a partner, complete the expressions for dealing with objections in the checklist. Then listen again and check your answers.

Useful expressions: Dealing with objections

Welcome objections and establish agreement

I know exactly what you _____.
There's always too much to do, _____?
You don't want …, _____ you?

Redirect the objection

I'm glad you _____ that _____.
So _____ me, is the membership fee the only _____ to signing up?
So, if I can …, are you _____ to sign up today?

'Feel, Felt, Found'

I understand _____ you _____. A lot of our customers _____ that way at _____. _____, they soon _____ they were saving money.

Check that the customer agrees

Does that make _____?
Are you _____ with that?
Does that _____ your question?

Internet research

Search for the keywords *how to make customers love you*. Take a class vote for the top ten ideas.

6 Match objections 1–6 with the answers used to redirect them a–f.

1 Your price is too high.
2 We haven't budgeted for it.
3 I like your main competitor's offer.
4 I'll think about it.
5 I only work with one supplier.
6 Your lead time is too long.

a) You're probably wondering what's different about our service, aren't you?
b) Do you mean, why are our prices higher than the competition?
c) You are wondering if this merits a budget extension, is that right?
d) Is the delivery date the only obstacle to ordering today?
e) If I can offer the terms you need, could you make a decision today?
f) Can I ask if there's a particular reason for only using them?

7 With a partner, write responses to each objection, starting each sentence with the words given. Then change partners and practise dealing with them.

1 We have a freeze on new investments. Call me back in six months' time.
   Is the freeze the only _____?
2 Your competitor offered us the same service for 20% less.
   I'm glad you _____. But have you asked yourself _____?
3 I have doubts about your product's reliability and durability.
   I understand how _____. A lot of our customers _____. But later, _____.
4 I can't afford the insurance on a new car.
   If I can _____, would you _____?
5 I'm not sure that Head Office will be very pleased if we change our procedures.
   You're probably wondering _____. Are you comfortable _____?
6 We need the parts now. We can't wait two weeks for delivery.
   Do you mean that if _____?

Brainstorming

8 Work in small groups. You have started a company which organizes study trips for students and young business people to learn about business and culture in another part of the world. Brainstorm the following details about your study trip, as well as your own ideas.

> cost   destination   length of stay   social activities
> travel and accommodation arrangements   type of organizations visited

9 Predict at least five objections you expect your clients to raise. Think of answers to these objections and practise overcoming them.

eWorkbook
Now watch the video for this unit.

Negotiation

10 Meet other groups and take turns to try to sell your study trip.

5 Selling more

- paragraph function and content
- the tripling technique
- writing a mailshot

5.5 Writing Mailshots and sales letters

Discussion

1 Choose the correct answers, then discuss your choices.

A good mailshot should
- be *as short as possible / neither too long nor too short / as long as necessary*.
- put the most important point *at the beginning / in the middle / at the end*.
- be written in *first person style (I) / second person style (you) / third person style (it)*.
- focus on *features / benefits / costs*.
- *always have a PS / never have a PS / have a PS and a PPS*.

Model

2 Read the sample mailshot below and choose a label for each paragraph.

Action   Benefits   Credentials   Hook   Promise   PS

Dear Reader,

New Business View multimedia magazine

1 How do today's business leaders keep up to date without trawling through hundreds of pages of newspapers and magazines?

2 They rely on New Business View – the only digital multimedia magazine to bring you all the latest business news, trends and opinions on one handy, multi-format disk. Subscribe to NBV, and we guarantee you'll never need to buy another magazine!

3 Be the first to know about mergers and takeovers, marketing trends and management tools. Watch, listen and read, on DVD, in the car, or on your PC. NBV gives you a deeper understanding of the issues that matter, whoever you are, wherever you are and whenever you want. 'Better than an MBA' – NBV is your private briefing from the world's best business specialists.

4 NBV is used by executives in leading companies, large, medium and small, all over the world. Over half of America's top business schools recommend it as part of their programmes.

5 You too can enjoy a better view of the world of business. Subscribe now for twelve months or more, and receive three issues totally free of charge. Just fill in the attached form, or subscribe online at www.newbusinessview.com.

Sincerely yours,

Jim Bradley

6 **PS Reply within fifteen days, and get free access to NBV's new daily podcast!**

Glossary PAGE 155
briefing
credentials
grab someone's attention
handling
PPS
PS
trawl through
USP

Analysis

3 Decide which paragraphs these tips on writing mailshots and sales letters refer to.

1 Don't forget to make it clear what you want – 'if you don't ask, you don't get!'
2 Give references which will persuade the reader that your product really delivers what it promises.
3 Tell the customer your USP – what only your product or service will deliver.
4 Provide additional motivation to act on the message.
5 Give readers details of the advantages they will enjoy.
6 You have less than five seconds to grab the reader's attention and make them want to read your message.

Internet research

Search for the keywords *advance fee fraud* to find out how dishonest writers persuade their victims to give them money.

4 Decide which part of a sales letter or mailshot you would put these sentences in.

1 Can you honestly say you would never prefer to stay in bed than to go to work?
2 I will call you early next week to arrange a demonstration of the software.
3 Over 20% of Fortune 500® companies are already using our system.
4 Please feel free to call me for more information or to arrange an appointment.
5 There are only two kinds of company – market leaders and market followers. Which is yours?
6 This offer is available for a limited time only; call early to avoid disappointment!
7 Within six months you can expect a return on investment that no other consultancy can deliver.
8 Your company will enjoy significant gains in productivity, reliability and staff morale.

Language focus

5 Sales letters and mailshots frequently build persuasive arguments by tripling: describing features and benefits in threes. Find and highlight four more examples of tripling in the letter in Exercise 2. What patterns of words are used in each group: verbs, nouns, adjectives, etc.?

… all the latest business news, trends and opinions.
Be the first to know about mergers and takeovers, marketing trends and management tools.

6 Use the tripling technique to build these arguments. Add two more ideas to each sentence.

1 The multimedia dictionary is ideal for students, _____ and _____.
2 Regular sessions in your mini-gym will make you fitter, _____ and _____.
3 Our office software helps you improve productivity, save _____ and increase _____.
4 In this seminar you'll learn how to plan, _____ and _____ a presentation.
5 The new Porsche has improved handling, a redesigned _____ and _____.
6 In less than an hour, you'll be able to start using home architect software; in less than a day _____ and _____.
7 The Norisko investment plan means you can save for a new house, _____ and _____.
8 By the end of this CRM course, you'll have learnt how to handle difficult customers, how to _____ and _____.

Output

7 In small groups, write a mailshot for an electric bicycle, timeshare flats, a book club or a mail order catalogue. Start by deciding the following features:

- who the target market is
- what the USPs of the product are
- what its benefits are
- what its credentials are
- how you can grab the reader's attention
- what you want the reader to do
- what you can put in your PS.

8 Write your mailshot. Remember to build persuasive arguments by tripling.

9 Give copies of your mailshot to other groups. Each group should choose the most persuasive mailshot (excluding their own). The group that makes the most 'sales' is the winner.

5 Selling more

- mobile phones for a courier firm
- negotiating a deal

5.6 Case study   Backchat Communications

Discussion

1 The first hand-held mobile phone was marketed in 1983. It weighed half a kilogram and cost $3,500. How have they changed since then? How will they continue to evolve?

Reading for implication

2 Read the introduction to the case, and answer questions 1–4 below.

'Min Su, have you any idea where Jung Ju is?' asked Thomas Ibáñez, Seoul Deliveries' office manager.
    'No, I'm sorry, I don't know,' replied
5 Min Su, looking up from a bank of computer screens. 'He should have been back from a delivery an hour ago, but there's no sign of him.'
    'I see.' The Frenchman was frustrated.
10 Running an efficient courier and delivery service was not easy in a city of ten million people and three million vehicles, but became especially difficult when drivers went missing. The old saying that
15 'time is money' was never truer than in the courier business.
    'I suppose you've tried calling his mobile?' asked Ibáñez.

'Yes, Mr Ibáñez,' said Min Su, 'but
20 he's on voicemail. Or more likely it's the battery. The drivers' mobiles are so old, the batteries are flat by the middle of the afternoon.'
    'All right. Thanks, Min Su,' said Ibáñez.
25 'Let me know as soon as you find out where he is. Oh, and listen, could you get in touch with Backchat Communications, and ask them to send us a proposal to renew our mobile phone fleet? They had
30 an ad in the subway for phones with GPS. If we had those, we wouldn't have this problem. We desperately need to upgrade our technology.'

1 Why is Thomas concerned about Jung Ju?
2 Why do you think the saying 'time is money' is important in the courier business?
3 Jung Ju's mobile is on voicemail. How does Min Su explain this? What other explanations can you think of?
4 Thomas thinks GPS may help. Why is this useful for a courier firm?

Glossary   PAGE 155

Bluetooth™
courier
flat
fleet
GPS
handset
keep up with
won

3 Read the advertisement, then answer the questions.

BACKCHAT COMMUNICATIONS
Most popular mobile phone deals   Monthly price plans and line rental

Basic ★★
400 minutes/month
20,000 won/month*
Handset features:
voice and text,
built-in camera

Smart ★★★
800 minutes/month
40,000 won/month*
Additional features:
mp3 player, video
games, Bluetooth

Hi-tech ★★★★
1,200 minutes/month
60,000 won/month*
Additional features:
email, PDA, FM radio,
TV, GPS

* 12 months minimum   Discounts negotiable for 18- and 24-month contracts

1 Why are the Smart and Hi-tech plans more expensive than the Basic plan?
2 Why are Backchat prepared to negotiate discounts for longer contracts?
3 Which phone deal seems best for Seoul Deliveries' a) drivers? b) admin staff? c) managers?

KOREA EXPRESS

Listening for detail

4 🔊 **2:18** Listen to a conversation at Backchat between the Sales Manager, Harry Lim, and his assistant. Complete the notes.

Customer	Seoul Deliveries
Contact name	(1) _____
Position	(2) _____
Approx. number of units required	(3) _____
User profiles and needs	Admin staff – would like (4) _____ Managers – need (5) _____ Drivers – management want to motivate drivers with something (6) _____
Possible objections	Drivers may object to (7) _____ (remind them about (8) _____) Managers may object to drivers (9) _____ and (10) _____.

Brainstorming

5 Divide into two groups, sellers with Backchat and buyers with Seoul Deliveries. Your goal is to negotiate the best possible deal. Discuss your strategy and what your main negotiating aims will be.

Negotiation

6 Work in small groups of two to four, with at least one buyer and one seller. Negotiate a deal. Write what you agree on the order form below.

Internet research

Search for the keywords *future of mobile phones* to find out more about what we can expect in the future. Hold a class vote to decide on the most useful and the most useless applications.

ORDER FORM

Plan	Number of contracts	Period of contracts	Discounts
Basic (20,000 won/month)			
Smart (40,000 won/month)			
Hi-tech (60,000 won/month)			
Extras	Number (paid)	Number (free)	
Spare battery			
Bluetooth™ headset			
Game and TV pack			

7 When you have finished your negotiation, calculate your score. Sellers: turn to page 118. Buyers: turn to page 120. Compare your score with other buyers/sellers to see who negotiated the best deal.

6 New business

- building a brand
- ideas for a new business

6.1 About business Developing a business

Discussion

1 Decide which of the motivations below is the most and least important when you start a business. Number the factors from 1–5 (1 = most important; 5 = least important).

- [ ] The fun of creating new products or services
- [ ] The freedom of being your own boss
- [ ] Making money quickly so that you can sell the business
- [ ] The satisfaction of providing quality goods and services
- [ ] The excitement of taking risks

Scan reading

2 Read the article opposite and match the headings below with paragraphs 1–5.

a) Go with your instinct
b) Follow your heart
c) Stay involved
d) Start small
e) Partner up

3 Complete the chart with the main milestones in the company's development.

Fresh – Milestones			
1991–1994	1991 *Opened first store, Nuts About Beauty*	2000–Soon	

4 Read the article carefully and mark these statements *T* (true), *F* (false) or *?* (don't know).

1. Fresh produces special beauty products for shoulders.
2. LVMH has a controlling interest in Fresh.
3. Fresh only sell their products in their own stores.
4. Lev Glazman and Alina Roytberg founded Fresh in 1991.
5. The products are all made from exotic ingredients.
6. The founders share the same skills.
7. Turnover in 2001 was $14 million.
8. The couple do not spend every day managing the company.

Listening

5 2:19–2:22 Listen to four successful entrepreneurs reacting to the article. Match speakers 1–4 with the summaries a–d. Which do you agree with?

a) The founders were simply lucky.
b) Fresh is where it is now because the company has always moved forward.
c) The key to their success is enthusiasm.
d) They made a wise decision giving up a majority stake in Fresh.

Discussion and presentation

6 In small groups, brainstorm some possible ideas for a new business. Choose the best one and present it to the class. Think about the following issues:

- why the product or service will be a success
- how much investment you will need and how you will raise the money
- whether you will manage the business yourself or bring in experts
- whether you will keep a majority stake or sell the company
- what the medium- or long-term outlook for the business is

Internet research

Search for the keywords *bootstrapping business* to find out more about do-it-yourself financing. Can you find any examples of companies that bootstrapped at the beginning?

Five simple rules for building a blockbuster brand

By Rosalind Resnick

When Lev Glazman and Alina Roytberg founded their company in 1991, they never imagined that one day their cosmetics brand Fresh would be rubbing shoulders with companies like Louis Vuitton, Christian Dior and Moët & Chandon.

But today, with 15 stores, 400 retail distribution outlets and 180 employees worldwide, Fresh has matured into an internationally-known brand. Sold in Barneys and other high-end retail stores, Fresh enjoys the backing of majority owner LVMH Group, the Paris-based luxury goods marketer.

Glazman and Roytberg hired a CEO to run day-to-day operations in 2007, but remain co-presidents and continue to guide Fresh's creative and product development strategies. The husband-and-wife team owns a minority stake in the company and works closely with LVMH's corporate management. 'Having LVMH as our strategic partner gives us the opportunity to open new markets and to develop R&D,' Glazman says. 'We still have complete autonomy in terms of creative control and continuous development of the brand.'

Many entrepreneurs would like to emulate their success story. Here are the couple's five simple rules for product and brand development.

1 _____ Growing up in St. Petersburg, Russia, Glazman saw that women like his mother yearned for beauty products in their Soviet-era homeland. 'She would buy a lot of things on the black market, and if she'd got caught, she would have gone to jail,' Glazman recalls. 'But by introducing me to things that weren't so available, she created in me a passion for fragrance.' When he later moved to the US, he met Roytberg, an aspiring fashion designer, and married her in 1990. With a small investment from friends and family, Glazman finally realized his passion in 1991, when he and his wife opened their first store, Nuts About Beauty, in New York. Two years later, they changed the name to Fresh.

2 _____ Initially selling products made by other companies, the couple decided to launch their own line of soaps in 1992. 'Soap was the easiest to start with because we could create the formula,' says Glazman, who initially found a manufacturer in the South of France to produce small batches. Fresh got its big break when its soaps were picked up by Barneys department store in 1994 and celebrities began singing their praises. Before long, the company had 500 products, including shower gels, fragrances, lotions and other beauty products made from soy, sake, sugar and Umbrian clay.

3 _____ Unlike some beauty-product companies, Fresh doesn't rely exclusively on market research for ideas. Instead, Glazman and Roytberg create products they would want to use themselves. It helps that Glazman has a nose for fragrances and Roytberg a knack for packaging. 'You have to trust your instincts,' Glazman says. Adds Roytberg, 'We found the best market research happens while listening to our customers in the store.'

4 _____ As Fresh began to grow, its founders quickly realized that they could only go so far on their own. They told *Entrepreneur* magazine they borrowed $10,000 from family members to open their first store and rang up $14 million in sales in 2001. In 2000, they signed a deal with LVMH, giving it a majority stake in their company. In return, they acquired the capital, management talent and distribution channels necessary for expansion without sacrificing the autonomy they had enjoyed. 'Our focus is on expanding distribution and opening new markets like Asia,' Glazman says. Roytberg says the company plans to enter China next fall.

5 _____ Glazman and Roytberg remain as passionate as ever about nurturing their home-grown brand. Freed from day-to-day management responsibilities, the duo can now focus exclusively on creating new products. Says Roytberg, 'If you're a gardener and you put a seed in the ground and water it and take care of it, you want to see it flower. The opportunity to get your products into the hands of people globally makes it more exciting to come to work every day.'

Glossary   PAGE 155

- batch
- knack
- nurture
- ring up
- rub shoulders with
- sing somebody's praises
- stake
- yearn

6 New business

- types of funding
- steps in a funding application
- phrasal verbs

6.2 Vocabulary Funding a start-up

Discussion

1 Work in small groups. You are financial advisors to start-ups and small companies. What sources of funding would you recommend in the following situations?

1 BUSYBODIES is a temping agency providing clerical help to other companies. It needs a new photocopier/printer but it does not have the cash available to buy it.

2 FIXA is a start-up providing home help for all sorts of everyday tasks or problems: gardening, household repairs, cleaning, ironing, etc. It needs £8,000 to cover start-up costs.

3 DON BEAL is an inventor. He has patented a new type of car engine which is 50% more efficient than existing engines. He needs money to produce a prototype but wants to keep control of his business.

4 ASC is a small engineering company that has temporary cash flow problems. It needs £1,500 to pay for raw materials. They are expecting to be paid £5,000 in outstanding bills in the next two weeks.

Defining words

2 Read the advice leaflet about business funding. Match the types of funding in the box with the correct descriptions.

| bank loan | equity finance | friends and family | grants | leasing | overdraft | self-funding |

1 _____

👍 Drawing on personal savings and credit cards can cover start-up costs without having to wait for other people's decisions.

👎 The downside is that using credit cards can be expensive in the long term.

2 _____

👍 Regular repayments can make it easier to budget.

👎 On the other hand, repayment schemes can cause cash flow problems. You may also need to provide security, such as business assets, or a guarantor.

3 _____

👍 This can be a very flexible option for short-term or day-to-day requirements.

👎 The disadvantage is that they usually bear a higher interest rate than other loans.

4 _____

👍 They might be willing to provide an interest-free loan or not require security.

👎 On the other hand, funding from this source can put strain on your relationships.

5 _____

👍 You get your funding, while the investor only realizes their investment when the business is doing well. You also get their expertise.

👎 On the downside, it's hard to raise this finance, and your own influence and share of the profits will be smaller.

6 _____

👍 These appear to be a source of cheap financing.

👎 However, there is often strong competition, and you may be required to provide matching funds. You may also need to prove a wider benefit to the community.

7 _____

👍 You can spread the cost of acquiring assets and maintenance may be covered.

👎 But it's more expensive than if you buy outright, and you don't own the assets until the end of the agreement.

3 Look back at your answers in Exercise 1. Would you change any of your recommendations?

4 Find words or phrases in the advice leaflet that mean:

1 the amount of money you pay back each month
2 money coming into and out of your business
3 an item you agree to give if you fail to pay
4 a person who takes responsibility if you fail to pay
5 debt which you pay back without any additional charge
6 money you provide alongside government funding
7 the cost of keeping something working

Scan reading

5 Read the seven steps in an application procedure. Number the steps in the correct order.

THE SEVEN STEPS TO HEAVEN

Seventh HEAVEN
Angel Investors Group

☐ **Screening meeting** If they didn't *turn you down* at Step 2, our review committee will invite you to a screening meeting. Be prepared to make a ten-minute pitch and answer any questions that *come up*.

☐ **Self-assessment** Before *putting forward* your business plan for our consideration, you must *work out* if angel capital – and specifically capital from our group – is right for your company.

☐ **Due diligence** If your presentation is successful, interested investors will *check out* the statements made in your business plan, presentation and financial projections. They will go over your team's background and track record in detail.

☐ **Funding** When all parties are happy with the terms and language contained in the term sheet, the deal can *go through*.

☐ **Online application** Once you have decided to submit a plan, complete our application online. This is designed to identify the most important details about your business so that our internal review committee can *weed out* the non-starters.

☐ **Term sheet** On successful completion of the due diligence process, interested angel group members will *draw up* a term sheet that *sets out* the structure of the investment deal, including type of equity and board of directors representation.

☐ **Presentation to membership** If you *get through* the screening meeting, you will be invited to make a 30-minute presentation to our full membership, the goal being to convince members that your proposal is worth investigating in detail.

6 Complete the sentences with the phrasal verbs in *italics* in Exercise 5.

1 Only two per cent of business plans _____ the complete funding process.
2 Problems often _____ in the early stages.
3 Business angels may _____ proposals for no apparent reason.
4 Angels always _____ an entrepreneur's background thoroughly.
5 It's worth getting a lawyer to _____ any contracts rather than trying to write them yourself.
6 The term sheet _____ all the conditions of the deal.
7 A lot of hard work is necessary before the deal finally _____.
8 In your pitch, you should _____ clear and convincing arguments.
9 Get help if you can't _____ how much finding to apply for.
10 The screening meeting allows investors to _____ poor applications at an early stage.

Listening

7 🔊 2:23–2:26 Listen to four entrepreneurs explaining why their proposals were turned down. Decide which reason from the box each person mentions.

> financial forecasts based on assumptions   inadequate financial returns
> lack of market awareness   lack of skills in the management team
> lack of trust   no clear exit route   no growth potential
> no track record or proof of concept   too complex

Discussion and presentation

8 Work in small groups. You work for a corporate finance firm bringing together investors and entrepreneurs. Using relevant phrases and vocabulary from the previous exercises, draw up a list of Dos and Don'ts for start-ups looking for funding.

9 Work with a partner from a different group. Present and compare your lists.

Glossary PAGE 155

asset
household
outstanding
pitch
raw materials
temping agency
track record
weed out

Internet research

Search for the key words *business angels* to find out more about their role in financing start-ups.

6 New business

- will be doing
- will have done
- will have been doing

Refresh your memory

Future continuous *will be doing*
Actions in progress at a future time.
I'll be driving home at six.

Future perfect *will have done*
Looking back on events from a time in the future.
We *will have merged* by 2020.

Future perfect continuous
Emphasizing actions before a time in the future.
I'll have been working all week.

▶ Grammar and practice pages 132–133

6.3 Grammar   Future continuous and future perfect

Future continuous

1 Work with a partner. Think about your work/study schedule for the next few weeks. Ask your partner what he/she will be doing:

- this time tomorrow
- at 5 o'clock tomorrow afternoon
- this time next Monday
- the week after next.

Try to find similarities in your schedules and continue the conversation.

A: *What will you be doing this time tomorrow?*
B: *I'll be flying to Munich for a meeting at head office.*
A: *What a coincidence! Me too. Will you be taking the eight-thirty flight?*
B: *No. I'll be leaving around noon.*

Listening for detail

2 🔊 2:27 Linda Griffin, Business Development Manager for an American company, is on a business trip to Europe looking for possible joint venture partners. Listen to Bob Stone, Linda's assistant, leaving a message on her voicemail, and complete her schedule.

Time	
7:00 AM	
8:00	Arrive Paris
9:00	
10:00	
11:00	
12:00	Lunch with Alain Giroud
13:00	
14:00	
15:00	
16:00	Arrive Macon
17:00	
18:00	
19:00	
20:00	

3 With a partner, take turns to ask and answer questions about what Linda will be doing at different times.

A: *What will she be doing at 9 o'clock?*
B: *She'll be travelling to head office by taxi.*

Future perfect

4 With a partner, look at Linda's to-do list and say what she will ✓ or won't ✗ have done by Friday.

To do (by friday?)
call Bob ✓
write up trip report ✗
do PowerPoint slides ✗
email Alex ✓
prepare pitch to new investors ✗
speak to CFO ✓
buy birthday present for Jamie ✓
book flight to Rome ✗

Language focus

5 Sustain is a UK company offering environmentally sustainable solutions to the building industry. Read Sustain's company history and complete sentences 1–6 below.

sustain COMPANY HISTORY

YEAR 1	started trading | opened warehouse in Staines | John Gregor named as managing director
YEAR 2	opened offices in Richmond | bought Housesmart, an interior design company
YEAR 3	began selling solar panels | started exporting products to Europe
YEAR 4	started receiving government grants for sustainable development

By the time Sustain reaches its fifth anniversary,
1. it _____ for _____ years. (trade)
2. John Gregor _____ managing director for _____ years. (be)
3. it _____ solar panels for _____ years. (sell)
4. it _____ offices in Richmond for _____ years. (have)
5. it _____ government grants for _____ year. (receive)
6. it _____ Housesmart for _____ years. (own)

Glossary   PAGE 156
black tie
fancy dress
plant
sustainable

6 Sustain is holding a party next week to celebrate its fifth anniversary. Read the invitation to the party. Complete the sentences about the guests' activities.

1. At 7.15, _____
2. At 8.00, _____
3. At 10.00, _____
4. At midnight, _____

sustain
FIFTH ANNIVERSARY BALL

5 November
Start 7pm
Huntingdon Hotel*
Bring a guest
Black tie or fancy dress

7.00–7.30 Cocktails on the lawn
7.30–9.30 Three course dinner (vegetarian options available)
9.30–10.30 John Gregor gives company awards
10.30–11.30 Jazz band
11.30–2.00 Disco

*Hotel parking must be booked in advance, if needed

7 Read the conversation between Sue, the event planner, and John Gregor. Complete the conversation with the questions she asked. Use the future continuous.

Sue: Mr Gregor, I was wondering whether I could just ask you a few questions so that we can get all the planning right.
John: No problem. What would you like to know?
Sue: Firstly, what time (1) _____?
John: Personally, not until 7.30. I'll miss the cocktails unfortunately.
Sue: And (2) _____ a parking space?
John: No, I won't. I'm coming by train.
Sue: Fine. And how many awards (3) _____?
John: Three. Half an hour should actually be long enough.
Sue: Fine. Just a few practical things. (4) _____ the vegetarian option?
John: No, not for me, thanks.
Sue: OK. And finally, (5) _____ fancy dress?
John: Certainly not. Black tie. But I think some of the younger staff may enjoy dressing up.

Discussion and presentation

8 Work in groups. Sustain would like to expand, but will require a bank loan to do so. You have been asked to make a business plan for years 6–10. Complete the table with your own ideas. Say what you will be doing in each year, and what you will have achieved by your tenth anniversary.

Plan	
Year 6	
Year 7	
Year 8	
Year 9	
Year 10	

Internet research
Search for the keywords *environmentally sustainable solutions* to find out more about changes in the construction business.

9 Present your business plan to the rest of the class. Vote to decide who has the best plan.

6 New business

- listening for advice on fielding questions
- expressions for commenting on questions
- giving a 60-second talk

6.4 Speaking Presentations: taking questions

Discussion

1 Work in small groups. The question and answer session is an important but unpredictable part of most presentations. Decide whether you agree or disagree with the statements on the right.

- If there are no questions, it means that you've given a really good presentation.
- It's better to answer questions during the presentation rather than waiting till the end.
- There's only one type of question: awkward!
- The question and answer session is an opportunity, not a threat.
- When answering a question, keep it brief.
- Never admit that you don't know the answer to a question. Bluff if necessary.

Listening for detail

2 🔊 2:28 Juliette Duncan, a presentations specialist, is giving a seminar on Perfect Presentations. Listen to the first part of her talk. What four pieces of advice does she give for fielding questions?

1 _____
2 _____
3 _____
4 _____

3 🔊 2:29 Listen to the second part of Juliette's seminar. She mentions five types of question. Complete the list.

Five types of question
1 _Useful_   2 _____   3 _____   4 _____   5 _____

4 🔊 2:29 Match each type of question in Exercise 3 with the advice below. There is one extra piece of advice. Then listen again and check your answers.

a) Make sure the question is irrelevant, be diplomatic and go on. ☐
b) You've already answered these questions in your talk. Remind the questioner and go on. ☐
c) Elicit questions by answering one of your own. ☐
d) They clarify what you're saying. Thank people for asking them. ☐
e) Ask somebody in the audience if they can answer the question. ☐
f) Don't bluff or lie. If you don't know the answer, offer to find out. If you don't want to answer, say so. ☐

Glossary PAGE 156

awkward
bluff
do your homework
field
nod
recap
threat

Internet research

Search for the keywords *presentations taking questions* to discover more tips on handling a question and answer session.

Presentation skills

5 With a partner, find suitable words to complete the expressions in the checklist for commenting on questions. Use the words in the box.

asked   assure   get   glad   question   raises   recap   relevant   remember   words

Useful expressions: Commenting on questions

Useful questions

That's a very good _____.
I'm _____ you raised that point.

Awkward questions

I'm afraid I don't have the figures with me. Can I _____ back to you on that?
So, in other _____ you're asking …
I understand your position, but I can _____ you we've done our homework.

Irrelevant questions

To be honest, I think that _____ a different issue.
I'm not sure that's really _____ to the discussion today.

Unnecessary questions

I think I covered that in Part Two, but let me just _____.
Well, you may _____ in the slide about growth forecast, I mentioned …

No questions

A question I'm often _____ is: 'Where do you see the firm in five years?'

Speaking

6 Imagine your partner has given a talk about a company. Write five questions about the company using the prompts below.

1. last year's profit figures
2. when the company was founded
3. the reasons for their successes
4. who invented the company logo
5. what colour they prefer

7 Work with a partner. One of you is the presenter and the other is the questioner. The questioner starts by saying that they have no questions, so that the presenter has to start the session. The questioner asks his or her questions from Exercise 6. When you have finished, swap roles.

Explaining and reformulating

8 A speaker is answering questions after a presentation about a new wind turbine. Complete his answer using the expressions for explaining and reformulating in the box.

In other words   It's quite simple   so   That's why   To be precise   To put it into perspective

(1) _____, really. Our turbine is the most efficient on the market.
(2) _____, 20% more efficient than any of our competitors'.
(3) _____ we're convinced that we'll meet our sales targets next year.
(4) _____, we will sell more than 450,000 units in the European market in the next twelve months. (5) _____ that's twice as many units as this year,
(6) _____ the future is rosy.

Presentation

9 Work in groups of three. Each member of the group should prepare a 60-second talk on one of the following topics.

- your future career plans
- a business idea you think will work
- the economy of your home town/country
- a subject of your own choice

10 When you are ready, tell the class the subject of your talk so that they can prepare at least three questions each to ask you. Then take turns to deliver your talks and answer the questions with appropriate comments.

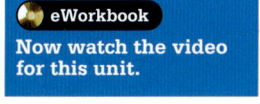

6 New business

- structure
- impact collocations
- writing a company profile

6.5 Writing   A company profile

Reading and discussion

1 Read the article below and answer the questions.

1. What are the three key points to remember about writing for publication online?
2. How would you adapt your writing style, the content and the format for the six contexts in paragraph 1?

Writing a winning company profile

Sooner or later you're going to need a company profile, whether it's for your website, a customer proposal, a social media site, a business plan, a brochure or a magazine article. You'll adapt your style, the content and the format depending on who you're writing for, but in today's business environment, it's increasingly likely that you'll be writing for publication online.

The F-pattern
Research shows most people read online text in an F-pattern. At first they read complete lines, but as they move down the page, they read two thirds, half, then only a quarter of each line. By the end of the text they're only reading the first word or two of each line – if they're still reading at all! So put your key ideas in the F if you want them to be read: use impact words and collocations in the first two paragraphs and in the first few words of subsequent sentences.

An elevator pitch in writing
Your company profile is a written version of your elevator pitch, so keep it short and snappy. Customers will only remember three main ideas; one of the three must be why your company is different from the rest.

Winning hearts
Finally, a winning company profile builds trust by making an emotional connection with the reader: highlight the human side of your business to win their hearts as well as their minds.

Model

2 Read the company profile opposite and mark these statements *T* (true) or *F* (false).

1. Bowie's is different because it combines one-on-one consulting with online merchandising. ☐
2. Bowie's core values are trust, integrity, commitment and high value products. ☐
3. Bowie's keeps stock to a minimum by using a just-in-time production system. ☐
4. If a customer receives the wrong size or colour, they just take it back to their salon. ☐
5. Fear of making a fashion mistake is not a sufficient reason for a customer to return goods. ☐
6. Bowie's annual fun day out brings employees' family and friends together. ☐

Analysis

3 Complete the structure guidelines with the words from the box. Refer to the company profile opposite to help you.

competitive	financial
guarantees	history
management	~~mission~~
technology	USP values
vision	

Writing a company profile: structure guidelines

Section	Key content
Why	Our (1) *mission* – now Our (2) _____ – the future Our (3) _____ – our guiding principles
How	Our market & our (4) _____ advantage Our (5) _____ & our skills Our (6) _____ & our (7) _____ summary
What	Our solutions Our products Our (8) _____
Who	Our (9) _____ Our people Our partners Our clients
Close	Our (10) _____ Next step Our contact information
Other optional information	Legal & administrative details Company news Business plan Financial statements Current or completed projects Certificates Maps

82   *The* Business 2.0

Bowie's Clothing Company
'PERSONAL FASHION CONSULTING'

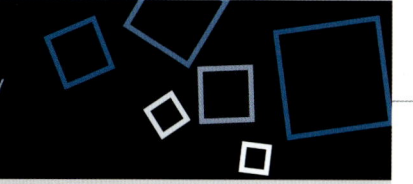

Bowie's Clothing Company brings a fresh and innovative approach to fashion distribution. Unlike other online boutiques, we offer personal fashion consulting via our partner network of hair and beauty salons. Providing a high-end shopping experience with top quality textiles and designer fashion at unbeatable Web prices is our mission. Building on customers' existing relationships with trusted fashion and beauty professionals, we aim to exceed customer expectations and develop a 'customer once, client forever' model. To achieve this vision, our business model is based on trust, integrity and a commitment to providing added value for our customers, partners and staff.

As acknowledged experts in the latest fashions, our partner salons showcase Bowie's designs and make personal recommendations to their clients. Sophisticated predictive merchandising and production software enables us to run a lean, highly efficient on-demand supply chain. Customers pick up orders from the salons, which reinforces the client-advisor relationship and allows us to provide a fast turnaround on returns and exchanges. With a proven track record for innovation, we are continually finding ways of improving quality and reducing costs. Since starting business in 2004 with just five partner salons, our turnover has risen to over £12m; next year will see our network go international with new partner salons in Belgium, France and Germany.

We offer a constantly updated online catalogue of jeans, jackets and T-shirts for both men and women. We offer an unconditional no quibble guarantee and free returns service, whatever the reason. Most of all, our customers can rely on the expert opinions of their personal fashion advisers to ensure they never make a fashion faux pas.

Bowie's is a family business, founded and managed by Sam Marques; once a year the whole production family meet up with our friends from partner salons all over the country for a fun day out. This is one way to remind ourselves that the fashion business is all about people. When our customers look good, they feel good; when we achieve that goal, we feel good too.

Long-term personal customer relationships coupled with exceptional design, production and IT expertise make Bowie's stand out from the crowd. We would be delighted to welcome you into our family.

Thank you for taking the time to read this profile. If you have any questions or comments, please feel free to contact Kerry Clarke, our public relations officer at k.clarke@bowies.co.uk.

Glossary   PAGE 156

elevator pitch
faux pas
high-end
quibble
showcase
snappy
track record
turnaround

Internet research

Search for the keywords *F-pattern reading* to find out more about Web page design and how people read Web content. Check your favourite sites and blogs to see how well they accommodate F-pattern readers.

Language focus

4 Common collocations carry important information and give your text more impact. Match the impact collocations in each set.

1	no quibble	a)	experts
2	proven	b)	updated catalogue
3	acknowledged	c)	guarantee
4	constantly	d)	track record

5	customer once,	e)	business
6	exceed	f)	client forever
7	family	g)	customer relationships
8	long-term personal	h)	customer expectations

9	added	i)	service
10	free returns	j)	the crowd
11	fast	k)	value
12	stand out from	l)	turnaround

13	fresh and innovative	m)	Web prices
14	high-end shopping	n)	supply chain
15	on-demand	o)	approach
16	unbeatable	p)	experience

Output

5 Write a company profile for a real or fictitious business of your choice. Choose a context (web page, customer proposal, business plan, etc.) and use the structure guidelines and impact collocations to help you.

6 New business

- starting a new business
- presenting a one-minute pitch for a new business

6.6 Case study Angels or demons?

Discussion

1 Answer the quiz below about starting a business.

ARE YOU CAPABLE OF MINDING YOUR OWN BUSINESS?

Could you start your own enterprise? Sure, you may have spotted a gap in the market and even devised a cunning business plan for filling it. But do you personally have what it takes to turn a commercial idea into a profitable reality? Take our test to find out. Answer *Yes* or *No*.

1. Are you ready for a complete change?
2. Are you up for learning hard and fast?
3. Are you willing to take advice from others?
4. Can you stay self-motivated, even when faced with disappointment and difficulty?
5. Can you be emotionally resilient?
6. Are you able to think laterally?
7. Are you able to build up good working relationships?
8. Can you manage your time?
9. Can you work under stress?
10. Are you good at financial management?

2 Compare your answers with a partner. Say what would be your strongest and weakest points.

Reading

3 Kate Shapiro and Luis Hernández are friends and former co-workers living in Montreal, Canada. Read Kate's email to Luis and answer the questions.

1. Why was Luis depressed?
2. What does the winner of the fast pitch competition receive?
3. Why does Kate want to meet in a restaurant?

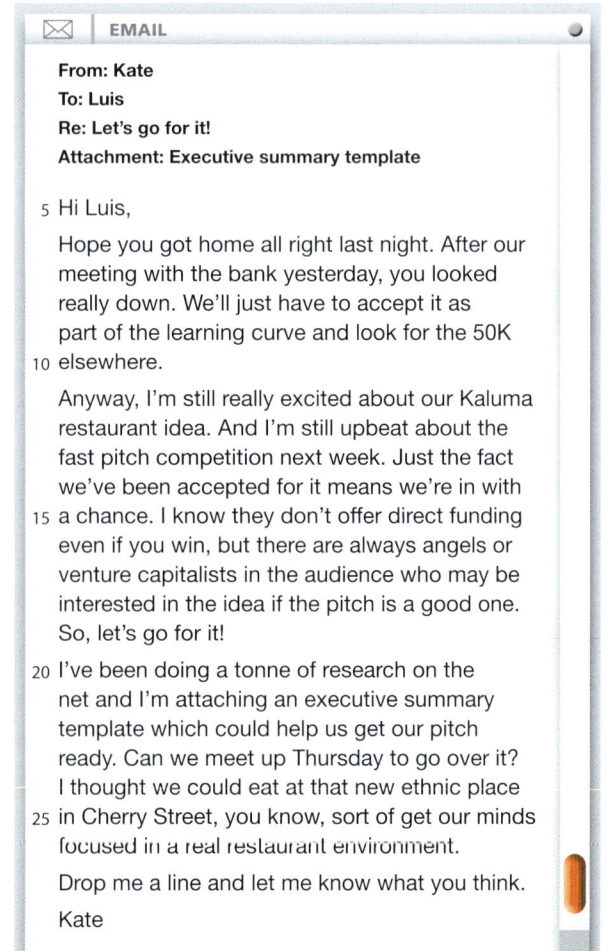

✉ EMAIL

From: Kate
To: Luis
Re: Let's go for it!
Attachment: Executive summary template

5 Hi Luis,

Hope you got home all right last night. After our meeting with the bank yesterday, you looked really down. We'll just have to accept it as part of the learning curve and look for the 50K
10 elsewhere.

Anyway, I'm still really excited about our Kaluma restaurant idea. And I'm still upbeat about the fast pitch competition next week. Just the fact we've been accepted for it means we're in with
15 a chance. I know they don't offer direct funding even if you win, but there are always angels or venture capitalists in the audience who may be interested in the idea if the pitch is a good one. So, let's go for it!

20 I've been doing a tonne of research on the net and I'm attaching an executive summary template which could help us get our pitch ready. Can we meet up Thursday to go over it? I thought we could eat at that new ethnic place
25 in Cherry Street, you know, sort of get our minds focused in a real restaurant environment.

Drop me a line and let me know what you think.

Kate

4 Before you listen, complete any information you can in the executive summary template.

Business name:
Outline:
Target customers:
Core products and services:
Management team:
Keys to success:
Financial summary:
Mission:

Listening

5 🔊 2:30 Two days later, Kate and Luis meet at the restaurant. Listen to their conversation and make notes to complete the rest of the template.

Preparation

6 Work in teams of three. Play the roles of Kate, Luis and Mario. Read the extract from the rules and, using the information on the template, prepare your pitch for the competition.

1 Pitches must be a maximum of 60 seconds, including any self-introductions and remarks. The microphone will be cut off automatically at the end of the 60 seconds, whether the pitch has finished or not.
2 Scoring is on a scale of 1–10 (1 = the lowest; 10 = the highest) for each of the following criteria: interest, clarity, persuasion and response to questions. The team with the highest combined score is the winner.
3 Each pitch will be followed by a three-minute question-and-answer session.

Internet research

Search for the keywords *angel fast pitch competition*. How many fast pitch competitions can you find? Watch or listen to some of the winning pitches and choose the best one. Report back to the class.

Listening

7 🔊 2:31 Pitch coach, Darren Larkins, interrupts your preparation session to give you some last minute tips on making the perfect pitch. Listen to his advice and adjust your pitch if necessary.

Presentation

8 Each team has one minute to make their pitch, followed by a three-minute question-and-answer session. Other teams ask questions and act as judges. Use the score card to note down the points you give, but do not reveal them.

Glossary PAGE 156

be up for
boost morale
cunning
drop someone a line
grab
hype
resilient
upbeat

Fast Pitch Score Card

Team	1	2	3	4	5
Interest					
Clarity					
Persuasion					
Response to questions					
TOTAL					

9 When every team has made their pitch, add up the points. The team with the highest total is the winner.

Review 5

Selling more

1 The words in bold are all in the wrong sentences. Move them so that the sentences make sense.

1 Michelle Hudson thinks dishonest digital marketers **bundle**.
2 'Get paid to **praise**' is a popular search on Google.
3 Users can receive a fee for following particular **sidelines**.
4 Dodgy companies can sell you a **double-edged sword** of 10,000 Twitter followers.
5 But does this damage a system which is based on **dashboards**?
6 Review sites are a **tweet** for the hotel industry.
7 Unsure how to react, hotels have been sitting on the **tracks**.
8 Revinate **suck** key words in blogs and discussion forums.
9 Medimix provides **Twitizens** for the medical industry.
10 These tools help companies respond to consumer complaints and **trust**.

2 Complete the text with the words in the box.

| coherency | convenience | cycle | environment |
| marketing | mix | place | price | product | promotion |

The marketing mix is often defined as being the 'four Ps'. But seen from the customer's point of view, these should perhaps be the 'four Cs'. So (1) _____ becomes customer solution, (2) _____ becomes cost, (3) _____ becomes communication, and (4) _____ (distribution) becomes (5) _____.
This basic (6) _____ can be expanded to include sub-mixes. For example, the promotion variable can be further broken down into advertising, sales promotion, personal selling, publicity, direct (7) _____ and e-marketing.
The elements of the mix have to blend together, and this is called (8) _____. Further, the mix has to be adapted to a changing business (9) _____, to changes in the organization's resources and to changes in the product life (10) _____.

3 Complete the text with the expressions in the box.

bring the product to market	face a declining market
flood the market	market leader	market research
market segmentation	market share	niche market

Start with some serious study – do some (1) _____.
Then you might discover how the market is divided up: the (2) _____. If you have an innovative but specialized product, don't worry, there will be a (3) _____ for it somewhere. Once you've found a manufacturer, it's time to (4) _____. Your aim initially will be to capture (5) _____. To do this, you might have to (6) _____ with a large number of cheap products – even below cost. But if your product is a good one, and your competitors weak, then hopefully you will soon become the (7) _____. However, here is a word of warning. Consumer tastes change very quickly and unless you continue to innovate you will soon (8) _____.

4 Add a question tag to the end of each sentence.

1 Sales are up again this quarter, _aren't they_?
2 It's not just because of our new advertising campaign, _____?
3 Profit margins look good as well, _____?
4 The new line of products won't be available until April, _____?
5 She's told Mike about the delay, _____?
6 Let's break for coffee now, _____?

5 Change the statements to negative questions to make them more persuasive.

1 It's time you looked at some alternatives.
   Isn't it time you looked at some alternatives?
2 You've been looking for a competitive edge.
   _____
3 Your customers ask for more functionality.
   _____
4 They would appreciate this model.
   _____

6 Read the customer's statement. Then fill in the missing letters to complete the salesman's possible replies (1–5).

Customer: The price is very high.

1 If I could po_____ne your first payment until next year, would you be r_____y to s_____ up today?
2 I'm g_____ you me_____ that. You're probably wo_____g why the price is higher than our competitors.
3 I understand how you fe__. A lot of our customers f__t that this was m___ th__ they wanted to sp___. But after using the product they fo__d that the be_____s through increased productivity really justified the investment.
4 Is the price the o___ re_____ you're not re___ to sign up now?
5 Yes, I know ex____y what you m___. It's a big decision to make. But have you as___ yo_____ why the price is set at that kind of level?

7 Match the sentences in Exercise 6 with the uses below.

a) Welcoming the objection ☐☐
b) Finding out the customer's position ☐☐
c) Use 'Feel, Felt, Found' ☐

8 Match the paragraphs from a mailshot with their descriptions below.

1 Hook ☐   3 Credentials ☐   5 Action ☐
2 Promise ☐ 4 Benefits ☐   6 PS ☐

a) saying what will happen if you use the product
b) saying how you will get an advantage in your life
c) finishing with a final reason to buy or act quickly
d) saying what the reader should do next
e) giving examples of existing users to establish credibility
f) getting people interested in the product

Review 6

New business

1 Fill in the missing letters to complete the article about creating a blockbuster brand.

It's not easy building a blockbuster (1) b_ _ _ d but if you have passion, (2) cr_ _ _ _ _ _ ty and a fantastic product, you too could be (3) ru_ _ _ _ g sh_ _ _ _ ers with famous (4) en_ _ _ _ _ _ _ _ urs in the years to come.
Daley Okren, an (5) asp_ _ _ ng chef, opened his first sandwich bar in London in 2009 with a small (6) in_ _ _ _ m_ _ t from family and friends. Initially selling basic sandwiches, he decided to (7) la_ _ ch a line of nutritionally-balanced, 'meal-in-one' rolls which soon had regular customers (8) s_ _ g_ _ g their pr_ _ _ _ s. With a (9) k_ _ ck for developing new recipes, over the next two years Okren opened (10) ou_ _ _ ts across Britain. In 2012, the company (11) r_ _ g up a profit of £1.2 million.
Now, with a CEO handling the (12) d_ _ -to-_ _ y operations, Okren is able to concentrate on what he does best – creating new recipes. In the near future, he hopes to get the (13) b_ _ k_ _ g of an international chain, in the form of a (14) ma_ _ _ _ _ y st_ _ e in the company. This will give him the (15) c_ _ _ t_ l and management expertise necessary to take the company to the next level.

2 Complete the sentences with the correct form of the phrasal verbs in the box. The clues in brackets will help you.

check out	come up	draw up	get through
go through	put forward	set out	turn down
work out			

1 When the new health and safety laws _____, we'll have to change the way the factory operates. (be officially approved and accepted)
2 They rejected all the proposals we _____. (suggest an idea so that people can discuss it and make a decision)
3 In her report she _____ her plans for reorganizing the department. (explain in a clear and detailed way)
4 It's a very confusing situation. I can't _____ what to do. (solve a problem by considering the facts)
5 Our brainstorming meetings usually generate a lot of ideas for new products, but only a few _____. (reach a good enough standard to pass to the next stage)
6 Something important _____ in the meeting this morning. I need to tell you about it. (be mentioned or suggested)
7 We agreed the deal in principle; now our lawyers have to _____ the contract. (prepare and write)
8 We should _____ his story carefully – I don't know whether we can trust him. (make sure that something is true or correct)
9 We were very reasonable during the negotiations, but they _____ our final offer. (refuse)

3 Complete the sentences with the most likely form of the verb in brackets and either *will* or *will be doing*. Use contractions.

1 When I retire, I _____ (travel) around the world.
2 I won't be in the office on Monday – I _____ (travel) between Frankfurt and Berlin.
3 Is this seat free? No? Don't worry, I _____ (sit) over there.
4 This time next week I _____ (sit) under a palm tree drinking piña coladas.

4 Complete the sentences with the most likely form of the verb in brackets and either *will be doing* or *will have done*. Use contractions.

1 By the time he retires, he _____ (work) here for over thirty years.
2 I don't think Marcus will join us in the pub – he _____ (work) late to finish the report.
3 By six o'clock we _____ (interview) more than a dozen candidates.
4 You won't be able to reach me on my mobile this afternoon – I _____ (interview) candidates for the new sales job.

5 Cover the box at the foot of the page. You can use expressions 1–7 to answer questions after a presentation. Try to complete them without looking at the box. Then uncover the box and compare your answers.

1 I'm _____ I don't have the _____ with me. Can I _____ _____ to you on that?
2 I think I covered that in Part Two, but just let me _____.
3 To be _____, I think that raises a difficult _____.
4 I understand your position, but I can _____ you that we have done our _____.
5 _____ me explain. It's quite _____, really.
6 Our turbine is the most efficient on the market. To _____ _____, it's twenty per cent more efficient than any of our competitors'.
7 We will sell more than 450,000 units in the next twelve months. To _____ it into _____, that's twice as many units as this year.

afraid	assure	back	be	figures	get
homework	honest	issue	let	perspective	
precise	put	recap	simple		

7 Financial control

- accountancy as a career
- opinions on accountancy

7.1 About business   Accountants

Discussion

1 With a partner, match the beginnings of these accountant jokes with their endings.

1. How many accountants does it take to change a light bulb?
2. Why do accountants get excited on Saturdays?
3. Why did the auditor cross the road?
4. There are just three types of accountants.

a) How much money do you have?
b) Those who can count and those who can't.
c) They can wear casual clothes to work.
d) Because he looked in the file and that's what they did last year.

2 What image does each joke give of accountants? What reasons can you think of for the image accountants have?

Listening

3 2:32 Listen to a careers consultant talking about changing perceptions of accountancy and answer the questions.

1. What three reasons does the consultant give for accountancy's traditional image?
2. What three reasons does the consultant give for accountancy's image improving?

Reading

4 Read the title, first paragraph and last paragraph of the article opposite and answer the questions.

1. Do you think the 'future accountant' T-shirt really exists?
2. Why does the author think it might be ironic?
3. Is the author positive or negative about accountancy in general?

5 Read the whole article. According to the author, which three personal characteristics do forensic accountants require?

6 Complete the sentences with the correct option a–d.

1. According to current perception, the accountancy profession
   a) contains more attractive members.
   b) is better paid than in the past.
   c) has too many job applicants.
   d) seems less boring than before.
2. The difference between forensic accountants and most other accountancy professionals is that their work always
   a) involves attendance at major crime scenes.
   b) relates to information used in legal proceedings.
   c) requires greater technical knowledge.
   d) ensures that financial criminals get convicted.
3. Al Capone was finally sent to prison because
   a) he was involved in a variety of crimes.
   b) his financial affairs were exposed.
   c) the Supreme Court convicted him.
   d) his criminal gang betrayed him.
4. In the future, forensic accountants will
   a) show how terrorist crimes get funding.
   b) change attitudes to white-collar crime.
   c) replace fingerprint experts on crime teams.
   d) reduce levels of support for terrorism.

Internet research

Search for the keywords *extreme accounting*. What does this involve? What do you think this idea is intended to achieve?

Discussion

7 In small groups, discuss the questions.

1. How far are you convinced that accountancy's image is improving?
2. To what extent do you think accountancy is a good career choice? Why?
3. Is technology likely to make accountancy easier or more difficult in the future? Why?

I RECENTLY SAW a student on a university campus wearing a T-shirt with the phrase 'future accountant'. Given the profession's traditional image problem, it must have been ironic, mustn't it?

Perhaps not. There are signs that accountancy is putting its traditional image problem behind it. Increasing numbers of graduates are applying to join the profession, motivated not just by the prospect of high salaries but also by a change in perception. Ironically, it is partly its association with the twenty-first century's biggest financial scandals of Enron and WorldCom that has made accountancy become, well, trendier.

At the forefront of this image makeover is the specialism of forensic accounting, with its suggestion of crime scene investigators and technicians in white coats. In reality, a forensic accountant's work is chiefly concerned with any investigation of financial data which will eventually be used in some form of litigation. Some of them work for law enforcement agencies gathering evidence to support fraud and bribery charges. Others are expert witnesses who testify on either side in financial dispute cases.

While it might not always be *CSI Miami*, forensic accountants do need to develop some special skills which relate to their roles as investigators. For instance, a forensic accountant's work can make them crucial figures in high-profile criminal cases like Enron, so a confident manner in court can be helpful. In addition, a systematic and analytical mind is essential. For example, in a fraud case, they may need to search financial records thoroughly, looking for patterns of similarities and coincidences that might indicate a cover-up. Imagination – not a characteristic traditionally associated with accounting – is also part of their skill set, as they dig deeper and try to get into the mind of suspected fraudsters.

Although the term 'forensic accounting' is relatively recent, the importance of accountants in legal matters has a long history. The most famous case in which forensic accountancy has provided the pivotal evidence was in the conviction of the notorious Chicago gangster Al Capone. While Capone's criminal activities had included protection rackets and murder, he was finally convicted on the apparently lesser charge of tax evasion. Elmer Irey, an official at the US Inland Revenue Service, believed that Capone's conviction could be obtained on the basis of a Supreme Court ruling that the income from organized criminal activity was also subject to taxation. A team of investigators spent several years gathering evidence on Capone's net worth and expenditure, sometimes working undercover as members of his criminal gang. They ultimately succeeded in assembling the documentary evidence needed to convict him.

Many believe that future demand for forensic accountancy services will only get bigger. Stories of scams and frauds emerge daily in the media and, against the background of Enron and WorldCom, the problem of white-collar crime is being taken increasingly seriously by policy-makers. The US Sarbanes-Oxley Act is just one example of this change in attitude.

But it's not just in the area of white-collar crime that forensic accountants will find future employment. Terrorists require money for their activities but need to conceal their sources of funding to avoid capture. The role of the forensic accountant will be to reveal the money trail from terrorist suspects back to their sponsors. Their importance has recently led one senior British politician to liken forensic accountants to the fingerprint experts of previous generations.

The future looks bright for accountancy, and there are enough exciting roles in the profession to ensure that its image is not quite what it once was. So, in case you run into someone wearing a 'future accountant' T-shirt, think before you congratulate them on their irony. They might just be serious.

Glossary PAGE 156

bribery
forefront
fraudster
makeover
protection racket
scam
undercover
white-collar crime

Why it's trendy to be a future accountant

7 Financial control

- P&L account, balance sheet, cash flow statement
- accounting terms
- verbs for enabling and preventing

Glossary PAGE 157
depreciation
pellet
snapshot

7.2 Vocabulary Financial documents and regulation

Discussion

1 With a partner, discuss the following questions.

1 How do you keep track of your personal finances? Do you keep accounts, use a computer program to track your income and expenditure, or simply look at your bank statements?
2 Do you know today whether you are in credit or in debt?

Defining words

2 Match the three main accounting documents 1–3 with the best description a–c.

1 profit and loss account
2 balance sheet
3 cash flow statement

a) to indicate inflow and outflow of money over a specific period, in particular to make sure it does not run out
b) to show managers whether a business made or lost money over a specific period
c) to provide a snapshot of a business's value at a particular point in time, showing what it has and what it owes

3 Match the three main accounting documents to the simplified examples below. Why are some numbers listed in brackets?

a _____
2012
Cash receipts (a)
Cash sales	€175,000
Loans	€40,000
Total cash receipts	€215,000

Cash payments (b)
Rent	€102,000
Admin	€85,000
Total cash payments	€187,000
Net cash flow	€28,000

b _____
2012
Net sales (c)	250,000
Cost of sales	(80,000)
Gross profit	170,000
Selling, general and administrative expenses	(65,000)
Operating profit (d)	105,000
Other income	20,000
Earnings before taxes	125,000
Taxes	(25,000)
Net income	100,000

c _____
April 1 2012
Assets
Current assets (e)
Cash	€75,000
Accounts receivable	€150,000
Total current assets	€225,000

Fixed assets (f)
Land	€150,000
Total fixed assets	€150,000
Total assets	€375,000

Liabilities (g)
Current liabilities
Taxes payable	€100,000
Payroll	€125,000
Total current liabilities	€225,000

Long-term liabilities
Loans repayable	€50,000
Total long-term liabilities	€50,000
Total liabilities	€275,000
Net assets (h)	€100,000
Owners' equity (i)	€100,000

4 Complete the sentences with terms a–i in the accounting documents above.

1 A business's _____ are the sums that it will have to pay at some time in the future, such as loan repayments or taxes.
2 All funds going out of a business in a specific period are known as _____.
3 The amount of profit after general running costs are deducted is known as _____.
4 Businesses often have money in the bank or money owed to them, known as _____.
5 The total income from all of a business's normal trading activity is known as _____.
6 All money coming into a business in a specific period is known as _____.
7 Some things that a business owns cannot be turned easily into cash: these things are its _____.
8 The difference between what a business owns and what it owes are its _____, which are equal to the _____.

Internet research

Search for the keywords *financial statements beginners' guide* to find further information about the main financial statements. Which site presents the statements most clearly? Compare your findings and vote for the best site.

5 Match the accounting categories 1–6 with the examples a–f.
1 depreciation
2 plant and machinery
3 raw materials
4 accounts payable
5 payroll
6 extraordinary income

a) Cherubs Pre-school Nursery employs five carers who get paid weekly.
b) Focal Photography Shop owes €3,000 to its suppliers.
c) Speedier Deliveries owns six vans. Last year, the resale value of each van fell by 20%.
d) Jonson Manufacturing has just raised €1.6 million from the sale of part of its site.
e) Stronglite Engineering has a small factory with a range of heavy-duty metalworking tools.
f) KJK Products spent €10,000 on plastic pellets for manufacturing.

6 Answer the following questions about the categories in Exercise 5.
1 Where on the cash flow statement would you put **raw materials** and **payroll**?
2 Where on the profit and loss account would you put **depreciation** and **extraordinary income**?
3 Where on the balance sheet would you put **plant and machinery** and **accounts payable**?

Enabling and preventing

7 Read the articles by three business owners who describe how financial documents have helped improve their business. Complete them with the correct form of the verbs in the boxes.

discourage   encourage   let   make

SALLY SANTANA I run a clothing business in Barcelona called Tangerine. The balance sheet is an invaluable document for me. Because it's a snapshot, I find it (1) _____ me to really think about whether my business is in the best shape. The profit and loss account is helpful, but the balance sheet (2) _____ me see what I actually owe in the short and long term. It has also (3) _____ me from developing bad habits: for instance, it has (4) _____ me pay my creditors sooner rather than later, so that the balance sheet looks better and improves our position with the bank.

allow   force   help   prevent

JAIME TRIER When we started up, I used a cash flow forecast as part of our application to the bank and it (5) _____ us get a start-up loan. Our bakery business, Kernel, has gone from strength to strength since then, but keeping an eye on cash flow has always been important to (6) _____ cash imbalances. If we got this wrong, it might even (7) _____ us to go out of business. I used to use a spreadsheet, but I've invested in some accounting software now which (8) _____ me to present the information in the form I need.

compel   enable   permit   prohibit

DANA SOARES I set up DS Engineering ten years ago, with the help of investment from a group of business angels. Obviously, they demand detailed reporting on our finances. And, whilst their rules of investment don't (9) _____ certain practices in the way some accounting regulations do, they're understandably quite strict: they certainly wouldn't (10) _____ us to take any unnecessary risks. The profit and loss account (11) _____ the investors to see that we are making a profit and (12) _____ us to make better decisions on what to do next.

8 Work with a partner. Use the verbs in Exercise 7 to write short explanations of what the following business documents are used to enable, help, prevent, etc.

- health and safety guidelines
- a business plan
- an annual report
- a meeting agenda

7 Financial control

- verbs and phrases for talking about cause and effect
- verbs for describing ability
- *a/an*, *the* and no article

Refresh your memory

Cause and effect
Verbs and prepositions: *lead to, result in, arise from*, etc.
Phrases: *owing to, due to, as a result of*

Ability
can/could for general ability to do something in the present/past
was able to/managed to/succeeded in for specific cases of ability in the past

Articles
a/an: non-specific or not previously mentioned
the: specific, unique or previously mentioned
no article: generalizations, abstract qualities, uncountable nouns

▶ Grammar and practice Pages 134–135

Glossary PAGE 157

admin
knock-on effect
misery
notably
raw materials
spiralling
stem from

7.3 Grammar Cause and effect, ability, articles

Cause and effect

1 With a partner, put the expressions in the correct column in the table.

arose from	As a result of	Because of	brought about	~~Due to~~	gave rise to
~~led to~~	On account of	originated in	Owing to	resulted from	resulted in
~~stemmed from~~	was/were due to

cause + **expression** + effect	effect + **expression** + cause	**expression** + cause + effect
led to	*stemmed from*	*Due to*

2 Fantastik is a manufacturer of air-conditioning equipment. Look at the graph of last year's sales figures for fans. With your partner, take turns to explain why sales were good or bad throughout the year, using the expressions in Exercise 1.

The freezing weather in February led to a sharp drop in sales. or
Low sales in February stemmed from the freezing weather. or
Due to freezing weather in February, sales were low.

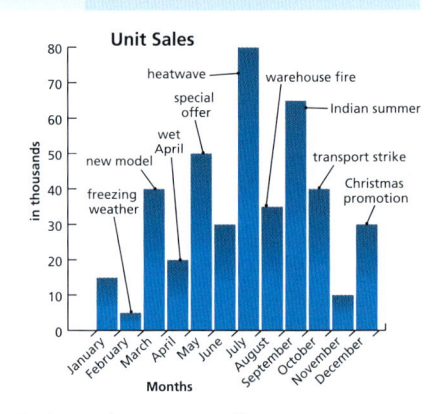

Describing ability

3 Work with a partner. Look at the graph in Exercise 2. Say what Fantastik:
- **can** or **can't** do in general each year.
- **were able to** do/**managed to** do/**succeeded in** doing last year.
- **couldn't** do last year.

*In the summer, the weather is hot so they **can** sell a lot of fans.*
*Last August, they **couldn't** sell as many fans due to the warehouse fire.*
*But they **managed to** sell more than usual in September because of the good weather.*

Articles

4 Work in small groups. You have $300 to bet on whether each sentence is correct or incorrect. The minimum bet on each sentence is $10. If the sentence is incorrect, correct it by adding, deleting or changing the articles *a/an* or *the*. For every sentence you get right, you keep the money you bet. For every sentence you get wrong, you lose it. Which group has the most money?

1. Sue gave me a useful information about the new regulations.
2. Bob's a real technophobe: he just hates the computers!
3. The company was criticised for aiming products at the young.
4. To become accountant, Geri spent three years studying.
5. They bought a new machinery to help them meet the order.
6. HR are finding it difficult to find candidates with the intelligence.
7. Tina felt she didn't have the confidence to succeed in France.
8. Luke resigned after he was accused of an unethical behaviour.
9. When completing your expenses form, remember to claim for the entertaining.
10. The CFO asked me to do a research to establish why our losses had increased.

Reporting performance

5 Read Fantastik's targets for a set of key indicators and the firm's actual performance. Which targets did the company meet?

	TARGET	ACTUAL
Unit sales	400,000	420,000
Value of sales	€10 million	€9.8 million
Repeat business	+ 5%	+ 5%
Admin costs	– 2%	– 3%
Raw materials (plastic)	– 4%	– 2%
Payroll	€2.5 million	€2.35 million
Operating profit	€220,000	€255,000

6 Complete the sentences with verbs for describing ability and your own words.

1 Fantastik hoped to sell 400,000 units, and *managed to sell 420,000*.
2 Fantastik planned net sales of €10 million. In fact, they only _____.
3 Fantastik planned to increase repeat business by 5%, and they _____.
4 Fantastik set a target to reduce admin costs by 2%. They _____.
5 Fantastik hoped to reduce raw material costs by 4%, but _____.
6 Fantastik planned _____.
7 Fantastik hoped _____.

Explaining performance

7 Read the articles. Make notes on factors which might explain each of Fantastik's results.

HOTTEST ON RECORD
Yesterday, temperatures topped 38°C for the fourth time in July. This means that we are having the hottest July since records began. Several offices have sent staff home after complaints about staff feeling ill at work. It's not all bad, though: sellers of refrigerated products and air-conditioning ...

COST RELIEF FOR BUSINESSES
After several years of spiralling costs, there are signs that businesses in Western Europe are finding it cheaper to operate. Labour costs have dropped slightly due to the availability of migrant workers from new European states. However, the picture for manufacturers is mixed: the price of oil is high. Consequently, petroleum-derived products are expensive, with knock-on effects on ...

EXCHANGE RATE MISERY FOR EXPORTERS
Unfavourable exchange rates mean that exporters have struggled to remain competitive, say industry analysts. 'We've also seen a big increase in unpaid bills,' said one manufacturer yesterday ...

8 Write a paragraph about Fantastik's performance. Use expressions from Exercise 1 for describing cause and effect.

*Hot temperatures **resulted in** some sickness among staff. This **brought about** complaints and ...*

9 Complete the extract below from the CFO's speech to staff with *a/an*, *the* or no article.

Since I became (1) _____ accountant, I can't remember (2) _____ better year for (3) _____ air-conditioning business. We received (4) _____ information early in (5) _____ summer that (6) _____ hot weather was coming, and we increased (7) _____ production accordingly. Some people have found (8) _____ weather uncomfortable, notably (9) _____ elderly and (10) _____ very young. Many people have ended up in (11) _____ hospital. But (12) _____ demand for (13) _____ air-conditioning products has risen well in (14) _____ commercial sector, our main market. Congratulations to (15) _____ sales team, who had (16) _____ intelligence to sell effectively, and did (17) _____ great work all round. And I've got (18) _____ good news for you: all staff will receive (19) _____ bonus of €500 with (20) _____ next month's salary.

Speaking

10 Think of situations in which you ...

- managed to do something unexpected.
- failed to complete an important task.
- succeeded in meeting an important target.
- weren't able to achieve what you had intended.

11 Work with a partner. Tell your partner about your experiences in Exercise 10, explaining the events that led up to this and what effects the situation brought about.

Internet research

Search for the keywords *causes of business failure*. Find a story involving a strange chain of events and tell the class about it.

7 Financial control

- identifying factors for successful meetings
- expressions for communicating in meetings
- roleplaying a meeting

7.4 Speaking Communicating in meetings

Discussion

1 Work with a partner. Read the descriptions about how people behave in meetings and decide where you would put your culture on the scales. Compare your ideas with your partner.

In meetings, people generally:

are clear	are unclear
admit they don't understand	never admit ignorance
stick to the agenda	don't stick to the agenda
summarize decisions clearly	don't summarize decisions
are direct and sometimes rude	are indirect and never rude
often interrupt	rarely interrupt

Listening

2 2:33 The American group, Mahler, has recently acquired the French packaging company Polystok. Listen to the meeting between Alice, Mahler's CFO, and two Polystok employees, Serge and David. Answer the questions.

1. How successful do you think the meeting is?
2. How much do you think David and Serge understand?
3. How could the meeting have been more effective?

3 2:34 Now, listen to a second version of the same conversation. Why is the meeting more productive?

Analysis

4 2:34 With a partner, find suitable words to complete the expressions in the checklist for communicating in meetings. Then listen again and check your answers.

5 Add each phrase below to the correct category in the checklist.

a) In other words, …
b) What exactly do you mean by …?
c) I'm not sure I follow you.
d) To recap, …
e) Let me start again.
f) So you mean …
g) Does that make sense?
h) Before we close, let me just summarize the main points.
i) Am I being clear?
j) If I understand correctly, …
k) Shall I go over the main points we agreed?
l) To sum up, …

Glossary PAGE 157

in good shape
iron out
starving
take stock
tweak

Useful expressions: Communicating in meetings

Asking for clarification

Could you be _____ ?

Clarifying

What I _____ is …

Checking you understand

So, what you're _____ is …

Checking other people understand

Do you _____ what I _____ ?

Summarizing

Can we _____ what we've decided?

eWorkbook
Now watch the video for this unit.

Internet research
Search for the keywords *ending a meeting*. List five pieces of advice on how to end a meeting well. Compare your advice with other students.

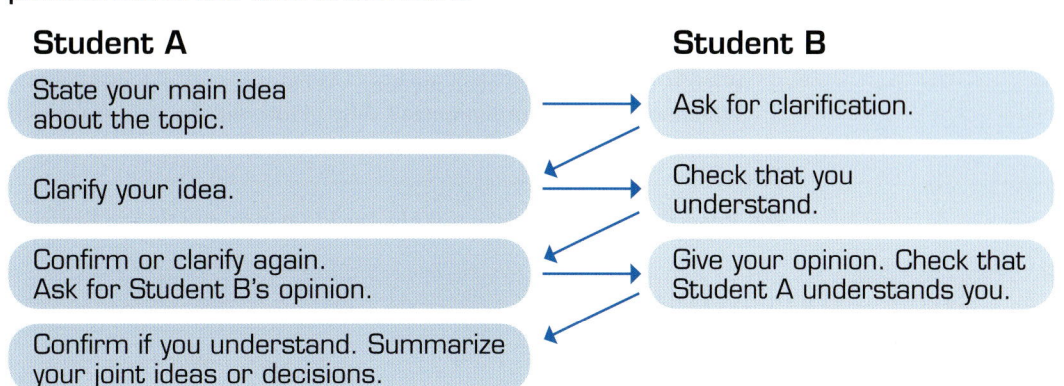

Speaking

6 Read the four situations below. Decide what action you would recommend in each situation. Make notes on your ideas.

1 Levels of executive pay have been rising in your industry. This makes recruitment difficult for your firm. How should you respond?
2 Your new CEO wants to introduce more American business practices. Some staff are resistant. What advice would you give the CEO?
3 Your country's education system doesn't produce the graduates you need. How could you improve the standard of job applicants?
4 Your firm has been criticised for employing too few women. How could you change this situation?

7 With a partner, hold short meetings on the issues in Exercise 6. Follow the structure provided below. Take turns to be A and B.

Student A
- State your main idea about the topic.
- Clarify your idea.
- Confirm or clarify again. Ask for Student B's opinion.
- Confirm if you understand. Summarize your joint ideas or decisions.

Student B
- Ask for clarification.
- Check that you understand.
- Give your opinion. Check that Student A understands you.

Roleplay

8 Work in groups of three. Take the roles of Alice, Serge and David and read the appropriate role card: Alice (page 115), Serge (page 117) and David (page 120). Hold a meeting to discuss the points on the agenda and remember to clarify your position if necessary.

Agenda

New accounting procedures
1 Introduction
2 Definition of new procedures
3 Schedule for implementation
4 Extra staffing requirements
5 Training on the new accounting procedures
6 Installation of new accounting software
7 Temporary project team requirements
8 Training on the new software
9 AOB

7 Financial control

- presentation and content
- action verbs
- writing minutes

7.5 Writing Minutes

Discussion

1 Work with a partner. Read about the meeting situations a–d and answer questions 1–3.

a) Hyperion Advertising office staff are meeting in a café to discuss their Christmas lunch.
b) Wells Engineering have just completed a major construction project. They are holding a one-off project review meeting today.
c) Living Colours is a printing company. The finance department are holding their fortnightly update meeting.
d) At Bitstore Electronics, two senior executives are meeting this afternoon to discuss which of four interviewees they will appoint as sales manager.

1 How formal will each meeting be?
2 What is the purpose of each meeting? What items do you think will be on the agenda?
3 Which meetings require minutes? Why? How will the minutes be different?

Model

2 Read the minutes below quickly. Decide which meeting in Exercise 1 they relate to.

MEETING MINUTES

Date: 11 June   Time: 15.30
(1) _____: Room 344
(2) _____: Enzo Falconi (EF)
(3) _____: Alice Keller (AK), Francois Weber (FW), Dylan Sanders (DS)

(4) _____	(5) _____	(6) _____
1 New staff	EF <u>announced</u> the appointment of Sally Collins as head of accounts payable.	
2 Office layout	FW expressed concern about the open-plan arrangement. We identified two main problems: telephone noise and lack of meeting rooms. AK proposed screens or full partitions. We agreed that EF (will investigate) the price of screens and FW will get quotations on full partitions.	EF and FW 25 June
3 Expenses claims	DS requested that all staff complete expense claim forms on time. We accepted that the form could be simpler. DS will prepare a new form by next meeting.	DS 25 June
4 Appraisals	We decided that the current appraisal system is not working, and we concluded that six-monthly appraisals would be better. AK to look into the practicalities of this.	AK 30 June

(7) _____: 25 June 13.00

Analysis

3 Complete gaps 1–7 in the minutes with these labels.

Action   Attendees   Chair   Discussion   Item   Next meeting   Venue

4 Answer the questions about the minutes in Exercise 2.
1 What do you notice about how names are presented?
2 What is the purpose of the Action column?
3 Which verbs in the minutes tell you what happened? The first one is underlined.
4 Which verbs in the minutes tell you what actions are planned? The first one is circled.

Internet research

Search for the words *writing clear minutes* and make a list of ten tips for good minute writing. Compile a class top ten.

Glossary PAGE 157

chair
open-plan office
partition
venue

Language focus

5 Summarize these extracts from the meeting using appropriate verbs from the box. The first one is done as an example.

confirm   congratulate   ~~discuss~~   explain   reject   suggest

1 AK: Basically, there are two options: either we install screens or full partitions. Of course, screens would be cheaper, but, on the other hand, full partitions would probably be much more effective …
We discussed the pros and cons of screens or full partitions.
2 EF: So, to summarize, we all agree then that we don't want to keep the existing open-plan arrangement, OK?
3 EF: Well done, Sally. You've really done a great job in accounts receivable.
4 DS: The reasons why the current appraisal system is not working are that the interviews take too long and they only happen once a year.
5 DS: I've spoken to all the department heads and I can assure you that they all think the current expense claim form is too complicated.
6 FW: Why don't we get three quotations for screens and three for partitions?

6 Match the decisions 1–6 with the action plans a–f, using an appropriate action verb from the box. The first one is done as an example.

arrange   chase up   contact   draw up   evaluate   ~~organize~~

1 EF suggested celebrating Sally's promotion. He will *organize* … – c
2 We decided to consult department heads on the new appraisal scheme. EF will …
3 AK proposed getting examples of screens and partitions so she will …
4 It was agreed that external advice on running appraisal interviews would be useful. FW will …
5 We concluded that a more detailed cost breakdown was necessary. DS to …
6 It was noted that only one quotation has been received to date. DS to …

a) … a visit to the suppliers' showroom.
b) … the other two suppliers.
c) … an after-work drink in the local pub for the accounts department.
d) … the best proposals and report back at the next meeting.
e) … a specialized management consultancy.
f) … a draft questionnaire before our next meeting.

Listening and note-taking

7 2:35–2:37 Three months later, the Living Colours finance team are holding another meeting. Look at the three main items on the agenda below. What issues do you think the participants might raise regarding each point? Listen to three extracts from the meeting and check if your ideas were mentioned.

Meeting agenda – Finance Department efficiency drive

Date: 16 September
Time: 14.30–16.00
Venue: Room 346

1 Minutes of last meeting
2 Chasing up late payers
3 Covering for absent colleagues
4 Reducing office waste
5 AOB

8 2:35–2:37 Listen to the three extracts again. Make meeting notes on what they decided for items 2–4.

Output

9 Use the notes you made in Exercise 8 to write the minutes of the meeting. Use the same format as the meeting minutes in Exercise 2.

7 Financial control

- honest and dishonest business activities
- agreeing on a plan of action

7.6 Case study Car-Glazer

Discussion

1 In small groups, answer the questions about the activities in the list.

1. Are these actions honest or dishonest, or is there a grey area in between?
2. For which actions should employers warn, reprimand or dismiss people. For which should they do nothing?

- making personal photocopies at work
- using the company phone to make private calls
- embezzling money from the company
- going to the dentist during working hours
- throwing a 'sickie'
- surfing the net during office hours
- borrowing money from the petty cash

Scan reading

2 Read the three documents below and answer the questions.

1. What business is Car-Glazer in and what services do they offer?
2. What does Emily Wyatt do and how long has she been working for the Czech subsidiary of Car-Glazer International plc? Write her name on the organigram opposite.
3. Who introduced Emily to Car-Glazer?
4. What problem is Car-Glazer facing with some of its technicians?

Glossary PAGE 157

bodyshop
chasing letter
dent
embezzle
reprimand
scratch
sickie
suspension

Car-Glazer International

Car-Glazer – Trade

Car-Glazer offers a comprehensive on-site windscreen and body glass replacement service to the motor trade throughout Europe. We visit your garage, showroom, forecourt or bodyshop to repair or replace all types of vehicle glass.

Hired Emily Wyatt, 20 Feb 2012 (Referred to us by Filip Novak - they met at business school)

Chief Accountant

- Reporting directly to the Director of Car-Glazer, Czech Republic
- Managing all aspects of the accounting function (accounts receivable and payable, budget, cash flow, tax)
- Establishing and maintaining accounting practices to ensure accurate and reliable data for business operations

Memo

Date: 8 October 2012
To: All technicians

We are receiving a growing number of claims from garages for damage to vehicles in the course of glass replacement: paint chips, minor dents and scratches, broken mirrors, etc.

Please ensure that you work carefully and follow company procedures, as such claims cost us (and indirectly, you) money!

Counting on all of you to see a reduction in claims.

Andy Webb
CEO Car-Glazer plc

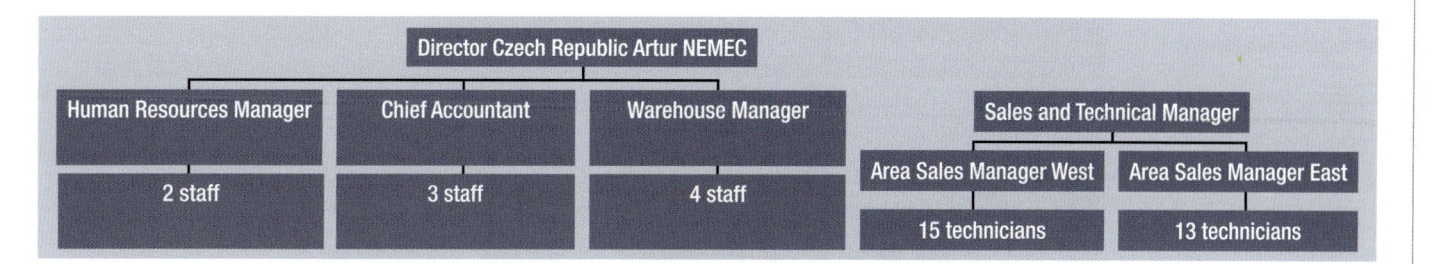

```
                    Director Czech Republic Artur NEMEC
    ┌───────────────────┬──────────────┬──────────────┬────────────────────────────┐
Human Resources    Chief Accountant   Warehouse            Sales and Technical Manager
Manager                                Manager        ┌──────────────────┬──────────────────┐
  2 staff            3 staff           4 staff        Area Sales Manager  Area Sales Manager
                                                      West                East
                                                      15 technicians      13 technicians
```

Analysis

3 Emily Wyatt arrives at work one morning to find this email waiting for her. Read the email and answer the questions.

1. What does Robert do in Car-Glazer? Write his name on the organigram.
2. What reasons could Nina Kovar have for being evasive?
3. What reasons could Garage Miler have for invoicing two separate bills and why might the technicians have caused more damage than usual?

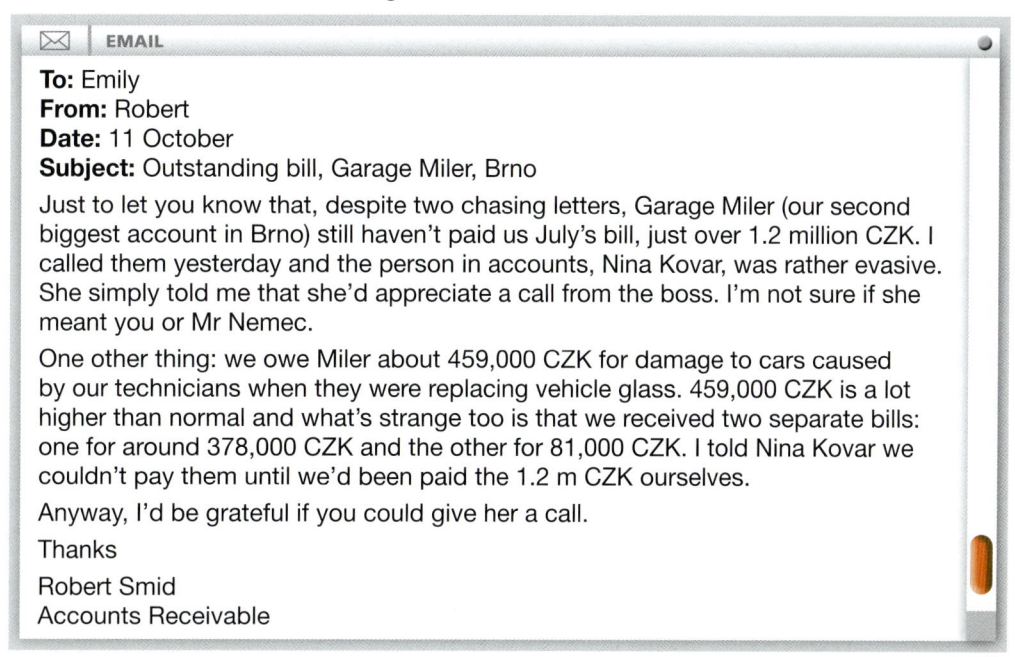

EMAIL

To: Emily
From: Robert
Date: 11 October
Subject: Outstanding bill, Garage Miler, Brno

Just to let you know that, despite two chasing letters, Garage Miler (our second biggest account in Brno) still haven't paid us July's bill, just over 1.2 million CZK. I called them yesterday and the person in accounts, Nina Kovar, was rather evasive. She simply told me that she'd appreciate a call from the boss. I'm not sure if she meant you or Mr Nemec.

One other thing: we owe Miler about 459,000 CZK for damage to cars caused by our technicians when they were replacing vehicle glass. 459,000 CZK is a lot higher than normal and what's strange too is that we received two separate bills: one for around 378,000 CZK and the other for 81,000 CZK. I told Nina Kovar we couldn't pay them until we'd been paid the 1.2 m CZK ourselves.

Anyway, I'd be grateful if you could give her a call.

Thanks

Robert Smid
Accounts Receivable

Listening for detail

4 🔊 2:38 Emily calls Nina Kovar. Listen to the conversation and answer the questions.

1. Who does Emily speak to in the end?
2. Who is Filip Novak? Write his name on the organigram.
3. What company car does Filip drive?
4. What car did Filip have repaired?
5. Why hasn't Garage Miler paid the outstanding bill?
6. In Emily's position, what would you do?

Discussion

5 Hold a meeting to decide what action Car-Glazer should take regarding Filip Novak. Consider the following courses of action:

- reprimand
- official warning
- temporary suspension
- dismissal
- other

Listening

6 🔊 2:39 During the meeting, Artur Nemec takes a call and announces some good news. Listen to what he has to say. How does this affect your decision?

Internet research

Search for the key words *famous whistleblowers*. What are whistleblowers in the business world and what scandals have been brought to light by them?

8 Fair trade

- the fair trade movement
- fair trade vs. free trade

8.1 About business Fair trade or free trade?

Discussion

1 Answer these questions.

1 What sort of products are traded under the label 'fair trade'?
2 When you buy a cup of coffee, what is 'a fair price'?
3 If you spent your holidays working on a coffee farm, how would you define 'a fair wage' and 'fair working conditions'?
4 If you owned a café, how would you define 'a fair profit' on a cup of coffee?

Predicting

2 Read the title of the article opposite and predict which of these points will be expressed by the writer. Then read the article and check your predictions.

1 Fair trade products make rich consumers feel guilty.
2 Free trade would help the poorest farmers more than fair trade.
3 Fair trade products are low quality.
4 Fair trade farmers are encouraged to modernize their production methods.
5 Big coffee chains force farmers to reduce their prices.

Reading for detail

3 Read the article again and answer the questions.

1 What must be paid to get fair trade certification?
2 Why might western consumers be attracted to fair trade goods?
3 Which consequence of fair trade has led Mexican producers to expand production?
4 Why do richer producers benefit most from fair trade?
5 Which processes of agricultural development has fair trade discouraged?
6 How have consumer attitudes to coffee changed?
7 Which producers have improved income without help from fair trade?

4 Find phrases in the article that imply these strong opinions.

1 Fair trade supporters know very little about economics. (paragraph 1)
2 Fixing fair trade prices unfairly deprives the poorest farmers of a way to make a living. (paragraph 2)
3 Fair trade supporters are naive to think they can solve all the problems of the developing world. (paragraph 3)
4 Fair trade supporters are out of touch with the realities of modern agriculture. (paragraph 4)
5 Fair trade prevents producers from increasing efficiency and revenue. (paragraph 4)
6 Coffee chains, unlike fair trade campaigners, benefit poor producers. (paragraph 6)

Listening

5 🔊 2:40 Listen to a radio phone-in about the article. What two benefits of fair trade does the speaker argue for?

Discussion

6 In small groups, discuss how far you think each of the statements below is true.

- Free trade rewards efficiency; fair trade rewards bad habits.
- Fair trade is the best protection some workers have against exploitation.
- Fair trade is just a fashion among rich western consumers.
- Free trade only looks to the short-term; fair trade looks at the bigger picture.

Internet research

Search for the keywords *fair trade vs free trade*. What values do the two movements share?

Why fair trade is a bad deal

IN THE NAME of fair trade, we are encouraged to pay more for everything from cups of coffee and chocolate bars to cosmetics and cut flowers. For a product to be certified as fair trade, the importer selling it in the West must pay a minimum price to producers. A voluntary price support scheme is entirely compatible with free trade: there is no conflict between altruism and the market economy. But while filling the shopping trolley with fair trade goods may relieve the guilt of middle class consumers, its wider effects may not really be so positive. A combination of economic illiteracy and misguided good intentions has created a monster that threatens the prosperity of the poorest producers.

Poverty relief would be much better served by a free trade and not a fair trade agenda. Fair trade policies, whether government-enforced or applied through ethical consumer schemes, distort the market. Producers in some countries may choose to produce certain crops only because they can get an artificially high price under fair trade schemes. This kicks away the ladder from the poorest producers who have no choice but to stay in the market. Take the example of Mexico, which produces a quarter of fair trade coffee. Because of the incentive of fair trade, Mexican producers have decided to keep producing coffee, even expand production. Without this incentive, Mexico could be producing other crops more efficiently. This distorting effect is unfair on poorer countries such as Ethiopia where producing other crops is not an option. As a result of fair trade policies, they are faced with greater competition.

Fair trade also punishes producers who are less good at quality – generally the poorest. Setting a minimum price for products encourages retailers to buy only from more affluent producers that can invest in higher quality. Poorer producers may be able to supply lower quality products more cheaply, but there is no incentive to buy these, because the retailers cannot call it fair trade. By simply pronouncing it 'unfair' to pay below a certain price, fair trade supporters seem to believe they can ignore market realities, wave a magic wand and make everything better. But fair trade is like all attempts to control prices: the poorest are cut out of the market.

Free markets and more open trade have lifted hundreds of millions of people out of poverty over the last quarter century. They work because they encourage producers to pursue higher living standards by becoming more productive through mechanization and modernization. By contrast, fair trade supports a romantic view of peasant farmers toiling in the fields, day in day out, rather than helping producers buy machinery and move into processing and packaging of products. The Fairtrade Foundation®, which promotes the scheme in the UK, admits it has no policy on mechanization. It has even been encouraging producers to become less efficient by growing other crops in between coffee plants. This limits producers' ability to mechanize, locking them into poverty.

In stark contrast, Starbucks™ has been running community projects to help producers construct coffee mills and climb up the economic ladder. Shops like Starbucks, Caffè Nero and Coffee Republic have encouraged consumers to appreciate coffee as a premium product. Consumers are dropping the cheap instant coffee they were drinking in the office in favour of cappuccinos and lattes made with high-price Arabica beans. Many producers, following this logic, are now commanding higher prices. This is not because of fair trade but because they are responding to the demands of the market.

Despite attacks from anti-globalization activists, the truth is that Starbucks has done more than anyone else in expanding markets and raising incomes for coffee producers in developing countries. It is the coffee chains that are the real superheroes of the coffee market, not fair trade campaigners.

Glossary PAGE 157

affluent
crop
deprive
distort
magic wand
misguided
pursue
toil

8 Fair trade

- collocations with *contract*
- expressions used in a contract
- types of unethical behaviour

8.2 Vocabulary Contracts and corporate ethics

Brainstorming

1 In what circumstances might you do the following? Give examples.

> amend a contract   award a contract   break a contract   cancel a contract
> draft a contract   negotiate a contract   renege on a contract   sign a contract

Defining words

2 Read part of the contract between Calisto Instruments and JZ Music to supply 500 tenor saxophones for the Christmas market. Find expressions that mean:

1 accepted
2 in this document
3 promises
4 not later than
5 later in this document
6 pay the bill
7 considered as
8 for whatever reason
9 inform
10 impossible to change

---

this agreement, made and entered into this fourth day of June by and between Calisto Instruments, the Seller, and JZ Music Ltd, the Buyer:
1. The seller hereby undertakes to transfer and deliver to the buyer on or before 1 November, the goods as specified hereinafter.
2. The buyer hereby undertakes to accept the goods and pay for them in accordance with the terms of the contract.
3. The buyer shall make payment within 30 days of reception of the goods.
4. Goods shall be deemed received by the buyer when received by him at the port of Southampton.
5. The risk of loss from any damage to the goods regardless of the cause thereof shall be on the seller until the goods have been accepted by the buyer.
6. The buyer shall have the right to examine the goods on arrival, and he must give notice to the seller of any claim for damages within seven business days after such delivery. The failure of the buyer to comply with these rules shall constitute irrevocable acceptance of the goods.

---

3 Complete the second extract from the contract with the expressions from Exercise 2.

9. The seller (1) _____ (2) _____ to provide maintenance and repair for one calendar year. The buyer shall be required to (3) _____ to the seller of any request for repair. On expiry of the warranty, an extension agreement may be (4) _____: the buyer shall (5) _____ of the annual fee before any repair work can be undertaken, (6) _____. Signature of the warranty extension shall constitute (7) _____ acceptance of the terms and conditions (8) _____ specified. Warranties not renewed (9) _____ 1 April shall be (10) _____ lapsed.

4 Choose the correct words to complete the paragraph about litigation.

A legally (1) *holding / binding / sticking* contract is one which can be (2) *obliged / inflicted / enforced* by the legal system. Many contracts include a (3) *penalty / punishment / price* clause which (4) *concerns / applies / effects* if deadlines are not met. A company which fails to respect its commitments can be (5) *charged / processed / sued* for (6) *violation / breach / breaking* of contract. However, in some cases the two (7) *participants / parties / factions* can avoid the expense of litigation by agreeing an out-of-court (8) *settlement / agreement / conclusion*. If the case (9) *moves / goes / takes* to court, the loser may be ordered to pay millions in (10) *payments / damages / expenses*.

Discussion

5 Calisto and JZ Music have now signed the contract. Discuss what will happen if:

1 Calisto deliver on 1 December.
2 Calisto deliver 500 alto saxophones instead of 500 tenor saxophones.
3 Calisto send JZ Music an invoice on 1 September.
4 the saxophones are delivered to Portsmouth.
5 some of the saxophones are damaged during shipping.
6 JZ inform Calisto of the damage in January after the Christmas holidays.
7 JZ refuse to pay.

Internet research

Search for the keywords *mission statement generator*. Hold a class vote for your favourite mission statement.

Listening for gist

6 Can you explain or give examples of these types of unethical behaviour?

| bribery   conspiracy   corruption   embezzlement |
| fraud   insider trading   money-laundering |
| nepotism |

7 🔊 2:41–2:48 Listen to eight cases. Name each offence, and discuss an appropriate punishment.

Reading

8 Match terms 1–6 with definitions a–f.

1. accountability
2. regulatory bodies
3. borderline ethics
4. corporate governance
5. empowerment
6. best practice

a) deciding objectives, means and standards for a company
b) being required to justify one's actions to a higher authority
c) organizations which investigate irregularities, such as the Securities and Exchange Commission
d) a process that has been shown to give excellent results
e) paying workers the minimum wage allowed by the law, for example
f) encouraging workers to improve the way they do their own jobs

9 Complete the book review with the terms from Exercise 8.

In her latest book, *Ethical Profits*, Hannah Shallanberger, who serves on the board of several corporations, argues that good (1) _____ is not incompatible with making profits. According to Shallanberger, values like honesty, fairness, transparency and (2) _____, when combined with commercial and manufacturing (3) _____, can help to make the world a better place.

Shallanberger blames Enron, WorldCom and other scandals first and foremost on spiralling executive pay. A world where six-figure salaries, stock options and golden retirements are a CEO's top priority encourages (4) _____ and leaves little space for global justice and social responsibility. Shallanberger advocates a third way. Companies which favour employee (5) _____, and which foster a sense of ownership and social responsibility throughout the organization, can not only obey the law, comply with and even exceed the requirements of (6) _____, but also give customers, employees, the environment and shareholders a fair deal. This book is a must-read for anyone involved in business strategy.

Glossary PAGE 158

amend
bend the rules (for someone)
beyond reproach
lapse
litigation
part and parcel
renege
wash your hands of

Discussion

10 Do the questionnaire, and then discuss your answers.

Ethical business *or* profit first?

1. **Lying, cheating and bending the rules is**
   a) unacceptable.
   b) OK, as long as you don't get caught.
   c) part and parcel of business.

2. **A company should**
   a) respect the spirit of the law.
   b) respect the letter of the law.
   c) be morally beyond reproach.

3. **The majority of corporate profits should go to**
   a) shareholders.
   b) top management.
   c) all company staff.

4. **Honesty and responsibility is the best policy**
   a) always.
   b) sometimes.
   c) rarely.

5. **Shallanberger's third way with ethical profits is**
   a) the key to twenty-first century business.
   b) a nice idea, but difficult to do.
   c) hopelessly idealistic.

6. **Making the world a better place is**
   a) a company's primary goal.
   b) something companies can contribute to.
   c) nothing to do with business.

8 Fair trade

- can, can't, must, mustn't, have to, don't have to, (not) be allowed to
- inversion in legal documents

8.3 Grammar Obligation and permission, inversion

Obligation and permission

1 In small groups, brainstorm a list of rules in your school or workplace relating to conduct and dress code. Use *can / can't / must / mustn't / have to / don't have to / be allowed to* and *(not) be allowed to*.

We're not allowed to use mobile phones during lessons/meetings.
We have to wear a company polo shirt in the office.

Obligation and permission in legal documents

2 Work with a partner. Read a formal agreement, highlight the formal language and explain the information to your partner in a less formal way. Your partner should ask for clarification if necessary.

Student A: Read the lease agreement.
Student B: Read the licence agreement.

Landlord hereby leases the Premises to Tenant for twelve calendar months.
→ The tenant is allowed to rent the offices for a year.

Refresh your memory

Obligation
In most cases, we can use *must*, *mustn't*, *have to* and *don't have to*. In more formal cases, you may encounter: *shall* and *shall not*.

Permission
In normal cases, we can use *can*, *can't* and *(not) be allowed to*. In more formal cases, you may encounter: *may* and *may not*.

Inversion
After certain negative phrases, subject and verb are inverted.
Not until all details were agreed did they sign the contract.

▶ Grammar and practice pages 136–137

Lease agreement

Property description: 100 m² in modern building. Open plan. Unfurnished.
Rent: €1,900 per calendar month.

1 **Term** Landlord hereby leases the Premises to Tenant for twelve calendar months. Tenant may renew the Lease by giving written notice to Landlord not less than ninety days prior to the expiration of the initial term of lease.
2 **Rental** Tenant shall pay to Landlord €1,900 per calendar month due in advance on the first day of each calendar month. Tenant shall also pay to Landlord a security deposit equivalent to one month of rent payable before first occupation of the Premises.
3 **Utilities** Tenant shall pay all charges for water, sewer, gas, electricity and telephone and other services used by Tenant. Landlord shall pay all reasonable air-conditioning and heating costs of the Premises.
4 **Repairs** During the Lease term, Tenant shall make, at Tenant's expense, all necessary repairs to the Premises. Repairs shall include routine repairs of floors, walls, ceilings, and other parts of the Premises damaged or worn through normal occupancy.
5 **Alterations** Tenant may with Landlord's written consent remodel, redecorate and make improvements to the Premises.
6 **Parking** During the term of this Lease, Tenant may use in common with Landlord, other tenants of the Building, their guests and invitees the non-reserved car parking area, subject to the rules and regulations for the use thereof.

Licence agreement

Property description: 70 m² in refurbished building. 4 large offices + reception area. Fully furnished.
Rent: €300 per person per month.

1 **Term** Licensor hereby licences Licensee to use the Premises for one calendar month. Licensee may renew the Licence or quit the Premises by giving written notice to Licensor not less than thirty days prior to the expiration of the Licence.
2 **Rental** Licensee shall pay to Licensor €300 per occupant per calendar month due in advance on the first day of each calendar month. Licensee shall also pay to Licensor a security deposit equivalent to two months' licence fee payable before first occupation of the Premises.
3 **Utilities** Licensor shall pay all charges for water, sewer, gas, electricity, air conditioning, heating and fixed charges for telephone and Internet connections. Licensee shall pay all charges for telephone calls and other internet pay services used by Licensee.
4 **Repairs** Licensee shall repair or pay for the repair of any damage to the Premises caused during occupancy and shall leave the Premises in the same condition as at the start of this agreement. Licensor shall take responsibility for normal wear and tear.
5 **Alterations** Licensee may not alter, remodel, redecorate or make improvements to the Premises.
6 **Parking** No on-site parking is provided but Licensee may rent reserved parking spaces for an additional monthly fee of €50 per space payable in advance at the same time as the monthly rent.

3 Work with a different partner. You run a thriving import export business and need to move to larger premises in the next three months.
You have a staff of five people (including you and your partner) and are planning to recruit an extra person in nine months' time. Look at the agreements in Exercise 2 and decide which premises would suit you best. Explain your reasons to another pair.

Setting guidelines

4 Managers often give guidelines to new employees on how to conduct themselves on company business. Complete the guidelines with modals of obligation and permission.

1 *You have to* obey the law and act ethically at all times.
2 _____ use video or audio recording equipment on the company's premises.
3 _____ use the Internet in an appropriate and responsible way.
4 _____ disclose sensitive information about the company's products.
5 _____ make negative claims about our competitor's products.
6 _____ get permission to download software onto office computers.
7 _____ accept small gifts from suppliers and other business partners.
8 _____ buy or sell the company's shares in expectation of a major announcement.

5 Sentences 1–4 are taken from a formal employment contract. Rewrite them in less formal English.

1 Employees shall not make expense claims in excess of €20,000.
   Remember that you _____ than €20,000.
2 All employees shall maintain company property in good condition.
   If you work here, you _____ after company property.
3 The Employer may terminate the contract with a one-month notice period.
   As the employer, I _____ the contract with just a month's notice.
4 Employees may not use the telephones for personal use.
   I think I ought to warn you that you _____ or family.

Listening and note-taking

6 🔊 2:49 Firms may also issue a code of practice to business partners as part of a contract. Listen to two managers discussing the terms of an outsourcing agreement in the Far East. Make notes on what they decide in these categories.

| Accommodation | Breaks | Minimum age | Safety | Working hours |

7 With a partner, use your notes from Exercise 6 to write formal guidelines for the suppliers in the Far East.

8 The clauses below were also included in the contract. Complete each sentence with a possible result.

1 Evidence of poor working conditions may *result in* …
2 Products not finished to agreed standards may …
3 Legal representatives appointed by us may …
4 Failure to use safety clothing may …

Inversion

9 Rewrite these sentences from the contract, using inversion to make them more emphatic.

1 Unless you can implement the full terms of the contract, don't agree to it.
   Under no circumstances should _____
2 We won't pay for the goods until the full shipment has been received.
   Not until the full shipment _____
3 The goods will be considered received when they arrive at our warehouse.
   Only once the goods _____
4 Health and safety must not be put at risk for any reason.
   On no account must _____

Writing

10 Choose five of the rules you identified in Exercise 1 and rewrite them in the style of a formal employment contract.

We're not allowed to use mobile phones during lessons/meetings.
→ **Under no circumstances shall** mobile phones **be used** during lessons/meetings.

Internet research

Search for the keywords *golden bull* to find examples of 'legal-speak'. Note down the most amusing or the worst example and report back to the class.

Glossary PAGE 158

at a stretch
landlord
notice
premises
refurbished
sewer
tenant
wear and tear

8 Fair trade

- identifying factors for successful negotiations
- expressions for negotiating a compromise
- negotiating a deal

8.4 Speaking — Negotiating a compromise

Discussion

1 Discuss what compromise might be found in these situations. How satisfactory is the compromise for each party?

1. Management at a car plant have offered a 5% pay increase in response to workers' demands for 10%. The workers have threatened to strike. Both sides are willing to discuss productivity and benefits. What compromise could they reach?
2. The top national newspaper has published evidence of corruption in a major company. Unfortunately, the company is the newspaper's most important advertising customer. How can the two parties reach an agreement to maintain their business relationship?
3. A dairy producer sells most of its products to a major supermarket chain which has been making late payments. The supermarket claims the suppliers' products have fallen in quality. What could each side do to improve their relationship?

Listening for detail

2 2:50 Leah works for an American fair trade chocolate manufacturer and Alfredo represents a workers' cooperative in Ecuador. Listen to a contract negotiation for cocoa beans and answer the questions.

1. What do they agree on within these topics?
   - the fair trade premium for top grade cocoa beans
   - prefinancing/advance payments
   - growing the crop under shade trees
   - children under fifteen
2. What went wrong in the negotiation?

3 2:51 Listen to the second version of the negotiation and answer question 1 in Exercise 2 again. Why is this version of the negotiation more successful?

4 2:51 With a partner, find suitable words to complete the expressions in the checklist for negotiating a compromise. Then listen again and check your answers.

Useful expressions: Negotiating a compromise	
Offering a compromise	**Accepting with conditions**
I am ready to …, on the understanding that you … I'm prepared to _____ you half way. Shall we split the difference?	We are _____ to agree to …, provided that … I'd be _____ to …, unless …
Accepting a compromise	**Rejecting a compromise**
That _____ fair. I can _____ with that.	I'm sorry, but I'm not sure that would work. I think we'll have to _____ to disagree on that. I'm afraid you put me in a difficult position.

Internet research

Search for the keywords *corporate barter*. Make a list of benefits companies can derive from this type of trade.

Practice

5 With a partner, suggest more appropriate expressions for this negotiation, and then practise the conversation.

A: I can pay ten per cent more, but you work Saturdays as well.
B: No way! I coach my local swimming team on Saturday afternoons.
A: How about 50–50? I pay five per cent more and you work Saturday mornings.
B: No. Not unless I can keep the company car at the weekend.
A: Deal!

6 Work with a partner. Using the framework below, take turns to be A and B and practise compromising in the following situations:

1. Student A wants to organize a two-day fair trade conference in Berlin. Student B prefers a week in Hong Kong.
2. Student A wants to sell fair trade chocolate in cheap 1kg bars. Student B wants to sell it in expensive, individually-wrapped squares.
3. Student A is a coffee grower and wants a five-year contract and a guaranteed minimum price. Student B is a manufacturer and wants a one-year contract and an index-linked price.
4. Student A wants to sell as many fair trade products as possible in their supermarkets at higher prices. Student B wants to sell the cheapest products at the lowest prices.

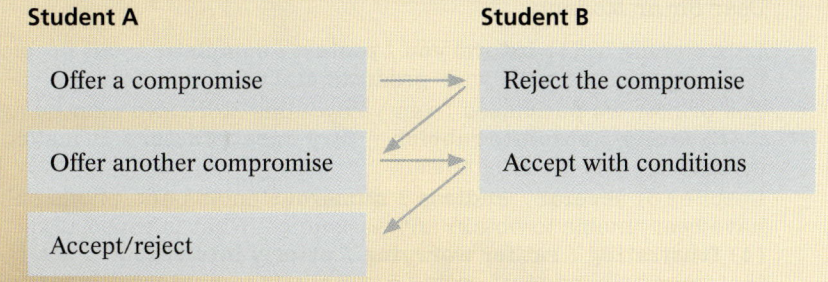

Student A
- Offer a compromise
- Offer another compromise
- Accept/reject

Student B
- Reject the compromise
- Accept with conditions

eWorkbook
Now watch the video for this unit.

Negotiation

7 Work with a partner. You represent small neighbouring countries in trade negotiations with each other. Student A: read the instructions and table below. Student B: look at page 118.

Student A
You have a surplus of some commodities and a shortage of others. Relations between your country and Student B's country are very friendly. Negotiate a deal with Student B to get the commodities you need.

	You have	You need	After negotiation, you have
Coal	4 million tons	1 million tons	
Gas	2 billion cubic meters	5 billion cubic meters	
Oil	0	200 million barrels	
Wheat	3 million tons	1.5 million tons	
Coffee	0	2,000 tons	
Tobacco	40,000 tons	25,000 tons	
Steel	8 million tons	6 million tons	
Gold	20 tons	20 tons	
Aluminium	200,000 tons	350,000 tons	
Chemicals	1 million tons	2 million tons	

8 Fair trade

- the tone of complaints
- assertive expressions
- writing a letter of complaint

8.5 Writing Assertive writing

Discussion

1 Decide which of these complaints is most likely to obtain a positive outcome in a restaurant, and why. Which complaint is aggressive, which is passive, and which is assertive?

1 'Sorry about this, but I'm afraid I'm a little disappointed with my meal.'
2 'The steak is overcooked and the vegetables are cold.'
3 'Your food is disgusting and your chef can't cook!'

Model

2 Read the letter of complaint. Use different colours to cross out the aggressive and passive options in **bold**, leaving an assertive letter.

Dear Sir or Madam,

I am writing to (1) **inform you / protest / complain** about problems we have experienced with your products and customer service.

The printer we purchased from your online store two months ago is (2) **faulty / absolute rubbish / very unsatisfactory**; it makes a continuous loud buzzing noise.

Despite (3) **several / endless / numerous** emails and phone calls, we have been unable to obtain any assistance. What is especially (4) **frustrating / rather worrying / utterly intolerable** is the fact that your helpline staff seem (5) **totally incompetent / insufficiently trained / somewhat inexperienced**.

(6) **Never in a million years / Very rarely / Under no circumstances** would such (7) **unprofessional / pathetic / disappointing** after-sales service be acceptable from a high-street store.

We (8) **demand that you / expect you to / would like you to** resolve this situation to our satisfaction within seven days of receipt of this letter. Failure to do so (9) **will result in the strongest / will leave us no option but to take appropriate / may lead us to consider** legal action.

Yours faithfully,
E. Lonamar

Analysis

3 Decide which of the adjectives in the box complete this description.

Writing assertively means being …

> aggressive   apologetic   confident   direct   evasive
> objective   personal   polite   rude   submissive

Language focus

4 Rephrase the sentences to make them more assertive. Use the prompts in brackets.

1 It seems we can't print our annual report. I'm afraid that's especially annoying! (What is …)
2 I'm sorry but I don't think the printer delivers what your website promises. (In no way does …)
3 Unless you fix the printer before the end of the week, I'm afraid we'll have to consider suing you. (Failure … legal action.)
4 People in the office find the constant buzzing noise annoying. (What people …)
5 Our Paris office needs a printer. I'm afraid I don't think it's very likely we'll recommend yours! (Under no …)
6 We might have to contact a consumers' association, as you don't seem to want to help us. (Unless …)

Glossary PAGE 159

assertive
evasive
submissive
sue

108 *The* Business 2.0

Internet research

Search for the keyword *assertiveness*. What are the rights the individual can assert? What assertiveness techniques are available?

5 Decide whether each expression implies that the speaker will give a *positive* or a *negative* response. Which 'negative phrase' suggests the speaker will negotiate?

as things stand	by and large	in principle
on the whole	regrettably	to be honest
unfortunately		

6 Choose the best expressions to complete the email opposite.

7 Using expressions from Exercise 5, write assertive one-line answers to these messages from your CEO.

1 We have a crisis. Can you fly to Canada tomorrow morning?
2 How would you feel about working two days a week from home?
3 I'd like you to get a couple of years' experience in the USA before taking on more responsibility.
4 We need someone to manage the night shift. Do you think you can handle it?
5 We think you should do an MBA. What's your reaction?
6 Next year's sales conference is in Siberia. You'll be organizing it.

EMAIL

Thank you very much for your email.
(1) *To be honest / On the whole / Regrettably*, the contract looks very fair. There are just two points which I'd like to clarify.
Firstly, you suggest we start shipping the full quota of flowers by the end of the year. (2) *On the whole / Unfortunately / By and large*, this would be very difficult for us, although (3) *regrettably / to be honest / in principle* we could start making small shipments in January and February.
Secondly, (4) *as things stand / in principle / by and large*, I'm afraid we would find it very difficult to freeze prices for so long.
(5) *Unfortunately / By and large / As things stand* I agree that eighteen months is normal for this type of contract. However, (6) *on the whole / regrettably / by and large*, we cannot commit to more than twelve months.

Output

8 Divide into two groups, A and B. Group A work for a fair trade clothing company in Bangladesh called Ganges Fashion. Group B work for AQX Logistics, a global transport provider that handles Ganges' logistics operation in Europe.

1 Read the following message from your boss and then discuss what to say.
2 Write a letter and deliver it to the other company.
3 Reply to the letter you receive.

Group A

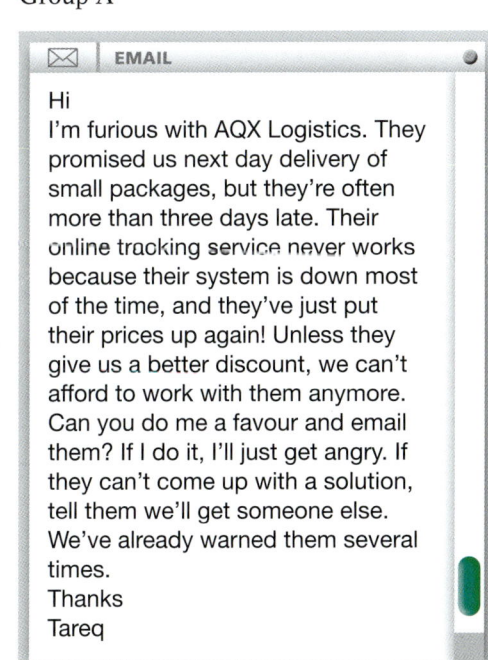

EMAIL

Hi
I'm furious with AQX Logistics. They promised us next day delivery of small packages, but they're often more than three days late. Their online tracking service never works because their system is down most of the time, and they've just put their prices up again! Unless they give us a better discount, we can't afford to work with them anymore. Can you do me a favour and email them? If I do it, I'll just get angry. If they can't come up with a solution, tell them we'll get someone else. We've already warned them several times.
Thanks
Tareq

Group B

MESSAGE

FROM: Clyde Lang, Finance

TAKEN BY: Annette

Please write to Ganges Fashion. They've finally paid last quarter's invoices, but they've deducted the tax again. We've already explained they have to pay us first, then they can claim the tax back. And they're only supposed to have 30 days credit, not 90! If they don't pay the tax by the end of the month, Clyde wants to suspend service.
NB Clyde was extremely angry, so he didn't want to write to them himself.

8 Fair trade

- supplier contracts
- negotiating a solution

8.6 Case study — Green Hills Coffee

Discussion

1 Explain these two quotations. Is there a place in business today for a gentleman's agreement?

An Englishman's word is his bond. – a sixteenth-century proverb
A verbal contract is not worth the paper it's written on! – Sam Goldwyn

Reading

2 Fiona Hills is President and CEO of Green Hills Coffee. Read the memo she received from her CFO and the attachment, and answer the questions.

1. What is the main problem, and what is the risk for Green Hills?
2. What does the CFO want Fiona to do?
3. What special circumstances might affect Fiona's judgement?
4. Which clauses of the contract are Green Hills concerned about?

MEMO

Re: Potential image problem

I heard yesterday that farmers in Guatemala are still employing child labour on coffee farms, although there are no contracts of course, so we can't prove it. I also discovered our biggest supplier is planting in virgin forest areas and using increasing amounts of pesticides – all clearly in breach of the terms of our contract (see attached). I know your father had a special relationship with the Cabrera family and used to turn a blind eye, but we have to sort this out quickly. There are other suppliers whose beans are just as good. We're already under pressure from fair trade brands. Fair trade sales grew 40% last year and we simply can't afford to be associated with these practices.

3.1 New planting in virgin forest areas is prohibited.
3.2 The supplier shall make continual reductions in the toxicity and use of agrochemicals.
3.3 Materials on the ICGA Prohibited Materials List may not be used.
4.1 All workers shall be employed under legally binding labour contracts.
4.2 Children below the age of sixteen may not be employed.
4.3 Working shall not jeopardize schooling or the social, moral or physical development of the young person.

Listening and note-taking

3 2:52 Listen to a conversation at Granos Cabrera between Fabio Cabrera and his wife Magda and complete the table.

	Fabio	Magda
Opinion of Gordon Hills		
Opinion of Fiona Hills		
Reasons for Granos Cabrera's problems		
Solutions to Granos Cabrera's problems		

Brainstorming

4 Green Hills and Granos Cabrera have decided to send representatives to meet and negotiate on neutral territory in New York. In small groups, A and B, prepare the negotiation. Group As should consider Green Hills' options; group Bs Granos Cabrera's.

	Green Hills	Granos Cabrera
What we would like to obtain (maximum)		
What we must obtain (minimum)		
Possible strategies		
Our best alternative if no negotiated agreement is possible		

Glossary PAGE 159

binding
breach
gentleman's agreement
jeopardize
practice
turn a blind eye (to something)

Reading

5 Read the two emails. Who are they from and to, and how do they affect the situation?

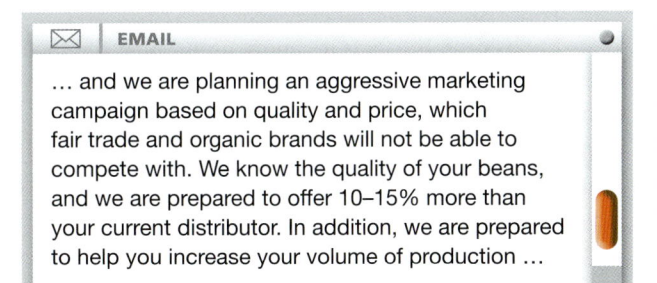

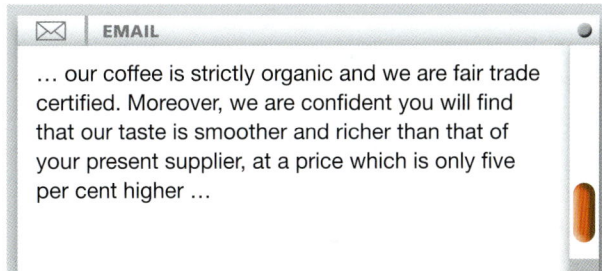

> ✉ **EMAIL**
>
> … and we are planning an aggressive marketing campaign based on quality and price, which fair trade and organic brands will not be able to compete with. We know the quality of your beans, and we are prepared to offer 10–15% more than your current distributor. In addition, we are prepared to help you increase your volume of production …

> ✉ **EMAIL**
>
> … our coffee is strictly organic and we are fair trade certified. Moreover, we are confident you will find that our taste is smoother and richer than that of your present supplier, at a price which is only five per cent higher …

Negotiation

6 Hold meetings between Green Hills (Group As) and Granos Cabrera (Group Bs) to try to negotiate solutions. Use the agenda opposite.

Discussion

7 Compare the outcomes of the negotiations. Which strategies produced the best results?

Internet research

Who buys fair trade foods? Search for the keywords *green consumers*. Draw up a customer profile for green, organic or fair trade products and services.

Agenda

Child labour
New planting in virgin forest areas
Pesticides
Organic farming
Fair trade certification
Investment
Prices
AOB

Review 7

Financial control

1 Match the words and expressions in the box with the definitions 1–8.

> bribery   fraudster   law enforcement agency
> litigation   protection racket   scam   tax evasion
> white-collar crime

1. use of the legal system to settle a disagreement (informal equivalent: 'to go to court')
2. the use of illegal methods to pay less tax
3. the crime of giving money to someone so that they will help you by doing something dishonest
4. *informal* a dishonest plan, usually to get money
5. an illegal system in which criminals threaten to harm you or your property if you do not give them money
6. someone who obtains money from other people by tricking them
7. crime in which people who work in offices steal money from the company they work for
8. an organization such as the police that makes sure that people obey laws

2 Complete the information on financial statements. Some letters are given to help you.

1. In the Income Statement, you start with the N_____ S_____s (income from trading activities), subtract the various costs and ex_____s, and you arrive at the O_____g P_____ (earnings from the trading activities of the business).
2. The basic equation in the balance sheet is: A_____ (things that the business owns) minus L_____s (things that the business owes) equals O_____s' E_____y.
3. In the old days, money owed to the company by its customers was referred to on the BS as 'debtors'; these days it is called acc_____ r_____. Equally, money owed by the company to its suppliers was referred to as 'creditors', while these days it is called acc_____ p_____.
4. A company's fi_____ a_____s are things that can't be turned easily into cash. They include pl_____ and m_____y (a factory and all its equipment), vehicles, etc.
5. The items in the previous sentence lose value over time. This is referred to as d_____.
6. A single word that means 'all the people that a company employs and the money that each of them earns' is p_____l.
7. An important item on the cash flow statement of a manufacturing company will be its payments for r_____ m_____s (physical inputs to the production process).
8. A company might have a one-time income from the sale of some land or the sale of a part of the business. This is referred to as ext_____y income.

3 Match an item from the first box with one from the second box.

> as a result   ~~brought~~   due   stemmed   led
> on account   owing   resulted   resulted
> were caused

> ~~about~~   by   from   from   in   of   of   to
> to   to

Now use these expressions in the correct sentences.

1. All the late payments by our suppliers *brought about* / _____ / _____ serious cashflow problems.
2. Serious cashflow problems _____ / _____ / _____ all the late payments by our suppliers.
3. _____ / _____ / _____ / _____ all the late payments by our suppliers, we had serious cashflow problems.

4 In each sentence, underline the correct option.

1. When I was younger, I *could play / succeeded in playing* tennis all afternoon without getting tired.
2. After five tries, I *could finally / finally managed to* send the fax.

5 Mark each sentence correct (✓) or incorrect (✗).

1. That's a very useful fact.
2. That's a very useful information.
3. That's very useful information.
4. Those are very useful facts.
5. Those are very useful informations.
6. In business, the facts are more useful than the theories.
7. In business, facts are more useful than theories.
8. I have the facts I was looking for.

6 Put the ten expressions into five matching pairs according to their function (how they are used).

1. Am I being clear?
2. Can we go over what we've decided?
3. Could you be more precise?
4. Do you see what I mean?
5. If I understand correctly, …
6. In other words, I …
7. Shall I go over the main points we've agreed?
8. So, what you're saying is …
9. What exactly do you mean by …?
10. What I mean is that I …

7 Put each pair of expressions from Exercise 6 into the correct category a–e.

a) Asking for clarification   ☐☐
b) Explaining your point more clearly   ☐☐
c) Reformulating to check you understand   ☐☐
d) Checking other people understand   ☐☐
e) Summarizing   ☐☐

Review 8

Fair trade

1 Match the verbs 1–8 with the phrases a–h to make expressions about free trade and fair trade.

1. relieve
2. threaten
3. pursue
4. set
5. ignore
6. lift
7. become
8. climb up

a) higher living standards
b) a minimum price for products
c) your guilt by buying fair trade goods
d) the prosperity of the poorest farmers
e) more productive through mechanization
f) people out of poverty
g) market realities
h) the economic ladder

2 The verbs 1–6 all collocate with a contract. Match the verbs with their closest synonyms a–f.

1. sign
2. negotiate
3. break
4. cancel
5. draft
6. award

a) discuss and finalize, draw up
b) produce a first version of
c) enter into, accept
d) give
e) end
f) be in breach of, renege on, violate the terms of

3 Match the legal words 1–10 (that you might read in a contract) with their meanings a–j.

1. irrevocable
2. give notice
3. hereby
4. undertake
5. make payment
6. deemed
7. on or before
8. hereinafter
9. lapsed
10. regardless of the cause thereof

a) settle the bill
b) impossible to change
c) promise
d) in this document
e) inform
f) no longer effective
g) for whatever reason
h) considered as
i) later in this document
j) not later than

4 Complete the sentences with the correct form of the legal words from Exercise 3.

1. The seller _____ _____ to provide maintenance and repair for a period of one year.
2. The buyer shall be required to _____ _____ to the seller of any request for repair.
3. The buyer shall _____ _____ of the annual fee.
4. Signature of the contract shall constitute _____ acceptance of the terms and conditions _____.
5. Warranties not renewed _____ _____ _____ 1 April shall be deemed _____.

5 Complete each sentence with a pair of items from the box.

goes to court/damages   legally binding/enforced
parties/out-of-court settlement   penalty clause/applies
sued/breach of contract

1. A _____ contract is one which can be _____ by the legal system.
2. Many contracts include a _____ which _____ if deadlines are not met.
3. A company which fails to respect its commitments can be _____ for _____.

4. In some cases the two _____ can avoid the expense of litigation by agreeing to an _____.
5. If the case _____, the loser may be ordered to pay millions in _____.

6 Match the expressions 1–6 with the words a–f to make collocations.

1. commercial best
2. money
3. requirements of regulatory
4. good corporate
5. insider
6. employee

a) bodies
b) practice
c) empowerment
d) trading
e) governance
f) laundering

7 Complete the definitions with words from Exercises 5 or 6.

1. must be obeyed according to the law _____ _____ (two words)
2. promises _____
3. be subject to a legal claim (in order that the other person can try to get money from you because you have harmed them) _____
4. people or group involved in a legal argument or legal agreement _____
5. process of taking a claim to a court of law _____ (not 'goes to court')
6. money that you pay to someone else as a punishment for harming them _____
7. putting money that has been obtained illegally into a legal business so that you can hide it _____
8. needs _____
9. the process of controlling and regulating an organization (formal) _____
10. giving someone more control over their life _____

8 Match the expressions that have the same meaning.

1. You mustn't do it.
2. You don't have to do it.
3. You shall do it.

a) You have to do it.
b) Don't do it.
c) You may do it if you want.

9 Put the words in the correct order to make expressions for negotiating a compromise.

1. I'm to meet half way you prepared.
2. Shall we difference the split?
3. I live that with can.
4. We are compromise to willing.
5. I'd do that to be reluctant.
6. I think to disagree to agree we'll have.

10 Match the pairs of expressions that have similar meanings.

as things stand   by and large   frankly   in principle
on the whole   regrettably   the way things are now
theoretically   to be honest   unfortunately

Additional material

1.2 Vocabulary: Education and career

Discussion (page 12, Exercise 7)

Student A
Read Jacky's description of her education and early working life. Some of the information is missing. Ask Student B questions and exchange information to complete the description.

> I wasn't a very motivated student when I was younger, so I (1) _____ my exams in 1999 and had to retake them the following summer. I'd already decided I wanted to (2) _____ then go to business school, so this time I (3) _____ and (4) _____ thoroughly: I passed easily. I spent a year abroad as an assistant in a secondary school and then went to business school - I'd already (5) _____ and successfully (6) _____ before resitting my exams.
>
> In my second year as (7) _____, I spent a semester as an intern at Hewlett Packard, which was very rewarding. In fact, I went straight into a job at HP after I graduated the following June. They encouraged me to do a (8) _____ by correspondence. I just have to finish writing my dissertation. I need a break now, but I may take a sabbatical to study for an MBA in a few years' time.

2.4 Speaking: Telephoning

Roleplay (page 29, Exercise 7)

Student A

Call 3
Your assistant has been on the phone with friends most of the morning. You have a lot to prepare for an important meeting tomorrow. Call your assistant to ask her/him to prepare a PowerPoint presentation for you. Your partner will start.

Call 4
You receive a call from your computer hardware supplier, who has recently sold you a large new computer system which isn't working very well. You are extremely busy preparing a business trip to Chicago next Tuesday, and you are not in a very good mood. You start by answering your phone.

Call 5
You work in Marketing in a large, very profitable manufacturing company. Your PC is three years old and very slow. Call your friend in the IT department to see if you can upgrade to a new machine. Your partner will start.

Call 6
You work in the HR department of an American factory. You have to be careful to respect legislation on employee rights and confidential personal information. You receive a call from the production supervisor. You start by answering your phone.

2.6 Case study: Meteor Bank
Discussion (page 33, Exercise 6)

> ### Student A
> You represent the HR department at the meeting. You feel Saul Finlay is the right man for the job and should be trusted to complete the work he has started. You believe high staff turnover is a good thing, because salary costs are falling and Saul is replacing older staff with new young technicians with more up-to-date skills. As the bank's IT expert, you think Saul should decide its IT policy. You recognize there are problems in the department, but you feel Saul is capable of dealing with them.

3.3 Grammar: Passive structures and *have something done*
Roleplay (page 41, Exercise 7)
Student A
Internal quality auditor
To comply with your company's ISO 9001 certification, the procedures below should be followed. Check that they are and ask any other questions you need to.

> Quality audit – points to raise
>
> Compliance with ISO 9001:
> * bottling lines to be checked before and during each shift
> * any problems to be noted in the shift log
> * at the end of each shift, the line supervisor should check if any problems have been reported and take any necessary action, e.g. ask the maintenance team to make repairs, change worn parts, etc.
> * all operators to receive quality training when they join the company
>
> Other issues:
> Quality tracking statistics show that the contaminated bottles were filled during the night shift on bottling line 3.

7.4 Speaking: Communicating in meetings
Roleplay (page 95, Exercise 8)

> ### Alice
> Introduce the subject of the meeting: the change from yearly to monthly reporting, which will enable management to run the business better.
> * You would like to see the new system in place in three months if possible, but you are willing to compromise if Serge and David produce valid arguments.
> * Mahler can provide training in US accounting procedures and on the new software that will have to be installed.
> * Other extra costs will have to be paid for by Polystok.

1.2 Vocabulary: Education and career

Discussion (page 12, Exercise 7)

Student B
Read Jacky's description of her education and early working life. Some of the information is missing. Ask Student A questions and exchange information to complete the description.

> I wasn't a very motivated student when I was younger, so I had to (1) _____ my exams in 2000 after I failed them the year before. I'd already decided that before (2) _____ I wanted to take a gap year. I (3) _____ easily because this time I completed all the coursework and revised thoroughly. I'd already applied and successfully attended an interview at a business school, so after resitting my exams I spent (4) _____ as an assistant in a secondary school.
>
> I spent a semester as (5) _____ at Hewlett Packard in my second year as an undergraduate, which was very rewarding. In fact, after I (6) _____ the following June, I went straight into a job at HP. I'm now writing (7) _____ for a Master's degree by correspondence, which HP encouraged me to do. I may (8) _____ to study for an MBA in a few years' time, but I need a break first.

2.4 Speaking: Telephoning

Roleplay (page 29, Exercise 7)

Student B

Call 3
You've just spent most of the morning on the phone with your company's IT department, trying without success to get them to repair your computer – the only application that works properly is Word. You receive a call from your boss. You start by answering your phone.

Call 4
You work for a computer hardware vendor. You recently set up a large new system for your customer, and you would like to show it to one of your prospects. Call your customer to arrange a visit next week. Your partner will start.

Call 5
You work in the IT department in a large manufacturing company. You are working night and day to install new security systems on all the company's sites – all other investments have been cancelled. You receive a call from a friend in Marketing. You start by answering your phone.

Call 6
You are the production supervisor in an American factory. You think it would be good for morale to celebrate your operators' birthdays with a cake. Call HR to ask for a list of dates of birth for everybody in your department. Your partner will start.

2.6 Case study: Meteor Bank
Discussion (page 33, Exercise 6)

> ### Student B
> You represent the foreign subsidiaries at the meeting. You think Saul Finlay is ignoring the facts – fast growth in the subsidiaries, need for a less centralized IT system, discontent in his department – because he is building his own personal empire. You feel his record is very poor, and that he should be replaced as soon as possible.

3.3 Grammar: Passive structures and *have something done*
Roleplay (page 41, Exercise 7)
Student B

Night shift supervisor
You are very busy at the moment. Two operators are off sick and three have received no training. You joined the company recently yourself and have had no time to read all the ISO 9001 procedures in detail. Last week, your production manager sent you this email:

✉ **EMAIL**

Hi
I'm aware you're busy at the moment. To save time, I suggest you:
- only check the bottling lines twice a week,
- report any problems directly to the maintenance team,
- tell the operators not to worry about filling in the shift log.

By the way, I heard that the filling machine on Line 3 is consuming a little more oil than normal. Have you noticed anything? I haven't told maintenance yet.

7.4 Speaking: Communicating in meetings
Roleplay (page 95, Exercise 8)

> ### Serge
> - You are not too happy about the proposed changes as they will mean a lot of extra work. However, you realize that you cannot oppose group policy, so you have decided to cooperate as long as things are done properly, and not in a rush.
> - You think that a realistic time frame to install the new accounting software, to train accounting staff and to start monthly reporting, is from six to nine months.
> - You would also like Mahler to provide training and to pay the extra staff you will have to employ. But you are willing to compromise.

5.6 Case study: Backchat Communications

Negotiation (page 73, Exercise 7)
Sellers
Follow the instructions below to calculate your score.

	Score
Give yourself 1 point for every Basic contract sold.	
Give yourself 2 points for every Smart contract sold.	
Give yourself 3 points for every Hi-tech contract sold.	
Give yourself 1 point for every 18-month contract sold.	
Give yourself 2 points for every 24-month contract sold.	
Give yourself 1 point for every extra sold.	
Deduct 1 point for every extra given free.	
Deduct 1 point for every 5,000 *won* discount given.	
Total	

8.4 Speaking: Negotiating a compromise

Negotiation (page 107, Exercise 7)
Student B
You have a surplus of some commodities and a shortage of others. Relations between your country and Student A's country are very friendly. Negotiate a deal with Student A to get the commodities you need.

	You have	You need	After negotiation, you have
Coal	1 million tons	2 million tons	
Gas	4 billion cubic metres	4 billion cubic metres	
Oil	300 million barrels	100 million barrels	
Wheat	1 million tons	1.5 million tons	
Coffee	6,000 tons	2,000 tons	
Tobacco	0	30,000 tons	
Steel	1 million tons	4 million tons	
Gold	0	20 tons	
Aluminium	400,000 tons	350,000 tons	
Chemicals	3 million tons	2.5 million tons	

Additional material

Business fundamentals

Reading (page 8, Exercise 2)
Breakeven analysis chart

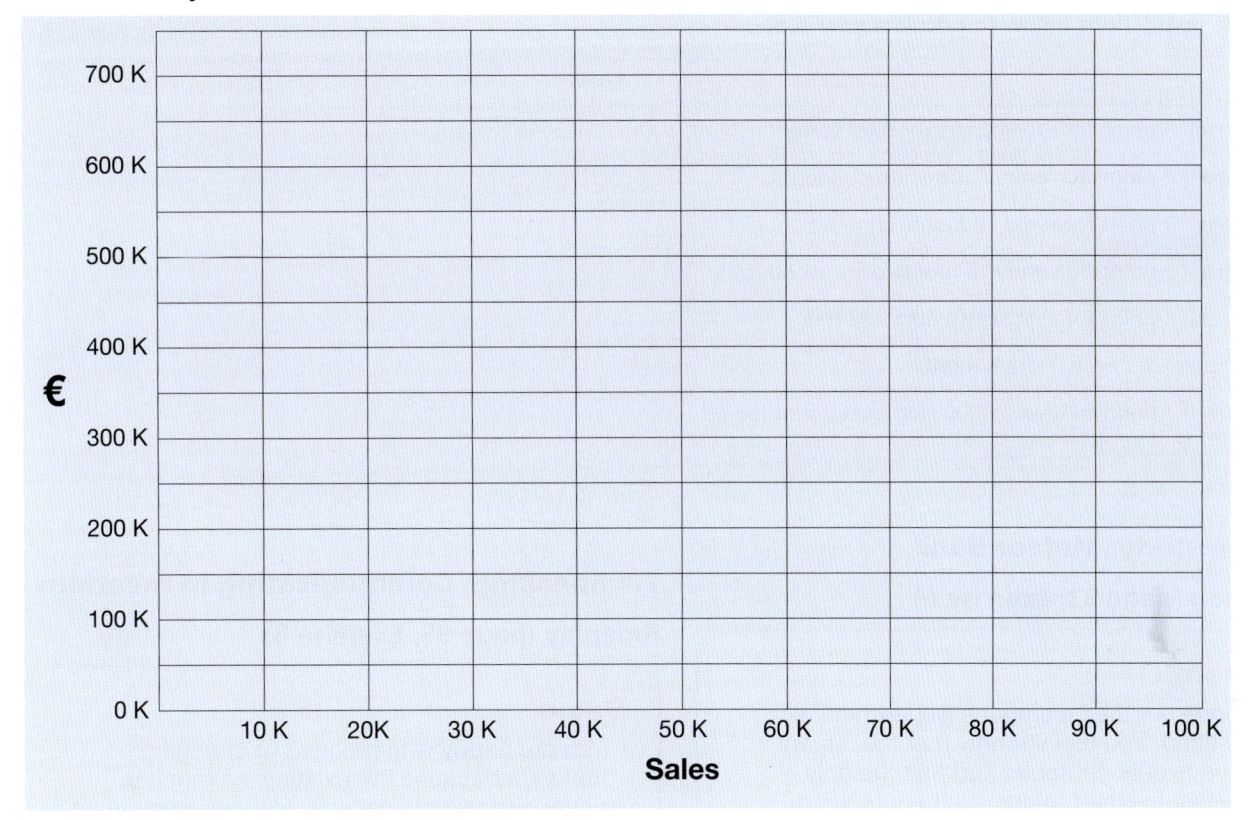

[Breakeven analysis chart: Y-axis labelled € with values 0 K, 100 K, 200 K, 300 K, 400 K, 500 K, 600 K, 700 K. X-axis labelled Sales with values 10 K, 20 K, 30 K, 40 K, 50 K, 60 K, 70 K, 80 K, 90 K, 100 K. Chart is empty grid.]

1.2 Vocabulary: Education and career

Listening and discussion (page 13, Exercise 13)

Speaker 1
Bob's situation is similar to that faced by Steve Jobs, who quit Apple Computer® in 1985. Jobs sold his shares and founded NeXT Computer. Although NeXT was never as successful as Jobs had hoped, in 1996 Apple® bought the company, and Jobs became CEO the following year. Under his guidance, Apple brought out the iMac® and the iPod; the rest, as they say, is history. When he died in 2011, Steve Jobs was thought to be worth over $8 billion.

Speaker 2
Lucy finds herself in a similar situation to JK Rowling, who wrote most of her first Harry Potter™ novel while she was unemployed or working part-time in Edinburgh cafés. After being rejected by twelve different publishers, Rowling's book was finally accepted, although her publisher advised her to get a part-time job as there wasn't much money in children's books. Her fortune is estimated at over $1 billion, making her the first person ever to become a $US billionaire by writing books.

Speaker 3
Mel's dilemma is similar to that faced by William Henry Gates III, now better known as one of the world's wealthiest individuals, worth over $60 billion. In 1975, Gates dropped out of Harvard to pursue a career in software development with Paul Allen, his high school business partner. Together, they founded Micro-Soft®, which was later to become Microsoft Corporation®.

5.6 Case study: Backchat Communications

Negotiation (page 73, Exercise 7)

Buyers
Follow the instructions below to calculate your score.

	Score
Give yourself 1 point for every Smart contract bought.	
Give yourself 2 points for every Basic contract bought.	
Give yourself 1 point for every 18-month contract bought.	
Give yourself 2 points for every 12-month contract bought.	
Give yourself 1 point for every extra obtained free.	
Deduct 1 point for every extra bought.	
Give yourself 1 point for every 5,000 *won* discount obtained.	
Total	

2.6 Case study: Meteor Bank

Discussion (page 33, Exercise 6)

> **Student C**
> You represent the Operations Department at the meeting. You feel strongly that the current situation is unacceptable, and that the only way to resolve the problems is to outsource the department, even if it means cutting jobs, including Saul Finlay's. This will immediately solve the problems of turnover, down time, unrest in the IT department and investment.

7.4 Speaking: Communicating in meetings

Roleplay (page 95, Exercise 8)

> **David**
> - You are happy with the idea of changing software because the existing system has never performed very well. However, you want to avoid any extra costs on your department budget.
> - You estimate that you will need to employ two external computer engineers on the project for at least six months. You would like Mahler to pay for this.
> - You would also like Mahler to pay for training for your staff on the new software. However, you may have to compromise.

1.5 Writing: Cover letters

Brainstorming (page 18, Exercise 1)

Dos

DO ask directly for an interview. Request an interview, and tell the employer when you will follow up to arrange it. It is imperative that you follow up.

DO follow the AIDA model used in advertising – attention, interest, desire, action. Write cover letters that are unique and specific to you, but consider using four paragraphs:

1 Get your reader's attention.
2 Give details of your accomplishments.
3 Relate yourself to the company, showing why the company should hire you.
4 Request action.

Don'ts

DON'T start your letter 'Dear Sir or Madam'. Address your letter to a named individual whenever possible.

DON'T write a formal introduction in the first paragraph. Use the first paragraph to grab the employer's attention.

DON'T write at least 400 words. Never write more than one page. Each paragraph should have no more than three sentences.

DON'T use sophisticated language to make a good impression. Use simple language and uncomplicated sentence structure. Eliminate all unnecessary words.

3.4 Speaking: Delivering presentations

Presentation (page 43, Exercise 9)

Use the table to give feedback on your colleagues' presentations.

1 = Poor, 2 = Acceptable, 3 = Good, 4 = Excellent

	1	2	3	4
Pauses				
Sentence length				
Signposting				
Speed				
Collocations				
Explanation of jargon				
Clarity				
Impact				

Grammar and practice

1 Building a career

Tense review

1 Read the conversation at a party and study the verbs in **bold**. Then answer the questions below.

A: I (1) **haven't seen** you for ages!
B: No, that's right. It's been a long time.
A: What were you doing the last time we met? Let me try to remember. Yes, you (2) **were working** as a sales manager somewhere. You (3) **had** just **finished** university.
B: Exactly.
A: I hope (4) **you're enjoying** the party. And who is the guy you came with? Is he your boyfriend?
B: Yes, he is. Actually, we (5a) **met** while I (5b) **was doing** that sales job. He was in the same department.
A: Really! How long (6) **have** you **been going out** together?
B: About two years.
A: That's great. And do you still work together?
B: No, he (7) **works** at that same company, but I don't. I (8) **decided** to have a change. Now (9) I'**m working** for an advertising agency. What about you?
A: (10) **I've quit** my job. I'm unemployed at the moment.
B: Are you trying to find something else?
A: Oh yes, of course. (11) **I've applied** for lots of jobs over the last few weeks, but it's so difficult to get an interview.

Find an example in the conversation of each of the following:

a) the present simple to show a permanent situation ☐
b) the present continuous to show a situation in progress right now ☐
c) the present continuous to show a situation in progress around now, but not right at this moment ☐
d) the past simple used alone to show a completed action ☐
e) the past continuous to show a situation in progress in the past ☐
f) the past simple followed by the past continuous to show a completed action and its background situation ☐
g) the past perfect to show a past event that happened before another past event ☐
h) the present perfect to show a situation that goes from the past up to the present ☐
i) the present perfect to show a series of actions from the past up to the present ☐
j) the present perfect to show an event in the past with a result in the present ☐
k) the present perfect continuous to show a situation in progress from the past to the present ☐

2 Put one verb into the past simple (*did*), one into the past continuous (*was/were doing*) and one into the past perfect (*had done*).

1. I _____ (work) in an IT company in Budapest at the time, but I wasn't happy and I _____ (already/decide) to give in my notice. Then, by chance, I _____ (find out) about a job in London.
2. I _____ (sit) at home one evening having my dinner when my friend Andreas _____ (call) me about the London job. He _____ (hear) that there was going to be a vacancy for a systems analyst.

3 Put one verb into the present simple (*do/does*), one into the present continuous (*am/are doing*) and one into the present perfect (*has/have done*).

1. An outside company _____ (design) all our sales materials. We _____ (use) the same one for many years and we're very happy with their services. We _____ (not/think) about changing right now.
2. This year we _____ (exceed) our sales targets by 8%. Congratulations, everybody. But there is no room for complacency. We _____ (go through) some big changes in the market at the moment, as you _____ (know).

4 Look back at *know* in Exercise 3 sentence 2. It is a 'state' verb (not used in a continuous form even for temporary situations). Identify six other state verbs from the list below.

| belong | contact | manage | mean | meet | motivate |
| seem | transfer | understand | want | weigh | worry |

5 Put each verb into the most appropriate form, present perfect (*has/have done*) or present perfect continuous (*has/have been doing*).

1. a) I _____ (apply for) jobs all week.
   b) I _____ (apply for) five jobs this week.
2. a) I _____ (write) the report. Here it is.
   b) I _____ (write) this report since three o'clock. I need a coffee.

6 In the example below both forms are possible.

I've worked/I've been working here for a year. ✓

Use this example, and Exercise 5, to complete the grammar rules below. Complete each sentence 1–4 with an ending a–c.

1. To talk about experiences up to now, use …
2. To focus on the action, not the result, use …
3. To focus on the result, not the action, use …
4. To say 'how many' use …

a) the present perfect
b) the present perfect continuous
c) the present perfect or the present perfect continuous

7 Put each verb in this email into the most appropriate form: present simple, present continuous, past simple or present perfect. The words in **bold** give you a clue.

Hi Estera! How are you? I (1) _____ (sit) in an Internet café in Milan **at the moment** – I'm here in Italy because I (2) _____ (visit) Stefano **for a few days**. I have some news to tell you. **A couple of weeks ago** I (3) _____ (go) to a reunion party of all the alumni from our Business School. **Since leaving**, I (4) _____ (lose) contact with most of them except you, so it was good to see everyone again.

We had a great night. As you know, **normally** I (5) _____ (not/like) going to discos, but **that evening** we (6) _____ (go) to a really good one with 70s music like Abba and the Bee Gees.

122 *The* Business 2.0

Conditionals

8 Read the conversation and study the verbs in **bold**. Then answer the questions below.

A: (1) **If** you **see** Marie-Flore, **will** you **give** her a message?
B: Of course, but I doubt that I'll see her until next week. She usually goes to her parents in Lyon at the weekend and (2) **if** she **goes** there then she **leaves** around 5pm. She's probably already left.
A: I need to speak to her as soon as possible. Do you know how I can contact her?
B: (3) **I'd help** you **if** I **could**, but I don't have any contact details for her at all. That's a shame. (4) If **I'd spoken** to you at lunchtime, I **would have been able to** give her your message before she left.

Find an example in the conversation of each of the following.

a) a zero conditional for something that is always or generally true ☐
b) a first conditional for an event that the speaker thinks is likely to happen ☐
c) a second conditional for an event that is imaginary, unlikely or impossible ☐
d) a third conditional for a situation that didn't actually happen ☐

9 Underline the correct form in **bold**.

1 I'm very confident, and of course if **I get/I will get** the job, **it is/it'll be** very convenient for me. It's just a short bus ride from my house to their offices.
2 I'm not very confident, and if **I got/I would get** the job **it will be/it would be** a miracle. I was twenty minutes late for the interview and I answered the questions really badly.
3 The interview didn't go well. If **I did/I'd done** some research on the company, **I would have performed/I would perform** better in the interview.
4 If **I know/I will know** that I have an interview coming up, **I go/I will go** to the Internet and do some research on the company beforehand.

10 Put each verb into the most appropriate form.

1 If I _____ (know) the answer, I _____ (tell) you, but it's not my field.
2 It's always the same. If I _____ (forget) my umbrella, it _____ (rain).
3 If you _____ (give) me the address, I _____ (find) it. No problem.
4 If I _____ (not/hear) from you within the next few days, I _____ (assume) you're not coming.
5 I didn't go to university, but if I _____ (go), I _____ (study) engineering.
6 Unless I _____ (hear) from you within the next few days, I _____ (assume) you're not coming.
7 I _____ (not/do) that if I _____ (be) you.
8 Let me see. What _____ (I/do) if _____ (I/be) Prime Minister?
9 It's midnight. What _____ (we/do) if _____ (the bus/not come)? Maybe we should phone for a taxi.

Will, be going to and present continuous

11 Match *will* in each sentence 1–5 with the best description of its use a–e below.

1 I imagine I'll get a pay rise in January. ☐
2 It's getting late. I'll give you a lift to the station. ☐
3 Next year **will** be the 25th anniversary of our company. ☐
4 It's hot in here. I'll open the window. ☐
5 I'll love you forever. ☐

a) simple fact about the future
b) prediction, often with I *think*, etc.
c) promise
d) offer, or willingness
e) decision made at the moment of speaking

12 Match *be going to* and the present continuous in sentences 1–3 with their use a–c below.

1 I**'m having** an interview with them on Friday. ☐
2 I**'m going to buy** a new computer in the sales. ☐
3 Is that the time? We**'re going to miss** the train. ☐

a) prediction with evidence in the present situation
b) intention, plan
c) fixed arrangement (it's 'in my diary')

Note: the uses given in Exercises 11 and 12 are guidelines, not rules. With the future, more than one form is often possible.

13 Underline the most likely form in **bold**.

1 This shop **will be closed/is going to be closed** on 24 and 25 December.
2 The interview went very well. I think **I'm getting/I'll get** the job.
3 Look out! **It will fall/It's going to fall**.
4 Wait a moment, **I'll open/I'm going to open** the door for you.
5 **I'll play/I'm playing** tennis with Ana on Saturday afternoon. I can meet you afterwards, around 5pm.
6 **I will start/I'm going to start** applying for jobs in other parts of the country – there's not much available here.

2 Information

Comparing solutions

1 Look at the prices of four items in a range: Aqua, Bounti, Cresta and Delite. Then complete each sentence with a form of the word in brackets plus any of these words that are necessary: *and, as, least, less, more, most, than, the*.

Aqua €100
Bounti €150
Cresta €150
Delite €200

1 Cresta is *cheaper than* (cheap) Delite.
2 Cresta is _____ (expensive) Delite.
3 Bounti is just _____ (expensive) Cresta.
4 Cresta is expensive, but not _____ (expensive) Delite.
5 Bounti is _____ (expensive) Aqua.
6 Aqua is _____ (cheap) of all the items.
7 Delite is _____ (expensive) of all the items.
8 Aqua is _____ (expensive) of all the items.
9 As you move from Aqua to Delite, the prices get _____ (expensive).
10 As you move from Delite to Aqua, the prices get _____ (cheap).

2 Complete this table of irregular comparatives and superlatives. Sometimes it is the spelling which is irregular.

	comparative	superlative
1 good	b_____	the b_____
2 bad	w_____	the w_____
3 big	b_____	the b_____
4 healthy	h_____	the h_____
5 far	fu_____	the fu_____

3 Fill in each gap with *as, of* or *than*.

1 X is far more expensive _____ Y.
2 X is almost as expensive _____ Y.
3 X is a little more expensive _____ Y.
4 X is a fraction of the price _____ Y.
5 X is slightly more expensive _____ Y.
6 X is a lot more expensive _____ Y.
7 X is not nearly as expensive _____ Y.
8 X is nearly as expensive _____ Y.

4 Now match two phrases from Exercise 3 with each set of prices below.

a) X costs €300, Y costs €100. ☐☐
b) X costs €120, Y costs €100. ☐☐
c) X costs €90, Y costs €100. ☐☐
d) X costs €30, Y costs €100. ☐☐

5 Underline the correct words in **bold**.

1 Excuse me, where's **the next/the nearest** post office?
2 Get ready – we have to get out at **the next/the nearest** stop.
3 Have you seen this amazing mobile phone? It's **the last/the latest** model.
4 That mobile phone company is being taken over. Your phone is probably **the last/the latest** model they will make using that brand name.

6 We often use a superlative with the present perfect. Rewrite the sentences beginning as shown.

1 I have never been to such a boring meeting.
That was *the most boring meeting I have ever been to* .
2 I have never used software as user-friendly as this.
This is _____.
3 I have never worked with such a friendly team.
They are _____.
4 I have never seen documentation as bad as this.
This is _____.

7 We can use a comparative form to say that a change in one thing is linked to a change in another. Put a tick (✓) if the form is correct, put a cross (✗) if it is not.

1 The older I get, *less* I want to go to the discotheque.
2 The older I get, *it's less* I want to go to the discotheque.
3 The older I get, *the less* I want to go to the discotheque.
4 The older I get, I want to go to the discotheque *each time less*.

8 Rewrite the sentences using *the … the …*

1 You pay more for your Internet connection depending on how fast it is.
The faster your Internet connection, the more you pay (for it).
2 We spend less time watching TV as we use the Internet more.
_____
3 How much can go wrong depends on the complexity of the network.
_____
4 I don't spend much time with my friends because I work so hard.
_____
5 The idea becomes less attractive as I think about it more.
_____

Getting help

9 Compare a) and b) each time, then study the notes in the box below.

1. a) When *is the meeting*?
   b) Can you tell me *when the meeting is*?
2. a) What time *does* the meeting *start*?
   b) Can you tell me what time *the meeting starts*?
3. a) Which room *will it be* in?
   b) Can you tell me which room *it will be* in?
4. a) *Will the meeting* start on time?
   b) Can you tell me *if/whether the meeting will* start on time?

> **Indirect questions**
> - Each example (a) is a direct question.
> - Each example (b) is an indirect question. Typical phrases to begin an indirect question are:
>   *Can you tell me …?*
>   *Do you know …?*
>   *Can I just check …?*
>   *Do you think you could let me know …?*
>   *I'm trying to find out …*
>   *I was (just) wondering …*
> - Notice how the word order changes in the indirect questions. The subject comes before the main verb, just like in a normal statement (*The meeting is* at 10.30; *The meeting starts* at 10:30; *It will be* in room 24; *The meeting will* start on time.)
> - Notice also how 2b has no auxiliary verb *does*, again just like in a statement.
> - In example 3a and 3b notice the position of the preposition *in*. The preposition comes at the end of a question (both direct and indirect). Be careful: in many other languages you would say *In which room …?*, but this word order is not common in modern English.
> - Example 4 is a *Yes/No* question, whereas the previous three were open 'Wh-' questions. Notice how we use *if* or *whether* with an indirect *Yes/No* question.

Now rewrite each direct question as an indirect question, beginning as shown.

1. How can I get to the station from here?
   Can you tell me _____?
2. What time does the train leave?
   Do you know _____?
3. Which platform will it leave from?
   I'm trying to find out _____.
4. Do I change in Cologne?
   Can I just check _____?
5. Can I get something to eat on the train?
   I was wondering _____.

10 Change each *Yes/No* question into a more open 'Wh-' question.

1. Are you thinking about your presentation?
   What are you thinking about?
2. Did you borrow this from Susan?
   _____
3. Is this dress made of linen?
   _____
4. Will you share your new office with Miguel?
   _____

11 Look at the patterns with 'mind', then study the notes in the box below.

a) **Do** you mind if I **open** the window?
b) **Would** you mind if I **opened** the window?
c) **Do/Would** you mind **opening** the window?

> **Questions with *mind***
> Examples a) and b) are asking for permission: a) is a regular first conditional and b) is a regular second conditional (both have the *if* clause at the end). Example b) is more formal and polite.
> Example c) is a request – we want the other person to do something.

Now make questions using the words in brackets.

1. (mind/call you back/later)
   _____?
2. (mind/called you back/later)
   _____?
3. (Would/calling me back/later)
   _____?

12 Study the notes in the box.

> **Replying to requests**
> To reply 'yes', simply repeating the auxiliary is not very friendly.
> *Can you give me a hand?*
> ~~Yes, I can~~ ✗   Yes, of course ✓   Sure ✓
> To reply 'no', give an apology and/or a reason.
> *Can you give me a hand?*
> *I'm sorry, I've got no idea how it works.* ✓
> Be careful! Questions with *mind* mean 'is it a problem for you?' So 'yes' means 'yes, it's a problem'!
> *Would you mind giving me a hand?*
> ~~Yes, I would~~ ✗   No, not at all ✓

Now put a tick (✓) by appropriate responses. Put a cross (✗) by inappropriate responses.

1. Can you show me how to use this software?
   a) Sure. No problem.
   b) Yes, I can.
   c) To be honest, I've never used it myself.
2. Would you mind showing me how to use this software?
   a) Yes, I would.
   b) No, not at all.
   c) Actually, I'm a bit busy right now. Perhaps later?

3 Quality

Passive structures: affirmatives

1 Look at the active sentence given first and then write the passive version below.

1. The Board usually takes strategic decisions.
   Strategic decisions _____ by the Board.
2. They announced the date for the talks yesterday.
   The date for the talks _____ yesterday.
3. A health and safety officer will visit the factory next week.
   Next week the factory _____ by a health and safety officer.
4. They are going to completely redesign the product.
   The product _____.
5. They are still considering the matter.
   The matter _____.
6. The garage was servicing my car last week.
   My car _____ last week.
7. The design engineer has finalized the plans.
   The plans _____ by the design engineer.
8. There was no point having the meeting – they had already agreed all the details.
   There was no point having the meeting – all the details _____.

When you have checked your answers, read the information in the box below.

- In examples 1–8 you formed the passive for each of the most common verb tenses. Notice the similarities: you used *be* + past participle in every case. Also notice how the form of *be* is the same as the tense in the active version.
- Is the person who does the action (the agent) mentioned in the passive version? Look back. The answer is 'yes' for sentences 1, 3 and 7. In the case of 1 and 3, the agent is necessary in the passive version – otherwise the meaning is not complete. In 7, the agent is not necessary – it could be left out if it is clear from the context (or not important) who finalized the plans.
- There were adverbs in sentences 1 (*usually*), 4 (*completely*), 5 (*still*) and 8 (*already*). Did you put them in the correct place?

2 Rewrite these active sentences in the passive, making the words in **bold** into the subject. Leave out the agent if it is not necessary.

1. We do **dozens of quality** checks every day.
   Dozens of quality checks are done every day.
2. Thousands of people use **our products**.
   _____
3. The secretary's just found **that file you were looking for**.
   _____
4. Last month the bank gave **us** more credit.
   _____
5. We will pay **all senior managers** a bonus at the end of the year.
   _____
6. They are never going to do **that**.
   _____
7. Highly-trained inspectors do **our quality checks**.
   _____
8. We are dealing with **the issue**.
   _____

3 Match each example of the passive 1–5 with the best description of its use a–e below.

1. First the beans are separated from the shells and then they are roasted over a low heat for two hours. ☐
2. Don't worry, the conference room was cleaned this morning. ☐
3. Keys and mobile phones must be placed on the trays provided. ☐
4. Yes, I can see that a small mistake was made on the invoice. I'll correct it and send out a new one. ☐
5. It was agreed that Inge should set up a working party to investigate the matter further. ☐

a) it is obvious or not important to say who did the action
b) avoiding mentioning a name in order to make the statement less personal
c) reporting formally (a decision, what someone said in a meeting, etc.)
d) describing a process
e) official announcements (often written)

4 Notice in Exercise 3 sentence 5c above that we often use *It* + passive to report things formally. Complete the sentences below with the words from the box. Several answers may be possible, but one solution uses all the words in the most appropriate way.

| agreed | announced | believed |
| estimated | reported | said |

1. It was _____ at the press conference that the CEO had resigned.
2. After some discussion it was _____ that Jim should be team leader for the forthcoming negotiations.
3. It is _____ that 'diamonds are a girl's best friend'. But I don't believe it. I think that chocolate is a girl's best friend.
4. It was _____ in yesterday's newspapers that the economy grew by 4% last year.
5. It has been _____ that fish stocks in the North Atlantic will decline to zero by the year 2050.
6. It is _____ that a gang of four armed men carried out the attack, but police are still unsure of the exact numbers.

Passive structures: negatives

5 Complete the second sentence so that it has the same meaning as the first. Use contractions (*n't* instead of *not*, etc.) where possible.

1. No one has serviced the machine since April.
   The machine *hasn't been serviced* since April.
2. They aren't going to pay us until June.
   We _____ until June.
3. The staff had been poorly trained.
   The staff _____ very well.

4 No one is monitoring the process.
   The process _____.
5 We still haven't shipped your order.
   Your order _____ yet.
6 People just don't do things like that around here.
   Things like that _____ around here.

Passive structures: questions

6 Put the words in the correct order to make a question with a passive form.

1 this machine is serviced regularly?
   Is this machine serviced regularly?
2 being at the moment is it serviced?
   _____
3 yesterday it was serviced?
   _____
4 will next week be it serviced?
   _____
5 it recently has serviced been?
   _____
6 it is serviced going to be soon?
   _____

Now use 1–6 above to make corresponding negative questions with a passive form. Use contractions where possible.

7 *Isn't this machine serviced regularly?*
8 _____
   at the moment?
9 _____
   yesterday?
10 _____
   next week?
11 _____
   recently?
12 _____
   soon?

7 Make the questions below less personal by changing them to a passive form and leaving out the agent.

1 Will you deliver the goods by next week?
   Will the goods be delivered by next week?
2 Has someone changed the password?
   _____
3 Are you using this photocopier?
   _____
4 Are they going to give us a meal when we arrive?
   _____
5 Did Robert give you any options?
   _____

Passive structures: modals

8 Study the active and passive forms in the box. Then rewrite 1–6 below as passives.

Somebody should do it right now.
It should be done right now.

Somebody should have done it yesterday.
It should have been done yesterday.

1 We must find a solution.
   A solution _____.
2 They must have found a solution by now.
   A solution _____ by now.
3 We could postpone the product launch.
   The product launch _____.
4 We could have postponed the launch, but it's too late.
   The launch _____, but it's too late.
5 The company might design it like that on purpose.
   It _____ like that on purpose.
6 The company might have designed it like that on purpose.
   It _____ like that on purpose.

Balance between active and passive

9 Complete this memo by putting the verb in brackets into the present perfect active (*has done*) or present perfect passive (*has been done*).

This memo (1) _____ (write) at the request of the Senior Quality Inspector. Regular checks over the last few weeks (2) _____ (show) that defects (3) _____ (reach) an unacceptable level of three per thousand pieces. It seems that this (4) _____ (cause) by incorrect set-up of the machine tools. The operators involved (5) _____ (now/told) that they must take greater care when preparing their tools for the manufacturing process.
Some operators (6) _____ (ask) us if they can have more time to set up their machines, and we (7) _____ (agree). They now have 30 minutes instead of 20.
You will see that some minor changes (8) _____ (make) to the Defect Report Form to allow us to identify the problems more rapidly.

> Notice the balance between active and passive forms. Too many passives make a text formal and difficult to understand.

have something done

10 When a professional person does some work for us, we can use *have something done*. Rewrite the sentences below using this structure in the same tense as the original.

1 A technician fixed this computer last week.
   I *had this computer fixed* last week.
2 PwC audit our accounts.
   We _____ by PwC.
3 The garage is servicing my car on Friday.
   I'm _____ on Friday.
4 The builders are going to install air conditioning.
   We're _____.
5 A girl at Gina's Salon does my hair.
   I _____ by a girl at Gina's Salon.

4 Feedback

Past modals (regrets and speculation)

1 Study the table about how to form modals in the past then do the exercise below.

can do	could have done
	couldn't have done
may/might do	may/might have done
	may/might not have done
must do	must have done
	mustn't have done
ought to do	ought to have done
	ought not to have done
should do	should have done
	shouldn't have done
will do	would have done
	wouldn't have done

A manager is talking about a project team he set up last month. Fill in the gaps using a form of the modal and main verb in brackets. Sometimes a negative is necessary.

'The team isn't working well, and it's my fault. If I had done things differently, we (1) _might not have reached_ (might/reach) the situation we are in today. The basic problem is my choice of team leader. I gave the job to Sonia, but I (2) _____ (should/do) that. She doesn't have enough experience. It (3) _____ (will/be) better to give the job to Angela. Yes, that's right, I can see that now – I definitely (4) _____ (ought/give) the job to Angela. What was I thinking at the time? I (5) _____ (must/be) crazy or something. But maybe I'm blaming myself too much. I know I took a risk, but at the time it seemed justified. I (6) _____ (can/know) that things would go so wrong.'

2 In each of 1–5, read the first sentence then complete the sentences with the phrases from the box so that the meaning is the same. Be very careful!

> could have been (x2)   might have been
> must have been   ought to have been
> should have been   would have been

1 I made a mistake when I appointed Sonia. My strong opinion now is that Angela was better for the job of team leader.
Angela _____ team leader.
OR
Angela _____ team leader.
2 Yes, I made a bad choice. Angela, not Sonia, had the real ability to be a good team leader.
Angela _____ a good team leader.
3 I wonder why I made that mistake. Perhaps I was focused on another project at the time.
I _____ focused on another project.
OR
I _____ focused on another project.
4 I wonder why I made that mistake. Almost certainly I was focused on another project at the time. I _____ focused on another project.
5 Yes, I'm certain. Sonia was a terrible choice and Angela was definitely the best choice.
Angela _____ better than Sonia.

Before you check your answers, read the information in the box below. Then go back and make any necessary changes in the exercise.

> ☐ For past regrets – when we are sorry about what happened – use *should have done*, *ought to have done* and *could have done*.
> ☐ These modals keep their normal meanings, so: *should/ought to* are used for strong opinions; *can* (*could* in the past) is used for ability.
> ☐ For past speculation – when we are wondering or guessing about what happened – use *may have done*, *might have done*, *could have done*, *must have done* and *would have done*.
> ☐ These modals also keep their normal meanings, so: *may/might/could* are used for possibility and uncertainty; *must* is used for very strong possibility, almost certainty; *will* (*would* in the past) is used for certainty.

3 Complete the sentences with an appropriate past modal + a form of the verb in brackets. Sometimes more than one modal is possible (e.g. *could* and *might*).

1 I did an MBA course but I was lazy and got a bad grade. It was a pity. I know I _could have got_ (get) a better grade.
2 My parents persuaded me to do business administration at college. But I regret it – I always wanted to be a firefighter. I _____ (listen) to them.
3 Imagine that I had decided to travel around the world instead of going to university. I _____ (get) a job anywhere.
4 Who was that in the cinema with Alex last night? No, it wasn't Joelle. Joelle is in Brussels at the moment. It _____ (be) Joelle.
5 Well, if it wasn't Joelle – who was it? You think it was Sandra? Yes, I think you're probably right. It _____ (be) Sandra.
6 Wait a minute! Alex already has a girlfriend, doesn't he? Her name is Ana. Ana _____ (be) very happy if she had seen Alex and Sandra together last night.

4 Make the question forms of past modals using the words in brackets.

1 You say that Angela would have been a better team leader. I'm not so sure. _Would she have consulted_ (would/consult) with the rest of the group before taking decisions?
2 I don't think this restaurant is very good. What do you think? _____ (should/go) somewhere else instead?
3 Mike and Sue aren't here yet. I wonder what's happened to them. _____ (could/get) lost?
4 I've made a few mistakes. But _____ (would/do) anything differently if I had another chance? No, I don't think so.

Third conditional

5 Look at four possible situations a–d. Match each situation with the sentences 1–4 below.

a) Stefan managed the project. And the result? We reached our targets.
b) Stefan managed the project. And the result? We didn't reach our targets.
c) Stefan didn't manage the project. And the result? We reached our targets.
d) Stefan didn't manage the project. And the result? We didn't reach our targets.

1 If Stefan **had managed** the project, we **would have reached** all our targets. ☐ d
2 If Stefan **had managed** the project, we **wouldn't have reached** all our targets. ☐
3 If Stefan **hadn't managed** the project, we **would have reached** all our targets. ☐
4 If Stefan **hadn't managed** the project, we **wouldn't have reached** all our targets. ☐

- Notice above how to form the third conditional: *If* + past perfect for the condition clause, *would have* + past participle for the result clause.
- We use the third conditional to talk about something that did not happen in the past. The word *If* means that we are imagining the opposite to what really happened.
- Because the third conditional is imagining the opposite of what happened, a positive clause means this thing didn't happen and a negative clause means this thing did happen.
- The condition and the result can be in the reverse order. In this case there is no comma in writing.
  We **would have reached** all our targets if Stefan **had managed** the project.

6 Look at each situation in **bold**. Then complete the sentence that follows using the correct form of the third conditional.

1 **I didn't take an umbrella, and so I got wet. But** …
   If I _____ (take) an umbrella, I _____ (get) wet.
2 **I did take an umbrella, and so I didn't get wet. But** …
   If I _____ (take) an umbrella, I _____ (get) wet.
3 **We didn't have enough people working on the project, and so we didn't meet the deadline. But** …
   If we _____ (had) enough people working on the project, we _____ (meet) the deadline.
4 **We had a lot of people working on the project, and so we met the deadline. But** …
   If we _____ (had) so many people working on the project, we _____ (meet) the deadline.

7 Underline the correct words in **bold**.

1 Yes, I'm sure. If we had given Murray a different job, he **wouldn't have / might not have** resigned.
2 Well, I'm not sure, but if we had given Murray a different job, he **wouldn't have / might not have** resigned.

Instead of *would*, we can use *might* or *could*. This shows an uncertain result.

used to, be used to, get used to

8 Match sentences 1–3 with their meanings a–c.

1 I **used to give** presentations in my job. ☐
2 I'**m used to giving** presentations in my job. ☐
3 I'**ve got used to giving** presentations in my job. ☐

a) I give presentations in my job. At first it was difficult but now it's OK.
b) I give presentations in my job. It's a completely familiar situation to me and there's no problem.
c) In the past it was normal for me to give presentations, but now I don't.

- *Used to* + infinitive describes a habit in the past. It suggests that the action or situation is no longer true, and so makes a contrast with the present.
- With negatives and questions, *used to* becomes *use to*. *Did you use to give presentations in your job? I didn't use to give presentations in my job.*
- *Be/get used to* are completely different. They mean you have done something many times before and it is no longer difficult.
- *Be/get used to* are followed by *-ing* or a noun, not an infinitive.
  I live in the UK now. I'm used to driving on the left, and I'm also used to the weather.
- *Be used to* is a state, *get used to* is a process. Compare with:
  I'm tired/hungry/fed up, etc. (state)
  I'm getting tired/hungry/fed up, etc. (process)

9 Complete the sentences using *used to, be used to* or *get used to* and the correct form of the verb.

1 I'm beginning to enjoy my new job. Slowly, I _____ (work) with my team.
2 I prefer being in a large company to working as a freelancer. I _____ (work) in a team.
3 Now I'm a freelancer and I prefer it. I'm my own boss. I _____ (work) in a team in my old job, but I got annoyed when other people did a bad job.

5 Selling more

Question tags

1 Complete each question by filling the gap with a question tag. Always use contractions where possible, so write *don't* not *do not*.

1. This is the newest model, *isn't* it?
2. This isn't the newest model, _____ it?
3. You're from Latvia, _____ you?
4. You haven't got this available in blue, _____ you?
5. She works in the sales department, _____ she?
6. You give discounts on large orders, _____ you?
7. You don't have this available in a larger size, _____ you?
8. You gave us a discount last time, _____ you?
9. You were selling this for a much lower price in the summer, _____ you?
10. Have you got my travel plans for Scandinavia? I'm going to Copenhagen and Oslo after Stockholm, _____ I?
11. You'll be bringing out a new model next year, _____ you?
12. You won't be late, _____ you?
13. It shouldn't cost more than about €100, _____ it?
14. I'm not late, _____ I?
15. I'm late, _____ I? Sorry!
16. The meeting's been going on for an hour and a half. Let's have a break, _____ we?
17. Turn the lights off, _____ you?
18. Everybody got a copy of the agenda, didn't _____?
19. Somebody will be here on Saturday morning, won't _____?
20. I know there were some problems at the beginning, but everything was OK in the end, wasn't _____?

Now study the following boxes and make any necessary changes to Exercise 1.

Question tags: general rules
- a positive sentence has a negative tag, and vice-versa
- if there is an auxiliary verb (*be, have, do*) or modal in the statement, repeat the auxiliary or modal in the tag
- if there is no auxiliary or modal, use a form of *do*
- the tense of the tag agrees with the tense of the main verb
- Question tags are common in British English but are not used in American English. Americans say *right?* for all tags.
- NB It is possible for a positive statement to be followed by a positive tag. This is used to express interest during a conversation.
  So you like working here, do you?
  This use is not practised in this book.

Question tags: special cases
- the tag for *I am* is *aren't I?* However, the tag for *I'm not* is *am I?*
- the tag for *let's* is *shall we?*
- the tag for an imperative is *will you?* It is also possible to use *won't you?*
- after *everybody/everyone* and *somebody/someone* use *they* in the tag (this is to generalize and avoid saying 'he or she')
- after *everything* and *something* use *it* in the tag

2 The intonation of a tag is different according to the meaning. Study the information in the box then answer the questions below.

Tags with a rising intonation
If the intonation of the tag rises at the end, then the person is asking for information and it is a real question
A: *You're from Latvia, **aren't you**?* ↗
B: *Yes, that's right. I come from a little town outside Riga. Have you ever been to my country?*

Tags with a falling intonation
If the intonation of the tag falls at the end, then it is not a real question. Instead, the speaker either wants to check information, or to persuade.
Checking:
A: *You're from Latvia, **aren't you**?* ↘
B: *Yes, that's right.*
A: *I thought so. Have you met Ilona? She's from Latvia as well.*
Persuading:
A: *It's not just a question of price, **is it**?* ↘
B: *No.*
A: *I thought not. Quality and design are also important.*

Note that in these two cases speaker A continues after B has made a short reply. This is because A's first line is not a real question.

For each mini-conversation, write ↗ at the end of A's line if the intonation goes up, and write ↘ if it goes down.

1. A: You haven't seen this kind of quality at such a reasonable price, **have you**?
   B: No, I haven't.
2. A: You don't happen to know where the spare paper for the photocopier is, **do you**?
   B: No, sorry, I don't. Have you looked in that cupboard over there?
3. A: I'm sending this to your main office, not the factory, **aren't I**?
   B: Yes, that's right.

Look at the two answers where the intonation went down. Which one is checking? Which one is persuading?

3 Look at the mini-conversations and underline the most likely answer in **bold**. Then read the information in the box below.

1 **A:** The negotiations are going well, aren't they?
  B: Yes, they are./No, they're not.
2 **A:** The negotiations aren't going well, are they?
  B: Yes, they are./No, they're not.

- A positive statement with a negative tag often expects the answer *Yes*.
- A negative statement with a positive tag often expects the answer *No*.
- A negative statement with a positive tag is also used to be polite, or indirect, or ask for a favour. The answer could be *Yes* or *No*.
  You haven't by any chance got a spare pen, have you?

4 Complete the sentences using a tag and any other necessary words.

You thought the meeting was good.
You say: 'That was *a good meeting, wasn't it?*'
1 You want to suggest that we go to the bar.
  You say: 'Let's go _____?'
2 You want to check if the train leaves from platform 4.
  You say: 'The train _____?'
3 You want to persuade someone that they can't afford to take a risk.
  You say: 'You can't afford _____?'
4 You want to make sure that the other person will speak to their boss.
  You say: 'You'll speak _____?'
5 You want to make sure your name is on the list.
  You say: 'I'm on _____?'
6 You can't reach the salt and want someone to pass it to you.
  You say: 'Pass _____?'
7 You're worried that the other person will be in danger.
  You say: 'Take care, _____?'
8 You feel a cold current of air.
  You say: 'Someone's left the door open, _____?'
9 You want to know if the other person has met Joelle. You expect the answer is 'no'.
  You say: 'You _____?'
10 You want to know if the other person has met Joelle. You expect the answer is 'yes'.
  You say: 'You _____?'
11 You want to ask a favour – for the other person to get you a sandwich from the shop.
  You say: 'You couldn't get _____?'
12 You want to ask politely if the other person will be passing a post box on their way home.
  You say: 'You won't by any _____?'

Negative questions

5 Match each negative question 1–4 with its use a–d. If several are possible choose the best one.

1 Don't you accept American Express? ☐
2 Don't you agree that anything that saves you time saves you money? ☐
3 Don't you eat meat? ☐
4 Don't you think that this proposal will just lead to increased costs and reduced efficiency? ☐

a) negative question to persuade
b) negative question to disagree politely
c) negative question to show surprise
d) negative question in social English to make it easier for the other person to say 'no'.

It is possible to use an uncontracted form with 'not' after the subject. This is formal and intensifies the meaning.
Do you not accept American Express? Do you not eat meat?
Do you not think that this proposal will just lead to increased costs and reduced efficiency?

6 Using the first sentence, add a tag question for a) and make a negative question for b). Look at the example.

  'There's a deadline'.
  a) *There's a deadline, isn't there?*
  b) *Isn't there a deadline?*
1 It'll be expensive to use Air Express.
  a) _____
  b) _____
2 It'd be better to ship via Rotterdam.
  a) _____
  b) _____
3 We've met somewhere before.
  a) _____
  b) _____
4 You spoke to our sales agent yesterday.
  a) _____
  b) _____
5 There's always room for compromise.
  a) _____
  b) _____
6 You don't have insurance cover.
  a) _____
  b) _____
7 You haven't seen one of these before.
  a) _____
  b) _____

7 Rewrite 6b and 7b from Exercise 6 with an uncontracted form of 'not'. Note how this intensifies the meaning.

1 _____
2 _____

6 New business

will do (future simple)

1 Match the main uses of will 1–5 with examples a–e.
1. simple fact about the future ☐
2. prediction, often with *I think*, etc. ☐
3. decision made at the moment of speaking ☐
4. promise ☐
5. offer ☐

a) Are you going to use UPS to deliver the package? I think it**'ll** be cheaper to use DHL.
b) We**'ll** be closed for one week over the Christmas period.
c) Don't worry, I**'ll** be at the airport to meet you.
d) **Will** you stay for lunch?
e) Do we need more copies of the agenda? No problem, I**'ll** photocopy them right now.

> The uses of *will* given above often overlap (e.g. decisions and promises), but it is helpful to remember that there are two basic categories:
> - *Will* used for information about the future.
>   *We'll be closed for one week over the Christmas period.*
> - *Will* used for social and functional language.
>   *Don't worry, I'll be at the airport to meet you.*
>   *Will you stay for lunch?*
>   *Do we need more copies of the agenda?*
>   *No problem, I'll photocopy them right now.*
>   This includes announcing decisions, giving refusals (*won't*), making promises and making offers. In these cases, *will* generally expresses 'willingness' or a strong intention.

will be doing (future continuous)

2 Read the notes in the box then do the exercise below.

> - The future continuous is formed with *will be* + *-ing* form of the verb.
> - All the continuous tenses are used for an 'action in progress'. The future continuous is no different. Compare:
>   **Past continuous**
>   *While I was at University I was working part-time in a restaurant.*
>   **Present continuous**
>   *At the moment I'm working part-time in a restaurant. I hope to get a proper job soon.*
>   **Future continuous**
>   *Next year I'm going to London to learn English. I'll be working part-time in the same restaurant where my friend works now.*
> - The future continuous often refers to the middle of an action. Compare:
>   *When you arrive we'll have the meeting.*
>   (You will arrive and then we will start the meeting)
>   *When you arrive we'll be having the meeting.*
>   (You will arrive in the middle of the meeting)
> - The future continuous is often used to show that something is definite. Compare:
>   *I'll speak to her tomorrow.* (decision, or promise)
>   *I'll be speaking to her tomorrow.* (definite fact)
>   *I'm going to speak to her tomorrow.* (intention)
> - The future continuous can be used to ask in a polite way about other people's plans:
>   *Will you be passing a post box on your way home?*
>   *How long will you be using the photocopier?*
> - Remember that there are no 'rules' for any future tense – just forms that are more common than others in certain circumstances.

Complete each sentence using the most appropriate form of the verb in brackets: either *will* or the future continuous. Use contractions.

1. If you give me the job of team leader, I _____ (work) night and day to make the project a success.
2. I can't go to the cinema on Saturday afternoon – I _____ (work) all day Saturday.
3. We _____ (launch) our new range of clothes at the end of March.
4. Yes, that's a great idea! We _____ (launch) our new range of clothes with an event featuring a footballer and a top model.
5. If you see me at the party tomorrow, I _____ (wear) my little black dress.
6. What shall I wear at the party tomorrow? I know! I _____ (wear) my little black dress.
7. No, I _____ (not/give) any more time to writing this assignment. It's good enough as it is.
8. I'll be at the conference, but I _____ (not/give) a talk this year.
9. This time tomorrow I _____ (sit) on an airplane somewhere over the Pacific.
10. Don't worry about your bag and coat while you go to the bathroom. I _____ (sit) here until you come back.

Check your answers before doing the next exercise.

3 In the previous exercise, the *will* form was most appropriate in sentences 1, 4, 6, 7 and 10. Write one of these numbers in each box:

a decision ☐4☐ and ☐   an offer ☐
a promise ☐   a refusal ☐

The future continuous form was most appropriate in sentences 2, 3, 5, 8 and 9. Write one of these numbers in each box.

referring to an action in progress ☐9☐
referring to the middle of an action ☐ and ☐
showing that something is definite ☐ and ☐

4 Rewrite these questions about people's plans using the future continuous.

1. Are you joining us in the bar later?
   _____ in the bar later?
2. Are you going to speak to your boss tomorrow?
   _____ to your boss tomorrow?
3. Will you visit Moscow again next year?
   _____ Moscow again next year?

The future continuous in these cases is more polite. It suggests 'I just want to know your plans – I don't want to put any pressure on you.'

will have done (future perfect)

5 Study the notes in the box.

> - The future perfect is formed with *will have* + past participle. It is often used with *by* or *by the time*.
> *I'll **have finished** the report by the end of the week.*
> *By the time you arrive, the meeting **will** already **have started**.*
> - All the perfect tenses are used for 'looking back'. The future perfect is no different. Compare:
> **Past perfect**
> *When I arrived at their offices, the meeting **had** already **started**.*
> (looking back from the past to an earlier event in the past)
> **Present perfect**
> *I'm sorry, I'm late. **Has** the sales meeting already **started**?*
> (looking back from now to an event in the recent past)
> **Future perfect**
> *Don't worry if you can't get to our offices until 9.30. The meeting **will** already **have started**, but it's scheduled to last until lunchtime and your presence will still be useful.*
> (looking back from the future to an earlier event in the future)
> - The future perfect is not common in English because it can often be replaced by a simple *will* form. This is easier and so speakers prefer it. Both of these are possible and there is no difference in meaning.
> *I'll **finish** the report by the end of the week.*
> *I'll **have finished** the report by the end of the week.*

Read the information about how a business person is going to spend her time over the next two weeks. Then answer the questions below using the future perfect.

Catherine is marketing director for a firm of publishers based in the UK. Over the next two weeks she is going to visit her most important markets in Western Europe: France, Belgium, the Netherlands, Germany, Switzerland and Austria. She's flying between the capital cities of each country, and of course flying out to Paris and back from Vienna at the end. She expects to have two meetings a day for each of her ten working days abroad. On trips like this she eats dinner in the restaurant in the evening – so that's no home cooking from Monday when she leaves to Friday afternoon of the following week – not even at the weekend.

1 How many countries will she have visited?
 By the end of the trip _she'll have visited six countries_.
2 How many flights will she have taken?
 Altogether _____.
3 How many meetings will she have had?
 When she finally gets to the end _____.
4 How many restaurant dinners will she have eaten?
 By the time she finishes _____.

6 Complete each sentence using the most appropriate form of the verb in brackets: either the future continuous (*will be doing*) or the future perfect (*will have done*). Use contractions.

1 I'm enjoying this course. I _____ (learn) a lot by the time it's finished.
2 I'm really looking forward to the course next year. I _____ (learn) about the world economy and its impact on financial markets.
3 I have to be careful with my money this month. I _____ (spend) a lot next week when my car is serviced, and I also have some bills to pay.
4 I haven't got much money left. If I go on like this, I _____ (spend) it all soon.

will have been doing (future perfect continuous)

7 Read the notes in the box then do the exercise below.

> - The future perfect continuous is formed with *will have been* + *-ing* form of the verb.
> - The future perfect continuous is used for 'looking back from the future at an action in progress'. In other words, it combines the meaning of the future perfect and the future continuous.
> - It is only very rarely that we need to express this meaning, and when we do it is usually to emphasize the duration and the repetitive nature of the action: *By the time he retires, he'**ll have been working** here for more than thirty years.*
> *By lunchtime, I'**ll have been replying** to emails for over two hours.*
> - Use the future perfect to emphasize a result, and the future perfect continuous to emphasize an action in progress:
> *By the end of her trip, she'**ll have collected** a lot of useful market information.* (result)
> *By the end of her trip, she'**ll have been travelling** non-stop for twelve days.* (action in progress, with emphasis on the duration and repetitive nature)

Complete each sentence using either the future perfect or the future perfect continuous. Use contractions.

1 Next year we _____ (make) cars on this same site for fifty years.
2 By the end of the year, we _____ (make) profits of over €3 million.
3 By Friday I _____ (write) the report. Then maybe I can think about something else for a change!
4 By Friday I _____ (write) this stupid report for two weeks and it still won't be finished. It's driving me mad.

7 Financial control

Cause and effect

1 Each item a–w can be used to complete just one of the sentences below. Write each letter in the appropriate box.

a) arose from
b) as
c) as a result
d) as a result of
e) because
f) because of
g) because of that
h) brought about
i) caused
j) consequently
k) developed from
l) due to
m) gave rise to
n) led to
o) on account of
p) originated from
q) owing to
r) resulted from
s) resulted in
t) since
u) stemmed from
v) thanks to
w) was caused by

Cause
1 The successful advertising campaign _____ an increase in sales. [h] □ □ □ □

Effect
2 The increase in sales _____ the successful advertising campaign. □ □ □ □ □ □
3 _____ we had a successful advertising campaign, sales increased. □ □ □
4 _____ the successful advertising campaign, sales increased. □ □ □ □ □ □
5 We had a successful advertising campaign and, _____, sales increased. □ □ □

- The verb *caused* can be replaced with *brought about, gave rise to, led to* and *resulted in*.
- The verb *was caused by* can be replaced with *arose from, developed from, originated in, resulted from, stemmed from*. (Do you know the literal meaning of a stem? Check in a dictionary.)
- The linking word *because* can be replaced with *as* and *since*. Note that *as* has a different meaning to its use in comparisons, and that *since* has a different meaning to its use as a time phrase.
- The linking phrase *because of* can be replaced with *as a result of, due to, on account of, owing to, thanks to*. Of these, *because of* is much more common than the others.
- The linking phrase *because of that* can be replaced with *as a result, consequently*.

2 Underline the correct words to make usage notes.

1 There is very little difference in meaning between 'because', 'as' and 'since'. However, **because/as and since** can emphasize the reason more strongly, while **because/as and since** can suggest that the reason is obvious.
2 In sentence 3 in the previous exercise, this word order is also possible: 'Sales increased because we had a successful advertising campaign'. In cases like this where 'because' comes in the middle, it is **equally common/much less common** to replace 'because' with 'as' and 'since'.
3 The phrase **owing to/thanks to** is more formal.
4 The phrase **due to/on account of** often refers to a problem or difficulty. For this reason it is *not* very natural in sentence 4 of the previous exercise because there is no problem (something good happened: a successful advertising campaign).
5 The phrase **due to/owing to** cannot come after the verb 'be'. (Example: The increase in sales was _____ the successful advertising campaign).
6 Study the difference between sentence 3 and 4 in the previous exercise. **Because/Because of** is used before a noun phrase (no verb), while **because/because of** is used before a clause (subject + verb).
7 In sentence 5 in the previous exercise the linking phrases come in the middle of a sentence after the word 'and'. It is **also very common/not so common** for them to come right at the beginning of a sentence, followed by a comma.

3 Look back again at sentence 5 in Exercise 1. What two-letter word is very common to express the same meaning, is more informal, and is written without commas?

We had a successful advertising campaign _____ sales increased.

4 Complete the sentences with a word or phrase from the box.

| arose from | as | as a result | due to |
| led to | so | | |

1 Changes in the market _____ the collapse of the company.
2 _____ there were so many changes in the market, the company eventually collapsed.
3 _____ the changes in the market, the company eventually collapsed.
4 The market changed completely _____ the company collapsed.
5 There were a lot of changes in the market, and, _____, the company collapsed.
6 The collapse of the company _____ all the changes in the market.

5 Cover all the other exercises on this page with a piece of paper. Complete each sentence below with one of these prepositions: *about, by, from, in, of, to.*

1 Our cashflow problems last year arose _____ late payments by suppliers.
2 Basically, all our cashflow problems have originated _____ late payments by suppliers.
3 On account _____ late payments by suppliers, we had a lot of cashflow problems last year.
4 Late payments by suppliers have brought _____ all our cashflow problems.
5 All those late payments by suppliers have given rise _____ a lot of cashflow problems.
6 Our cashflow problems are largely caused _____ suppliers paying us late.

Describing ability in the past

6 Underline the words in **bold** that are the most natural then read the information in the box.

1. In the old days **we could/we were able to** take our customers out for lunch all the time without worrying about the bill.
2. The new software arrived yesterday. **I could/I was able to** install it quite easily.

- To talk about general past ability (not limited to one occasion) we use *could*.
- To talk about one specific past action we use *was/were able to*.
- To talk about one specific past action we can also use *managed to*, *failed to* and *succeeded in*.

7 Complete each sentence with the correct ending, a) or b).

1. I was able
2. I managed
3. I succeeded
4. I failed

a) to install it
b) in installing it

8 Look at the second bullet point in the box above, and then look at the sentence below.

Her presentation was excellent. I could understand everything she said.

This seems to break the rule – is it correct?

To talk about one specific past action with verbs of the senses and thoughts (*see*, *feel*, *hear*, *think*, *understand*, etc.) we can use *could* as well as *was/were able to*.

Articles

9 Match the uses a–j in the box with the examples 1–10.

a/an
a) referring to something for the first time
b) used when you mean any person or thing of a particular type, but not a specific one
c) describing a type of job (*a teacher, an accountant*)

the
d) referring to something mentioned previously
e) referring to something for the first time when it is clear from the situation which one we mean
f) when there is only one of something (*the boss, the sun*)
g) nationalities and other groups (*the English, the young, the poor*)

no article
h) plural countable nouns (*facts, jobs, machines, animals*) used in a general way
i) uncountable nouns (*information, work, machinery, nature*) used in a general way
j) most countries, continents, cities, streets (*Italy, Europe, Geneva, Church Street*)

1. He's finished university and wants to work as **an** electrical engineer. ☐
2. Have you got **a** car? ☐
3. I have **a** suggestion. ☐
4. I've been thinking about **the** suggestion you made at the meeting yesterday. ☐
5. We sell these products all over **the** world. ☐
6. I think there should be more training for **the** unemployed. ☐
7. I think **the** project is going well. ☐
8. For me, football is like life. ☐
9. At our plant in Slovakia we make cars and trucks. ☐
10. Riga is the capital of Latvia. ☐

10 The word *advice* is uncountable. Decide if each sentence is correct (✓) or incorrect (✗).

1. He gave me a good advice.
2. He gave me the good advice.
3. He gave me good advice.
4. He gave me some good advice.
5. The advice he gave me was very good.

- A common mistake is to use *a* or *the* with uncountable nouns used in a general way. In these cases we sometimes use no article, but it is more common to use *some* or *a lot of*.
- In sentence 5 *the* is used because it is clear from the situation which advice we mean.

11 The word *computer* is countable. Decide if each sentence is correct (✓) or incorrect (✗).

1. He's a real techie – he loves the computers.
2. He's a real techie – he loves computers.
3. The computers we have at work are a bit out-of-date.

- A common mistake is to use *the* with plural countable nouns used in a general way. We normally use no article.
- In sentence 3 *the* is used because it is clear from the situation which computers we mean.

12 If the sentence is correct, put a tick (✓). If it is incorrect, add or delete the articles *the* or *a/an*.

1. In business, the up-to-date information is critical for success.
2. This is a very important information.
3. Thanks for information you gave me – it was useful.
4. I enjoy job I do in the evening.
5. It's hard to find jobs in the finance sector.
6. To become doctor you need to study at university for many years.
7. The love is not rational – you can't explain it.
8. The love I have for my cat is not the same as the love I have for my boyfriend.
9. We need to do a research.
10. We need to do some research.
11. We need to do the research to see if you're right.
12. We need to do a lot of research.

8 Fair trade

Obligation and permission

1 Match the forms in **bold** with their best descriptions a–e below.

1 You **have to do** it. ☐
2 You **must do** it. ☐
3 You **don't have to do** it. ☐
4 You **mustn't do** it. ☐
5 You **can do** it. ☐
6 You **can't do** it. ☐

a) You have permission.
b) It is not necessary.
c) It is prohibited (forbidden) *or* You do not have permission.
d) It is necessary. I am telling you.
e) It is necessary. The rules say so.

2 Read the notes in the box then do the exercise below.

> There is no real difference between *must* and *have to* in writing. In speech there is a very small difference:
> *must* can suggest that the speaker decides what is necessary.
> *have to* can suggest the necessity comes from the situation.

Complete the sentences with the most likely form, *must* or *have to*. Remember that this is not a 100% rule, and both are possible in all the sentences.

1 I _____ go on a diet – these trousers don't fit any more!
2 I _____ go on a diet – the doctor says that I am overweight.
3 This is the text the teacher gave us. We _____ read it for homework. We're going to discuss it in class tomorrow.
4 This book is really good – you _____ read it.

3 In very formal language (such as legal documents) you can use *shall* to express obligation. Match the words in **bold** below with some words in bold from Exercise 1 (so that the meaning is the same).

1 You **shall do** it. _____ and _____.
2 You **shall not do** it. _____ and _____.

> The most common use for *shall* is making suggestions, and in this case we only use it with *I/we*: *Shall we stop for lunch?* But in the formal use for obligation mentioned above it can be used with *you/he/she/it/they* as well.

4 The forms in **bold** below are other ways to express obligation and permission. At the end of each sentence write the words in bold from Exercise 1 that have the same meaning. You might write the same words twice.

1 You **need to do** it. _____ and _____.
2 You **needn't do** it. _____.
3 You're **allowed to do** it. _____.
4 You're **not allowed to do** it. _____ and _____.
5 You've **got to do** it. _____ and _____.

5 Be careful with the word *may*. It can indicate permission in a formal context, or it can indicate possibility (approximately a 50:50 chance of something happening).

Look at the use of *may* in the sentences below and write 'permission' or 'possibility' at the end.

1 Visitors **may** use the swimming pool between 5.30 and 7.30pm. _____
2 There **may** be an easier way of solving the problem. _____
3 **May** I use your phone? _____
4 You **may** go home now if you want. _____
5 You **may** be asked to show your passport. _____
6 Some chemicals **may** cause environmental damage. _____
7 You **may** not use this equipment unless you have been on a training course. _____
8 You **may** not believe me, but it's true. _____

> When *may* is used for possibility (as in 2, 5, 6 and 8 in Exercise 5) we can use *might* with the same meaning. We cannot do this for the other sentences.

6 Underline the correct words in **bold**.

1 I'm sorry, this is a non-smoking area – you **haven't got to/can't** smoke here.
2 You **mustn't/don't have to** come if you are busy, but it would be nice to see you.
3 Ethical behaviour is important – you **mustn't/needn't** accept bribes.
4 You **mustn't/needn't** take an umbrella – I've got a spare one in the car.
5 You **don't have to/can't** enter the USA without a visa.
6 This report is confidential – you **mustn't/needn't** show it to anyone.
7 You **must/aren't allowed to** maintain the equipment in good condition.
8 You **mustn't/don't have to** do that, I'll do it tomorrow.
9 You **mustn't/don't have to** do that, it's dangerous.
10 All payments **shall/mustn't** be made within 30 working days.
11 If you want to smoke, you **shall/may** go outside.
12 Don't worry, the law states that you **shall/may** receive all the money that is owing to you.

7 Complete each sentence with a form of *have to*. Choices include *has to, don't have to, had to, didn't have to, 'll have to, won't have to*.

1 If you want to do well in your exams, you _____ work a lot harder this semester.
2 I'm sorry I'm late, I _____ take my daughter to the hospital.
3 It's a drop-in service, you _____ make an appointment.
4 If we redecorate the offices this year, we _____ do it again for another five years.
5 Teresa can't fly direct from Brno. She _____ go via Prague.
6 Oh, you brought your own projector! You _____ – we have one in the conference room.

8 Complete b) and c) so that they have the same meaning each time as a). For b) use a form of *can*, for c) use a form of *allowed*.

1 a) When I was young, we had permission to park anywhere in the city centre.
   b) When I was young, we _____ anywhere in the city centre.
   c) When I was young, we _____ anywhere in the city centre.
2 a) I'm sorry, it's prohibited to smoke in here.
   b) I'm sorry, _____ in here.
   c) I'm sorry, _____ in here.
3 a) Yes, that's OK, taking pictures is permitted.
   b) Yes, that's OK, _____ pictures.
   c) Yes, that's OK, taking _____.

9 Look at the word *got* in these sentences. If it is correct, put a tick (✓). If it is not correct, cross it out.

1 Maria is busy – she's got to finish some work before tomorrow.
2 You could have gone to the restaurant. You didn't have got to wait for us.
3 Is that the time? I've got to go now.
4 What time have we got to be at the meeting?
5 Do I have got to sign in the visitor's book?
6 It's boring to have got to wait so long.

> Both *have to* and *have got to* express necessity. *Have got to* is a little more informal, and is mostly used in the present simple. Also, *have got to* cannot be used in the infinitive form (see sentence 6 above).

Inversion

10 Read the information in the box. Then rewrite each sentence 1–6 beginning as shown.

> - In formal speech and writing there is a special construction when the sentence begins with a negative adverb (like those underlined below).
>   *I have never in my life seen such bad service.*
>   → <u>Never in my life</u> **have I** seen such bad service.
>   *You shouldn't do that under any circumstances.*
>   → <u>Under no circumstances</u> **should you** do that.
>   *It is not only bad practice, it is also illegal.*
>   → <u>Not only</u> **is it** bad practice, it is also illegal.
>   *I wasn't able to see a doctor until Monday.*
>   → <u>Not until</u> Monday **was I** able to see a doctor.
> - Notice how the subject and the verb – in **bold** – are inverted (change places).
> - This structure emphasizes the negative adverb.
> - Words and phrases used with this structure include:
>   *never, no sooner, not once, not only, not since, not until, on no account, only after, only once, only then, rarely, seldom, under no circumstances.*

1 I have rarely tasted coffee as good as this.
   Rarely _____.
2 You shouldn't accept a bribe under any circumstances.
   Under no _____.
3 We won't pay them until all the work is completed.
   Not until _____.
4 The contract is not only badly worded, it is also incomplete.
   Not _____.
5 You should not talk to the media on any account.
   On no _____.
6 Work can begin only once safety checks have been carried out.
   Only _____.

> In 2 and 5 in Exercise 10 notice how the word *any* in the first sentence becomes *no* in the second.

11 Look at the list of negative adverbs in italics in the final bullet point of the box above. Complete each explanation below with items from this list:

1 '_____' means 'very rarely'.
2 '_____' and '_____' are both used to emphasize that someone must definitely not do something, for any reason.
3 '_____ had ... than ...' is used to say that something happened almost immediately after something else.

Recordings

Unit 1 Building a career

1.1 About business: The education business

1:01–1:04

Speaker 1: Education for all – what a ludicrous idea! It's an incredible waste of resources. In countries where anybody can go to university, at least half the students drop out after the first year. If resources are limited, which they obviously are, then we should use them wisely to train the brightest and best – those who can benefit most from a university education.

Speaker 2: I think it's unrealistic to keep pumping public money into universities. That way, there's no incentive for them to become more competitive. It makes much more sense to use government funding to provide loans to students, and let universities compete with private schools for their business. They'd soon sort out their finances!

Speaker 3: It's not right that students should have to mortgage their future. Article 26 of the Universal Declaration of Human Rights states that everyone has the right to education. Universities should remain not-for-profit. It would be disastrous if they were forced to become profit-making businesses.

Speaker 4: This whole debate is a complete waste of time. A university degree just isn't relevant any more. You spend three or four years learning outdated theories that have nothing to do with modern life, and there isn't even a guarantee of a good job at the end of it, or a job at all for that matter. You just waste three years when you could be earning money and gaining valuable real-world experience.

1.2 Vocabulary: Education and career

1:05–1:10

Speaker 1: I'm thinking of leaving actually. I've worked in China, Argentina and Alaska, and now they want me to go to South Africa for two years! But even if I resign, they'll make me work at least another three months. I'm just sick of being moved around all the time.

Speaker 2: When the company was modernized, they told me to stay at home for a week or two while they found me a different job – but they never did. So, in the end, they had to 'let me go', as they say. Replaced by a machine! Actually, I'm grateful – it was probably the best thing that could have happened to me.

Speaker 3: I've just been sent home for a week because I refused to wear a safety helmet – they're too hot and uncomfortable. They keep harassing me – I think they'd like to fire me actually!

Speaker 4: I was on the road for thirty years as a sales rep. Then I was lucky enough to get the job as sales manager here four years ago. I've just been made 'Director of Customer Satisfaction' – or as the boys in sales say, they've just kicked me upstairs! Well, at my age, I'm over the moon!

Speaker 5: I'm based in London for the moment. Actually, right now I'm doing audits in Paris for our French subsidiary – but it's just for three months. After that, they've asked me to move to the Vancouver office. It's a fantastic opportunity!

Speaker 6: Well, I'm not actually working at the moment. I'm an actor and I finished a movie a couple of months ago. I'm thinking about taking a year off to write a book.

1:11–1:13

Speaker 1: Hi. My name's Bob. A few years ago I started up an electronics company which has been very successful. So successful, in fact, that I had to hire a CEO to give me time for my creative work. I brought in Jack, a manager from a completely different business, a soda manufacturer in fact. I thought he would be the right man to help my company grow, but now I know I made a big mistake. Recently we disagreed about strategy. Believe it or not, the Board decided he was right and I was wrong, and stripped me of my duties. Of course, I resigned. Well, what would you have done? I still hold my shares in the company, but I think I'm going to sell them. I don't know what I'll do next. Maybe I'll invest the money from the shares and retire somewhere cheap and sunny. Or I suppose I could start over and build a new company. Or join a competitor. What do you think I should do?

Speaker 2: Hello, I'm Lucy, and my problem is that I've never really known what sort of career to choose. I studied languages at university, which was great, but it doesn't really qualify you to do anything. After graduating, I worked as a researcher for a charity, then I went abroad and worked as an English teacher for a while. Now I'm a secretary; or should I say I was a secretary, because I've just been fired for writing stories at work!
 I love writing – but it's not easy to make a living from it. I suppose I'd need to go back to school and do a creative writing course. Perhaps I could work part-time, waitressing or something. Or should I just look for another secretarial job? Or go back to being a researcher, or a teacher maybe … at least that's more creative. What do you think?

Speaker 3: Hi. I'm Mel. I've wanted to run my own business for as long as I can remember. When I was in high school, a friend and I designed a product which we managed to sell to local government departments. But my parents were really keen on sending me to business school, so now I'm in my third year at a really prestigious, expensive school. The thing is, my friend and I have a fantastic opportunity to start our own business: we have a new product and a big company is really interested in buying it. But to develop our idea, I'll have to drop out of school, and I know my parents will be really upset. What do you think I should do?

1.3 Grammar: Tense review

1:14

Jess: Fraser Orbell!
Fraser: Oh, hi.
J: Fraser, fancy meeting you here! You look great! Do you still go running?
F: Oh, thank you. Yes, I usually run two or three times a week. Um, I'm sorry, I'm afraid I always forget people's names …
J: It's Jess! Jess Tomey!
F: Oh, Jess, of course! I'm so sorry …
J: It's all right. People often don't recognize me. Too many business lunches, so I always tend to put on weight!
F: Oh, no, you look wonderful. As always!
J: Thank you, Fraser! So what are you doing these days?
F: Well, actually, at the moment I'm not doing very much. Sort of, job-hunting, you know …
J: Oh, I see. Well, I hope you find something soon. But what did you do after graduation?
F: Well, you probably remember that I dropped out in my final year, so I didn't actually graduate. But I worked for ITC in Manchester for twenty years.
J: Oh, did you?!
F: Yes, until they were taken over by Morgan-Hoenshell about a year ago. Twenty years of loyal service, but when Morgan-Hoenshell came along, I was made redundant without so much as a word of thanks.
J: Oh, how awful for you!
F: Yes, well, you know, that's life, isn't it? But, um, actually, I've just got back from Nepal.
J: Nepal? Wow!
F: Yeah, been, um, working on a book.
J: Oh, that's terrific, Fraser! So when can I buy it?
F: Well, I haven't finished it yet, but hopefully it'll be published next year – I promise I'll send you a copy. But anyway, that's enough about me – what have you done since you left Franklin? Did you get that job you wanted in finance?
J: Yes, I did. I worked in several firms, actually. I became a specialist in downsizing – cutting costs, streamlining, restructuring, you know …
F: I see. A bit like Morgan-Hoenshell!
J: Well, yes, a bit …
F: So where are you working now?
J: Oh, I'm currently managing one of our subsidiaries, um, up north.
F: Oh, yeah – anywhere near Manchester?
J: Um, yes … but I'm going to move down to London soon.
F: Oh, really?
J: Yes, I've just had some rather good news.
F: Uh-huh?
J: Well, if all goes well, I'm taking over as group CEO next year.
F: Wow, congratulations! Which company?
J: Um, you probably wouldn't be interested …
F: Come on, Jess. We go back a long way! No secrets between us, eh?
J: Well, it's Morgan-Hoenshell, actually …

1.4 Speaking: Interviewing: giving reasons

1:15–1:20

1 What inspires you in a job?
2 Describe a decision you made that was a failure. What happened and why?
3 How do you measure success?
4 What can you do for us that someone else can't?
5 If we don't hire you, why do you think that would be?
6 What do you feel this position should pay?

1:21

Interviewer: How do you measure success?
Olivia: Well, as regards measuring professional success, I think it's important not only to understand what the company expects from me, and to compare my own performance with those benchmarks, but also to listen very carefully to the feedback I get from managers and co-workers. As far as my personal life is concerned, I try to discuss my objectives regularly with my family. That way I can be sure that they approve of what I'm trying to do and, what's more, they share the success when I achieve an objective.

1:22

I: What can you do for us that someone else can't?
O: Well, it's true that lots of people have similar qualifications to mine but, on the other hand, not so many people have excellent people skills. I believe that my ability to get on with people will be very valuable to your company. For one thing, working as a team to achieve a common goal is essential in marketing and, for another, real quality is only possible when every member of the team is committed to adding value to the organization. I have a proven ability to get people to work together and, in addition, to share values like respect, honesty and hard work.

1.6 Case study: Mangalia Business School

1:23

First of all, I would like to thank you all for coming here today. We hope you will enjoy your visit, and experience for yourselves why Mangalia is such a wonderful place to live and study. As you know, institutions like MBS now compete in a global market. The days when we could rely on our contacts in Romania and Central Europe to fill our school are long gone. Today we compete with giants like Harvard and the London Business School. Small schools like MBS face a difficult choice: either we sit back and watch the brightest students and the best professors fly away to Massachusetts, Paris, Barcelona or London, or we take risks, invest and develop new ways to be more competitive in the global marketplace. Here in Mangalia, we are not used to sitting back and doing nothing. We have chosen to draw up a five-year plan to make MBS a truly international business school, and we have invited you here to help us. We are not only relying on your experience, your know-how and your creativity to help us make the right decisions, but we are also counting on you to identify and promote the USPs – the unique selling propositions – that will give us a competitive advantage in attracting the best students and the most influential corporate clients. As far as finance is concerned, some of you will already have heard the excellent news that the prominent businessman and multimillionaire Ion Bumbescu has offered to sponsor our school. This would have the immediate effect of doubling our budget. However, Mr Bumbescu's business methods are somewhat controversial, and his offer specifies that the school should be known as the Bumbescu Business School. Consequently, I must ask you to consider carefully all the implications of such a change.

1:24

In business news, controversial multi-millionaire Ion Bumbescu has again been accused of involvement in defence procurement for developing countries. Mr Bumbescu, who is believed to be travelling in Southeast Asia, was unavailable for comment, but in a short statement made earlier today, a spokesman for Bumbescu Holdings claimed that 'the group's companies had done nothing illegal.' Mr Bumbescu's business methods have been frequently criticised by his competitors. Recently his Bumbescu Foundation has been pouring millions into research and education projects, in what appears to be an attempt to improve his image.

Unit 2 Information

2.1 About business: IT solutions

1:25–1:28

Speaker 1: I'm not sure all this technology is a good thing. Take these BlackBerry® smartphones, for example. I was at a meeting last week where three of the six attendees spent most of the time doing email! People get really addicted to it – it's a drug! I heard about one executive whose wife got so fed up with him checking his emails all weekend that she flushed his BlackBerry down the toilet!
Speaker 2: IT? Oh, I love it! As soon as there's a new gadget, I have to have it. I think it's just amazing what you can do nowadays. Of course, you don't really save time, but you get so much more done in a day. I just cannot imagine how anyone can manage without a smartphone and an iPad.
Speaker 3: As far as I'm concerned, information technology is just another weapon in the class war. Management will use any way they can to exploit the workers, and increasing productivity with computer systems is just another way to get as much as they can. Not to mention the untold damage that the radiation and microwaves from all these electronic devices are doing to our eyes, our backs and our brains!
Speaker 4: Well, I have to use the computer at work sometimes, but I wouldn't have one in the house. All those viruses, spam and computer crime! Anyway, a lot of people at work seem to spend more time fixing computer problems than actually doing any work. I think we'd be better off without them!

2.2 Vocabulary: Information systems and communication

1:29–1:36

Speaker 1: Hello? Mr Skopelitis? Oh. This is Ebony Brooks in Accounts. Something went wrong with the system when I was in the middle of a backup. Everything just stopped. It wasn't just my computer. Do you think you could call me? Give me a ring as soon as you can.
Speaker 2: George, it's Maurice. I'm still having that problem making appointments on the website. I log in, then everything seems to freeze, and when I try to escape, I get the famous blue screen. Can you give me an update on what progress you've made on this problem? Just a quick report.
Speaker 3: Yeah, George, it's Martha here. Listen, could you contact me? I want to replace my department's laptops with something more modern. Our old ones are getting pretty tired, know what I mean? Please get in touch as soon as you have a moment.
Speaker 4: Hello, George. This is Lincoln Thigpen. I hope you can help me out. I seem to have done something stupid. I was cleaning up my hard disk, and well, now some very important presentation slides seem to have disappeared. I hope you have some way of rescuing them. If you could get back to me with an answer sometime today, I'd appreciate it.
Speaker 5: Hi, Mr Skopelitis. This is Camilla Ramsey from Customer Services. It's about that little software thingy you sent me. I've copied it into the database program like you told me to, but it doesn't seem to work. I know some other people were having the same problem. Do you think you could include me in the group of people to inform? You know, keep me in the loop. Thanks.
Speaker 6: George, Maurice again. Where are you?! Marketing are hassling me every five minutes because they still can't use the Internet. Will you please tell me when you're going to be able to get them online? Let me know asap.
Speaker 7: George, Marvin. Remember how you said you could get that software from the Internet to make my sound card work? I can't work without my music! I guess you're working on it, but can you keep me informed, maybe a regular progress report, OK?
Speaker 8: Good morning, Mr Skopelitis. This is Cara Bickerson in Marketing. I'm looking for a quicker way to get information from our market studies into the database – typing it all in is just too slow. I'm interested in voice recognition software. I wonder if you could fill me in on the details of what's available? You can reach me any time today before 4 p.m. Thank you.

2.4 Speaking: Telephoning

1:37

Lorenzo: Accounts?
Kelly: Lorenzo? It's Kelly, from Sales.
L: Uh-huh.
K: Listen, I'm with a customer and I need you to give me last year's billing figures.
L: What's the customer account number?
K: Um, I don't have it here. But it's Zimmer, in Warsaw.
L: Well, if you don't have the account number, I can't help you.
K: Oh, come on, Lorenzo. I really need this! I'm sure you can find it.
L: Look, Kelly, it's the end of the month and we're closing the accounts. I'd like to help you, but I'm up to my eyes in work here. I really haven't got time to look for your customer's records now. Try Marielle in Sales Administration. I'll put you through.
K: Thanks a million.

1:38

Cory: Cory Wilks.
Tabetha: Hello, Cory. It's Tabetha Pullman here.
C: Oh, hi Tabetha, how are you doing?
T: I'm fine, thanks. How are you?
C: Well, you know, mustn't grumble, I suppose. Things'll be a bit easier when the weather improves.
T: Oh yeah, it's been a really long winter, hasn't it? Anyway, have you got a couple of minutes?
C: Yes, sure.
T: Well, do you happen to know how to set up a WiFi connection to a laptop? I would've asked the IT department, but apparently they're all in some big meeting, so I thought you might be able to help me.
C: Oh, I'm sorry, Tabetha. I wish I could help you, but I don't know that much about it myself. Amanda does all my department's computer stuff and she's out of the office today. I'm sorry.
T: Don't worry. I just thought you might know, but it doesn't matter. Thank you anyway.
C: No problem.
T: Anyway, I won't keep you any longer – thanks once again.
C: You're welcome – sorry I couldn't help you more.
T: That's all right. Bye.
C: Bye.

🔊 1:39

Lauren: Hello?
Erich: Good afternoon. I wonder if I could speak to Ms Simpson, please?
L: Speaking.
E: Excuse me?
L: This is Lauren Simpson.
E: Ah, Ms Simpson. Erich Schrader, calling from Switzerland. We met at the conference in Nice last month.
L: Oh, yes, of course! How are you, Erich?
E: I am very well, thank you, Ms Simpson. And how are you?
L: Fine, thanks. Um, what can I do for you?
E: Well, I'm very sorry to disturb you, but I was wondering if I could ask you a favour?
L: Yes, of course …
E: Do you think you could possibly send me a copy of the slides you showed at the conference? They were most interesting.
L: Ah. Well, normally I'd be glad to help, but I'm afraid my hard disk crashed last week.
E: Oh dear, how very unfortunate. I trust you didn't lose too much important information.
L: Well, everything, actually. But there wasn't too much important stuff on it – except the slides, of course.
E: And you wouldn't happen to have a backup, or a hard copy, would you?
L: No, I'm afraid not.
E: I see. Well, I mustn't take up any more of your time. Thank you all the same, Ms Simpson.
L: You're welcome. Goodbye Erich, I mean, Mr, um …
E: Schrader.
L: Um, yes. Goodbye then.

🔊 1:40

Russell: Russell Pond speaking.
Mike: Hello, Russell – Mike.
R: Hello, mate. How's life?
M: Not so bad. And you?
R: Fine, fine. Looking forward to the weekend, though!
M: Yeah, me too. Er, Russell, you got a moment?
R: Yes; what's on your mind?
M: Well, I know this is asking a lot, but I've got this presentation on Monday and my laptop's got a virus. Any chance I could borrow yours for the weekend?
R: Ah. Look, it's not that I don't trust you or anything …
M: OK, just forget it. I shouldn't have asked.
R: The thing is, I've got some really important data on it and the anti-virus isn't up-to-date …
M: It's all right, Russell. I know what you mean. Anyway, I'd better get on. Are you going to the match on Saturday?
R: Yes, I expect so.
M: OK. I'll see you there, then. Bye.
R: Cheers.

2.5 Writing: Memos

🔊 1:41

Hello, Chris Webster here. I'm at the airport, just about to leave for my holiday, and I've just realized there's something important I've forgotten to do, so I wonder if I could ask you a favour? You know the new procedure we discussed for computer upgrades? Asking people to evaluate their computing needs for the next two years so we can budget for buying new equipment in advance? Well, do you think you could write a memo to everyone in the department, explaining the new system? Remind them that we've been dramatically over budget in the last two years, so, you know, some people who needed laptops didn't get one, while other people got an upgrade they didn't really need. I need to have the information in time for the budget meeting in October, so can you ask people to email me their evaluations as soon as possible, by the end of September at the latest? And make it positive and friendly please, because I know people complain about the amount of paperwork they have to do already. OK? I've got to go now: my plane's boarding. Thanks a lot, I really appreciate your help – and, see you in two weeks!

2.6 Case study: Meteor Bank

🔊 1:42–1:45

Tonye: Look, Astrid. We appointed Saul Finlay because he's a very bright, very ambitious young man. All right, he's irritated some of his colleagues – but as he says, you don't make an omelette without breaking eggs. Of course, I'm worried about staff turnover and down time costs, and so is Saul. But you have to remember that our transactions have increased by 40% since he joined us – our subsidiaries in Ivory Coast, Ghana, Cameroon, etc. are growing really quickly. We need to invest in the new equipment he's asking for.
Vincent: Well, if you ask me, I have to say that I think Saul is too ambitious – he's just empire-building. OK, he's increased our capacity. I suppose that's an achievement. But he's made our computer system too centralized. If the main server goes down, we're in trouble – not just in Nigeria, but all over West Africa. The trend today is towards grid computing: that way, if the server in Lagos goes down, we can just redirect transactions via Abidjan, Niamey or Dakar. I say we should decentralize our systems. And another thing, you can't explain the down time just by component failures and software errors. You have to wonder whether some of it isn't malicious …
Kehinde: The problem is simple. Everybody in IT is exhausted. Mr Finlay is a very demanding manager. He works fifteen hours a day and he expects us to do the same. That's why so many people are leaving! Frankly, I'm not sure that appointing a European IT manager was such a good idea. OK, Mr Finlay has raised salaries. But he's made the job too hard – and it's going to get more complicated if he invests in more sophisticated equipment. So now some people are pleased when the system goes down – you know what I mean? We need to recruit more experienced staff, a lot more.
Joseph: Look, I've nothing against Saul Finlay. I like him. He's a nice young man, and he's succeeded in getting rid of some older staff who just couldn't adapt to change. Of course he's made mistakes, like not understanding the work culture here, but that's almost inevitable when you bring in a foreign manager. I just want efficient service and no more down time – some of our big customers are getting very angry. It seems to me the simple answer is to outsource our IT services. That way we don't have any of the investment, HR or recruitment problems to worry about.

Unit 3 Quality

3.1 About business: What quality means

🔊 1:46

Well, over the years, in the household electrical goods industry, or *white goods* as it's often called, there's been a lot of talk about planned or built-in obsolescence. This means making products that are designed to last a limited time. It's true that we are seeing a general trend towards shorter product lifespans. A fridge, for example, that would once have lasted for twenty years, now lasts for around ten on average. However, I wouldn't go as far as to call it planned obsolescence. But it's true that manufacturers these days decide very carefully what build quality they're aiming for. Consumer behaviour is changing and people don't want to keep things forever. They want to upgrade more often, and there's not much point in producing machines that will last for twenty years when people will be tired of them after ten. So, most manufacturers design accordingly. And that's why it's often cheaper to buy something new than to have a product repaired. The cost of the spare parts and the labour time to repair a broken washing machine, for example, may well come to more than the cost price of a new one. I think another factor is recent legislation regarding recycling. This means that today's ethical consumer can buy electrical goods knowing that we can recycle them at the end of their useful life. And, of course, they can also argue that by upgrading regularly, they're investing in more efficient, more environmentally-friendly technology. Now, if you want to buy a quality product that will last, you can still go for the top brands and …

3.2 Vocabulary: Quality and standards

🔊 1:47–1:49

Speaker 1: Well, most of the time I'm looking for value for money, you know, for everyday things and that. So, a balance between quality and the price I'm paying. But, erm, if I'm splashing out on a pair of trainers or the latest mp3 player, I want something reliable that's going to last. And, of course, they've got to look great, too. Do you know what I mean?
Speaker 2: My job basically involves ensuring that the process is as efficient as possible and makes the best use of all the resources needed to make the final product. So, I'm constantly looking at ways to improve it, which means not only solving problems that come up, but also looking for new ways to do things even better. I let the design guys worry about pure product quality. Quality for me is really producing a part or a product which conforms to given technical specifications in the most cost-effective way.
Speaker 3: Erm, although I believe what I do contributes to the end quality of the product, it's not really my everyday concern. I check that the company has documented quality procedures in place and that they're being followed. So, erm, I suppose, in theory, the company might conform to the quality standards, but might be producing a product that is substandard in some way. We don't live in a perfect world, after all!

3.3 Grammar: Passive structures and *have something done*

🔊 1:50

Willi: Well, thank you all for coming. I know you're all very busy at the moment so we'll see if we can sort this out as quickly as possible. José, perhaps you can start and tell us the background from the Sales side?
José: Sure, Willi. Well, the problem is simple. Airbridge can't fix the pumps to the fuel tanks properly. The reason, it seems, is because they don't fit.

Birgit: What do you mean, they don't fit, José?
J: Basically, Birgit, your Production department put the wrong type of fitting on the pumps!
B: My Production department, José! Hold on! First of all, Sales didn't warn Production that they wanted things this early. That made things very difficult. We had to organize an extra shift.
J: Well, yes, I'm sorry about that. We'll try to give you more warning next time.
B: That was bad enough. And Stock didn't make things any easier. They shouldn't have sent two different parts to the workshop in the same delivery. And, to top it all, they delivered them at the last minute! OK, I'm prepared to admit that there may have been a problem, but you can hardly blame my people in Production if they didn't spot the difference!
W: But wait a minute, Birgit. The Stock department didn't make a mistake. If you remember, at the last Logistics meeting, we – yes, you, me and everybody else – decided to deliver different parts together to reduce stock movements!
B: OK, Willi. OK, I accept that, but Stock did deliver late. And Sales should've given us more warning!
J: More warning! How could we give you more warning? You know that Airbridge only increased their order two weeks before the final delivery date! It's always the same. The customer …
W: Now take it easy, both of you. We're not going to find a solution if we spend all our time blaming each other. We've all made mistakes but, as I see it, the underlying cause seems to be customer pressure. So, let's put our heads together and see how we can improve our reaction time without compromising our quality …

3.4 Speaking: Delivering presentations

1:51–1:54

Speaker 1: Anyway, the ACI has shown an increase on the marginal propensity gradient of 4.5% over and above the CDWLP.
Speaker 2: Well, that's as you can see an increase OK in the rate of sales growth over the quarter and this rate of growth OK continued OK into the new year which was completely unexpected OK and then …
Speaker 3: As is clear from the graph, there was … as is clear, there was an important development, erm … important change in the market structure during the previous … year.
Speaker 4: Obviously, we aim to do a profit. We always expect to do a profit, and I'm sure we will do a profit. The sales team are really making a great job.

1:55

So, this graph shows the PFR, that's the Part Failure Rate, per ten thousand over the first ten months of the year. As you can see, it was pretty high for the first four months, around seventy on average. And that's why we set up the quality improvement plan in April. By the way, I'd just like to thank Magda for her input on the plan. I think you'll all agree she did a great job. Anyway, the first results were very promising, with PFR falling to thirty-five in May and then twenty-eight in June. However, since then the rate has got worse again, rising to forty-four in August and forty-seven last month. So, we need to turn things around again. In other words, get the rate back down in the twenties, or better. And basically, that's why we're here today: to look at the reasons and some possible solutions. … Is that clear so far? … Good, well, I think that covers the basic problem, so now I'd like to look at some of the reasons we've identified. Let's look at the next table which shows …

3.6 Case study: Zaluski Strawberries

1:56

Piotr Sieberski: Piotr Sieberski.
Suzanne Van Peeters: Good morning, Mr Sieberski. This is Suzanne Van Peeters from Schuurman in Amsterdam.
P: Ah, morning, Ms Van Peeters. I imagine you're calling about the email we got from you yesterday.
S: That's right.
P: Something about a quality audit, wasn't it? I don't think you'll find much wrong with our strawberries in terms of quality.
S: I'm sure you're right, Mr Sieberski. We've always been very happy with your fruit. But, as I mentioned in my email, we're currently running audits with all our fresh fruit suppliers. Basically, it's a matter of looking at a wide range of issues which may impact fruit quality, and seeing where there may be room for improvement. You know, trying to sort out any potential problems before they happen.
P: Well, of course, you're welcome to come and see us if you want to, but I'm not sure what can be improved, really. Your purchaser comes here at least once a year and he's never had anything negative to say about our strawberries, apart from the price of course!
S: Yes, well, in fact I was calling to fix up a visit to you. Our supplier audits generally last a day or two and I was wondering whether you'd be free to see us towards the end of next week?
P: Next week? … That's rather short notice and we are pretty busy at the moment, but … hold on … Let me check my schedule …Yes, I guess I could see you on Thursday and/or Friday if that suits you?
S: Perfect, Mr Sieberski. Thursday would be fine. We'd probably be arriving the night before, so we could start as early as you like on Thursday morning.
P: Well, I get in around seven most days, Ms Van Peeters. That gives me time to look at the important matters before things really get going and I'm interrupted every five minutes!
S: Seven! Well, we'll give you a bit of breathing space, Mr Sieberski. How about eight-thirty?
P: Suits me fine, Ms Van Peeters. So that's eight-thirty on the fifteenth.
S: Great! Looking forward to seeing you next Thursday.
P: Yes! See you then. Thank you for calling! Goodbye.
S: Goodbye, Mr Sieberski.

1:57

Suzanne Van Peeters: Perhaps we could begin with harvesting, Mr Sieberski. Who does that?
Piotr Sieberski: Well, the farms hire their own workers each season, generally students or local people.
S: And, do they get any training?
P: That's the responsibility of each producer, but I know most of them do some. After all, it's in their own interests.
S: What about supervision and picking bonuses to make sure only sound fruit are picked?
P: Most farms pay a small productivity bonus if daily picking targets are met, but it encourages quantity rather than quality, I think. And I must admit, there's little supervision of the picking crews.
S: And how is the fruit packed for transfer to your cooler?
P: The pickers put them in standard wooden trays, ten centimetres deep. Then the trays are placed on trailers and, when the trailer is full, it's pulled to our shed by tractor.
S: Isn't that rather long, Mr Sieberski? I mean, how long do they take to get from the field to your cooler?
P: Oh, um, on average, I reckon, three or four hours. Maybe more if several trailers arrive at the same time. In the cooler, the berries are cooled to a temperature of three degrees. Then they're placed in the storage shed until we can pack them.
S: I presume the storage shed is chilled too?
P: Well, yes, it is. The thermostat is kept on two degrees but, to be honest, we haven't got time to keep records. The picking season is always such a mad rush you know, Ms Van Peeters!
S: Yes, I can imagine.
P: From storage, the strawberries go to the packing shed. But, I'll let Klara tell you about that. She's been our packing shed supervisor for seven years now and she knows the job inside out. Klara.
Klara Solak: Thanks, Piotr. Well, Ms Van Peeters, the packing shed is where we put the berries into the punnets for retail sale in outlets like yours. It's seasonal work, and most people imagine that it's unskilled. But I can tell you that good packers are not easy to find.
S: And what about training and bonuses, things like that?
K: Of course, we give them basic training when they're hired: fruit selection, careful handling to avoid bruising, that sort of thing. But they learn on the job otherwise. They're paid according to what they pack in a day so there aren't any bonuses. In fact, we've been looking at the idea of a bonus based on the quality of packing. You know, making sure that they don't put bruised or decaying berries in the packages, and so on. But, quite honestly, it's not very easy to measure that sort of thing.
S: Yes, but it would certainly be a good idea, I'm sure, and there'd be benefits all along the line. As supervisor, do you check the quality of fruit being packed?
K: Huh! Not as much as I'd like. You see, I'm usually packing too, covering for absent staff, that sort of thing.
S: I see. Now, what about shipping?
K: Well, the punnets are loaded onto trucks for shipping to customers around Europe. Now, we require the trucks to have refrigeration systems and be cooled to zero before loading, but we don't check them systematically.
S: Hm, well. Thank you for your explanations, Mrs Solak. Erm, let me see. Ah, yes. One last question for the moment, Mr Sieberski. I'm sure you're aware that the use of nitrogen fertilizers can lead to softer fruit, lower sugar content and less flavour. Do your farmers use nitrogen?
P: Yes, I'm aware of the problem, Ms Van Peeters, and at the moment a lot of them still use it. But it's an expensive operation anyway, and most of the producers in the region are planting new varieties of strawberry which don't need nitrogen. So, I reckon that the practice will have died out within the next two or three years.
S: Well, that's encouraging! Good, now perhaps we could go and look at …

Unit 4 Feedback

4.1 About business: The project team

🔊 1:58

OK. I think everyone's here apart from Mr Wong, who'll be joining us on the video link in half an hour. So, perhaps we can start? The purpose of today's meeting is to review the dam project schedule to date, look at why things have slipped and see what we can do to get things back on track. First, I'd like to take a look at the original schedule on the Gantt chart here, to put our current situation into perspective. I think you'll all agree, things ran pretty smoothly in Year 1 and we reached the first milestones, completion of the feasibility study and the geological survey bang on target at the end of August. Unfortunately, we got bogged down in bureaucracy – you know, the usual red tape – at the project approval stage. That set us back four months and we could only begin buying the land in May of Year 2. Land purchase went pretty much according to plan, despite some delays for legal reasons, but it still took twelve months. We were able to start population resettlement on time, but we had to postpone diverting the river for six months as it had to be done in the summer months, when the river was at its lowest, which meant starting June of Year 3. So, that's how things stand today. We've just completed the two tunnels to divert the river, so that's almost complete, and we're beginning excavations for the dam foundations next week – one year behind schedule! Which means we won't be able to begin work on the dam wall until at least September of Year 4. Of course, due to this schedule slippage, we're also facing considerable cost overruns. So, I'd like your suggestions on how we can crash the schedule – yes, I mean, accelerate things – to try to respect the original delivery date at the end of Year 7. Any ideas …?

4.2 Vocabulary: Managing people and projects

🔊 1:59

Lucy: Well, Andrei, thanks for finding time to see me. I know things are very busy, what with the annual appraisal interviews. Anyway, perhaps you can just give me your impressions of Anna, Bjorn and Katia before we go through the interview results in a bit more detail.
Andrei: Sure, Lucy. So, first of all, Anna. Well, on the positive side, she's hard-working. But she's very independent and single-minded: she tends to do her own thing and she'll pass the buck if she feels it's not her problem, so the others in the team see her as selfish and a bit of a loner. They often think she's not pulling her weight and that she's letting the team down, just because she doesn't see things the same way. And she can be pretty direct, which of course the others interpret as being over-critical, but I don't think she means to be.
L: OK, so Anna has her good and bad points. Now, what about Bjorn?
A: Yes, Bjorn! To be honest, he seems very stressed and I'm worried that he may burn out. He works long hours – he's often in the office long after everyone's gone home. He's definitely organized – some of the others would say obsessive – but I'm not sure he's always really clear about what needs doing and what is less important, so he tends to create work for himself. He could certainly do with taking it easy sometimes, you know.
L: Yes, sounds as if he needs to learn to pace himself a little better!
A: Yeah, that's right. He could do with some time management training, in fact, and I'd like to come back to that when we look at the interview results in detail.
L: Good idea. But first, let's just finish with Katia.
A: Ah, Katia. Well, the first thing is she's new but she's settling in really well. She's friendly and easy-going and gets on well with nearly everybody, except Anna! She's really helpful and she knows what it means to pull together in a team; and she's always ready to cover for somebody. On the other hand, she can be a bit messy, but she's definitely not incompetent. And I think she's very cooperative with her colleagues …

4.4 Speaking: Coaching

🔊 1:60

Mrs Gómez: Rafael?
Rafael: Yes, Mrs Gómez?
G: Do you have a moment?
R: Yes, of course.
G: Come in, Rafael. Have a seat. As you know, the last three weeks have been really busy. We could have lost a lot of business while Maria was off sick but, thanks to you, everything has gone really smoothly. So I just wanted to thank you for taking care of Maria's section and staying late while she was off sick.
R: Oh, it was no problem. I was glad to help.
G: Well, you've worked a lot of extra hours, and you've been very supportive of Maria's team. You're not only hard-working and conscientious, but you've shown that you can take initiative: these are qualities the company values highly.
R: Well, thank you.
G: I want to say how much I appreciate your dedication to the company and your solidarity with your colleagues. What's more, I'm very grateful for the support you have shown me personally by dealing with this difficult situation yourself.
R: It was my pleasure. And I enjoyed the chance to work with a bigger team.
G: Well, I'm sure there'll be opportunities for you to take on more responsibility in the very near future, and it's really good to know we can count on you. Well done, Rafael, and thank you!

🔊 1:61

Mrs Gómez: Rafael?
Rafael: Yes, Mrs Gómez?
G: Could I just have a word?
R: Yes, of course.
G: Come in Rafael. Have a seat. Now, it seems there was a problem with Mr Baitan last Friday. He called me to say he was very upset. Can you tell me exactly what happened?
R: I'm sorry, I messed up. I was really tired: it was 6pm, I had two sales assistants off sick and Mr Baitan was being really difficult. I just lost my patience. He wouldn't stop asking me the same questions!
G: Well, Rafael, you're a good supervisor, but you can't afford to forget your basic customer care skills, can you?
R: No, I understand. I realize I didn't set a very good example for the team.
G: Quite. Now, do you have any ideas as to why Mr Baitan was so upset?
R: Well, I understand that he expects VIP treatment. I'm afraid I was probably a bit rude to him.
G: Look Rafael, you've been with us for, what, three years now? You do realize that this kind of problem can have serious consequences, don't you?
R: Yes, of course.
G: All right then, so what do you think we can do to make sure this doesn't happen again?
R: Well, I've been thinking about doing the stress management course. I think it could help me a lot. And, perhaps Maria could let me have someone to help out in my section when things are really busy?
G: Right. I think that's a good plan. I know you've been under pressure, so if you need help, you will get back to me, won't you?
R: Yes, thank you.
G: Good. Is there anything else you'd like to add?
R: No.
G: So, before you go, let's just summarize what we have agreed. I'll book you on the course next week, and I'll ask Maria to give you some help during the really busy periods. OK? And let's meet again in a month's time to see how you're getting on. Are you comfortable with that?
R: Yes, that's fine Mrs Gómez. Thank you very much.

4.6 Case study: Trident Overseas

🔊 1:62

John Thorpe: Abeba, you've been a mechanic in Witu for five and a half years, is that right?
Abeba: Yes, sir, that's right.
JT: So you worked for two other dealers before Mr Mbugua – would you say that things have got worse since he became the Dealer here?
A: Yes, sir. Before Mr Mbugua arrived, we had a good team. Everyone pulled together and we enjoyed our work. Now, it's not at all the same. Morale is bad and the customers can see the difference. A lot of our regular customers have stopped coming. Mr Mbugua fired several good colleagues for no reason, just so he could hire his friends and relatives instead. They get the easy shifts and the rest of us do the hard work.
JT: Have you spoken to the sales rep about this?
A: Mrs Mohamed? Huh! We never see her. She's too busy with the development project. Anyway, she can't do anything – Mr Mbugua is Mr Wambugu's nephew, didn't you know? To be honest, I'd leave if there was any choice. But there aren't any other jobs around here, so I just have to put up with it.

🔊 1:63

John Thorpe: Mr Mbugua, I've been hearing accusations of favouritism – and that you've employed friends and members of your family in your service station?
Mr Mbugua: Oh, don't pay any attention to what Abeba says, Mr Thorpe. She's not a team player – she's only interested in herself. It would be better for her to leave, and the sooner she leaves, the better.
JT: But is it true that you employ members of your family?
M: Yes, of course it's true. As a Young Dealer, I work my fingers to the bone for Trident, Mr Thorpe, and I get very little thanks for it. I need staff who will work hard for the company too, and it's not easy to find them, I can tell you. I employ two of my cousins and a couple of friends because I know they're hard workers, like me. What's wrong with that?
JT: Does Mrs Mohamed agree with this recruitment policy?
M: I haven't asked her. Anyway, I don't think Mrs Mohamed is interested. Her big development project is far more important! I get absolutely no support from her, or

from the company, for that matter. Other companies look after their dealers much better. I have to do everything myself. Everything!

🔘 **1:64**

Mrs Mohamed: Thank you for taking the time to see me, Mr Thorpe. I really need to talk to someone. I don't think I can go on much longer like this.
John Thorpe: That's what I'm here for, Mrs Mohamed. The more you can tell me about the problems, the better – and I promise I'll do my best to help.
M: Thank you. It's just – I always wanted to become a sales rep. But it's turned into a nightmare. Mr Wambugu, the District Manager, delegates everything to me and I just can't cope. He gives me impossible deadlines, then blames me when we fall behind schedule. And that means I have no time to visit the dealers, so they're not getting any support.
JT: Yes, I've just been speaking to Mr Mbugua in Witu.
M: Oh, don't talk to me about Mbugua! The way he treats his staff is a disgrace, especially the women!
JT: So how did he become a Young Dealer?
M: Didn't you know? He's Mr Wambugu's nephew! I tried to stop his appointment, but there was nothing I could do. I think Mr Wambugu got to hear about it and he's never forgiven me. I think he's giving me too much work because he hopes I'll quit.

🔘 **1:65**

Mr Thorpe, this is Mr Wambugu. One of my sales reps, Mrs Mohamed, has just handed me her resignation. I intend to promote Mr Mbugua, currently the Young Dealer in Witu, to the position of sales rep. He is a hard-working young man with energy, ideas and enthusiasm who will do well in the job. As you are no doubt aware, I need you to authorize this appointment with the HR department in Nairobi. Personally, I think Corporate should stop interfering, and let us Kenyans manage our own affairs. However, since that's the procedure, I would appreciate it if you could deal with this matter as soon as possible.

Unit 5 Selling more

5.1 About business: Social media marketing

🔘 **2:01**

Interviewer: Our guest today is Michelle Hudson, who blogs on *Social Media Monitor*. Michelle, you claim that digital marketers are using trickery and deception. What's made you so indignant?
Michelle: Well, social networking is an incredibly powerful way of sharing information and influencing people's opinions. Inevitably I suppose, some marketers are trying to exploit social media in ways that vary from, let's say, less than honest, to downright illegal.
I: Can you give us some examples?
M: Sure. Buying friends and followers, for instance; sponsoring tweets; guaranteeing YouTube views …
I: But surely this is nothing new? I mean, these things go on in traditional advertising channels. What's wrong with paying to place your video somewhere people will see it? Or paying celebrities to endorse a product? They already do it on billboards and on TV, so why not on Twitter?
M: Well, the whole point about social media is that people share their opinions and links to the latest viral or whatever with friends or followers, so the whole thing is based on trust and loyalty. But when a company starts paying people to push its products or to follow a particular Twitzen, the whole idea of social networking breaks down, because you no longer know whether you can trust people. I mean, let's say you're a well-known blogger on high-tech products, and you recommend the latest gadget; now, I know you have thousands of followers, so I'm inclined to believe what you say. But if I suspect you're being paid by the manufacturer, I can't trust your opinion any more, can I?
I: I see what you mean. So, can you really buy friends?
M: Oh, yes! And the more you have, the more you'll get paid for your sponsored tweets! It's forbidden of course, but there are companies that have ways of avoiding detection, and they'll happily sell you ten thousand followers!
I: And are these real people or just made-up names with fake accounts?
M: Oh, they're real people with real Twitter accounts. They're paid a fee to follow clients of a particular service. The phrase 'get paid to tweet' is one of the most popular searches on Google!

5.2 Vocabulary: The marketing mix

🔘 **2:02–2:07**

Speaker 1: Determining market segmentation is essential when using media like TV. Football matches guarantee a large, masculine audience: every four years, the World Cup attracts an average 90 million viewers per match. It's the perfect opportunity for advertisers to try to flood the market with razors, deodorants and sports shoes.
Speaker 2: Entering a new market often means a 'hard sell'. If you want to promote your new alarm system to companies in Eastern Europe, don't waste money on TV or newspaper advertising: conduct a market study to identify suitable targets, send out a mailshot, then call any companies who show an interest in your product.
Speaker 3: New technology is providing new promotional tools. Sellers can use electronic databases to select suitable prospects, then address a personalized sales pitch by email or SMS. These techniques are often combined with telemarketing. Don't be surprised if the email you received about investing in a timeshare apartment in Spain is followed up a day or two later by a call on your mobile inviting you on a free holiday!
Speaker 4: In many western countries, tobacco and cigarettes are facing a declining market. Advertising is strictly regulated, so even market leaders have to resort to stealth tactics like getting their products in films. Smoking is all about image, and the subliminal messages delivered by Hollywood movie stars are strong motivators.
Speaker 5: A movie is a product with huge development costs. In order to guarantee successful box office, DVD and TV sales, it is crucial to capture market share in the first days after release. Producers encourage rumours about the love life of their stars in the weeks before they bring the movie to market – nothing attracts public interest more than a little scandal!
Speaker 6: A little market research soon demonstrates that one of the best ways to develop a niche market like skateboarding accessories is by releasing games or video clips featuring the products onto the net. Teenagers circulate them to their friends – it's a perfect 'soft sell' by word of mouth – or word of electronic messaging, to be precise.

5.3 Grammar: Questions for persuading

🔘 **2:08–2:09**

You don't happen to know how many you ordered last year, do you? ↗
You don't really want to run out of components, do you? ↘

🔘 **2:10**

1 You don't happen to know how many you ordered last year, do you? ↗
2 You don't really want to run out of components, do you? ↘
3 You couldn't possibly give me an order today, could you? ↗
4 You can't afford failure, can you? ↘
5 You'd agree that everybody needs to know how to use the system, wouldn't you? ↘
6 You wouldn't have any idea how many people need training, would you? ↗
7 You really should upgrade your software regularly, shouldn't you? ↘
8 You haven't upgraded to the new version yet, have you? ↗

🔘 **2:11**

A: You'd enjoy driving a nice new car, wouldn't you?
B: I probably would enjoy it, that's right.
C: I imagine your old car is costing you a lot in repairs, isn't it?
B: It certainly is.
A: And I expect you're going on holiday soon, aren't you?
B: Y … um, that's correct.
C: So this might be a good time to think about buying a new car, right?
B: Well, possibly …
A: Because you wouldn't want to break down in the middle of your holiday, would you?
B: Of course not.
C: You didn't say 'no' then, did you?
B: No, I said 'of course' … Oh, no!

5.4 Speaking: Dealing with objections

🔘 **2:12–2:14**

1 **Customer:** I want a 10% discount on my subscription.
   Salesperson: Well, I might be able to give you 5% …
   C: 10%. Take it or leave it.
2 **Customer:** Listen, your proposal for the pool looks great, but I'm worried it'll be too much work.
   Salesperson: Well, if you don't place the order, I'll have to bill you for the study.
3 **Customer:** $32,000?! I've had a quotation from another software developer for less than half that!
   Salesperson: Well, you know what they say: *you get what you pay for!*

🔘 **2:15–2:17**

1 **Customer:** I want a 10% discount on my subscription.
   Salesperson: Well, I'm glad you raised that point. We feel that if we gave discounts, we'd have to compromise on quality and service. And I'm sure you'd agree that would be a mistake, wouldn't you?
   C: Yes, I suppose so.
   S: So, tell me, is the membership fee the only obstacle to signing up?
   C: Well, yes. I've just bought a new car, you see.

S: Right. So, if I can postpone your first payment to next year, are you ready to sign up today? Does that make sense?

2 **Customer:** Listen, your proposal for the pool looks great, but I'm worried it'll be too much work.
Salesperson: I know exactly what you mean. There's always too much to do, right?
C: Yeah. Things are busy at work, and I don't have time for the garden, let alone a pool.
S: I understand. You don't want to spend all your time cleaning instead of swimming, do you?
C: Exactly.
S: Well, if we include the automatic chlorinator and robot pool cleaner options, I can guarantee that you will spend less than ten minutes a week on maintenance. Are you comfortable with that?

3 **Customer:** $32,000?! I've had a quotation from another software developer for less than half that!
Salesperson: I understand how you feel. A lot of our customers felt that way at first. However, they soon found they were saving money. After you start using the software, you'll reduce your annual operating costs by 25 to 30%.
C: As much as that?!
S: Yes, more in some cases, but that's the average saving. Does that answer your question?

5.6 Case study: Backchat Communications

🔘 2:18

Assistant: Mr Lim?
Lim: Yes?
A: I just had a call from Seoul Deliveries, you know, the courier company?
L: Yes?
A: They're interested in mobiles for about two hundred staff.
L: Are they now? Hm, we'd better send somebody to see them.
A: They said they'd like a proposal by fax.
L: Well, yes, but we need to know more about their needs before we can write a proposal. Let me note this down. Who's in charge over there?
A: The Office Manager is a Mr Ibáñez. He's French, apparently.
L: Ibáñez. Right. Two hundred, you say. Do we know who they want the phones for?
A: Well, there are three categories. Drivers, managers and admin staff.
L: Admin staff? Why do they want mobiles?
A: Well, it seems that they have to move about a lot between different offices. They only really need to call the drivers when they're out on the road, but they take a lot of calls from customers and they like the idea of Bluetooth™ headsets so they can work hands-free.
L: I see. Yes, that makes sense – I can imagine it would make their lives a lot easier. What about the managers?
A: They seem quite keen on smartphones. Email is very important for them.
L: Good. They'll need the high-tech price plan then. Do you think budget will be a problem?
A: They didn't say.
L: Good. We can try to sell some longer contracts. We need to secure our future cash flow, even if we have to give discounts.
A: They did say they were interested in giving the drivers a sophisticated phone to motivate them.

L: Sounds better and better! And the GPS would be really useful – then the office would always know exactly where they were.
A: I don't know if the drivers would like that very much!
L: You're right, I'll make a note – we have met some resistance in the past. But generally once they find out there's an mp3 player and they can also have TV to keep up with baseball and soccer games, they're happy.
A: Hm. But I guess the managers won't be very happy if they think drivers are wasting time watching TV and playing video games!
L: Well, that's where we come in. The sales team's goal is to show them why they need all these features – and to try to get some longer contracts and sell them some options too, of course! OK, thanks very much, I'll get someone over there as soon as possible.

Unit 6 New business

6.1 About business: Developing a business

🔘 2:19–2:22

Speaker 1: Personally, I admire the passion they obviously bring to the business. And I reckon that's the underlying key to their success. The cosmetics industry is dog eat dog and you have to love what you're doing to make it!
Speaker 2: If you ask me, I'd say they just happened to be in the right place at the right time … you know … like, jumping on the natural products bandwagon at the right moment.
Speaker 3: They're both definitely very much on the creative side, so I think they took a smart decision when they teamed up with LVMH. That allowed them to step back from the day-to-day hassles of running a business and focus on doing what they do best – product creation and development.
Speaker 4: I'm not sure I'd like to identify any one key factor behind their success. But their story does show that to build a blockbuster brand, you have to stay on your toes. You can't afford to stand still!

6.2 Vocabulary: Funding a start-up

🔘 2:23–2:26

Speaker 1: Well, basically the first angel we met turned us down because of the IRR – that's the Internal Rate of Return – we were forecasting: between 30 and 40%. Investors lose money on around 40% of deals and they need to make that up on the others. So, a rate of 50% per annum minimum would have been a better return on investment.
Speaker 2: The three of us were fresh out of college, full of enthusiasm, with a really good product. We had checked out the market and drawn up a good business plan. But there was just one problem. None of us had run a business before and I guess we just didn't have the sort of hands-on experience they were looking for.
Speaker 3: The venture capitalist we contacted went through our business plan in detail. When he'd finished working out the figures, he said that our niche market was just that – too 'niche' – not enough growth potential. Our target customers were specialists in their own field and there would've been a limit to what we could sell them.

Speaker 4: We'd done our homework and we knew that the financials needed to be set out in detail. But, in retrospect, I think we tried to be too realistic, taking all eventualities into account. The projections were peppered with 'if this, then that' and I think they were looking for something more concrete.

6.3 Grammar: Future continuous and future perfect

🔘 2:27

Hi, Linda. Bob here. Hope you're enjoying Munich! Linda, listen. Our email's down again so this is just to update you on tomorrow's schedule. Your flight gets into Paris at eight, local time. They're sending a taxi to meet you at the airport and it'll get you to head office in La Défense by around a quarter after nine. You won't be seeing the marketing manager as originally planned, because she's sick. But you'll be meeting with the rest of the marketing team from nine-thirty through eleven. Then you're seeing Alain Giroud from R&D for an hour. You break at noon and I guess he'll be taking you to lunch. After lunch, you have a train from the station at Lyon at two twenty-five, which will get you into Macon around four. Danielle Fernández will be taking you directly to the plant for a short visit from four-thirty to a quarter after five. Then she'll drop you at your hotel just round the corner from the plant and that's about all for … Oh, sorry, I nearly forgot, you have an invitation to dinner at half past seven with someone by the name of … Antonio …?

6.4 Speaking: Presentations: taking questions

🔘 2:28

Part 1

Last but not least that brings us to the question of … questions! A lot of inexperienced presenters are terrified of the question and answer session. After all, it's the part of the presentation over which, apparently, you have least control. But, with careful preparation, you can come out smiling. Put yourself in your listeners' shoes. What sort of questions could they ask you? What are the worst questions they could come up with and how can you answer them? And preparing for questions involves developing your general question-answering techniques, improving your skills in response to the five basic types of question. There are a couple of general points to remember. The first point to remember when you're fielding questions is listen to the questioner. For example, maintain eye contact with the questioner and use body language – nodding for example – to show that you're paying attention. The next thing to remember is: don't interrupt. That would make you look rude, and the questioner might feel he or she hasn't had a chance to get their point across. Next, comment on the question before you answer it. This signals your attitude to the audience, but, equally important, gives you a few seconds of thinking time. The final thing to remember is to reply to the audience. Yes, not just to the person who asked the question, but to the whole audience. Although one person asked the question, it might have been in everyone's minds. After all, you hope everybody wants to hear the answer …

🔘 2:29

Part 2

That brings me to the five basic question types and how to react to them. First, useful questions. They reinforce or clarify what you're saying. Thank people for asking them.

Second, awkward questions. Questions can be awkward for different reasons: they may be loaded – aiming to put you on the spot – aggressive, or just unclear. Or maybe you just don't have the answer. Whatever happens, you must avoid getting into an argument. Defuse the aggressive ones and clarify the vague ones. Be prepared to explain, reformulate or reassure. Be fair but firm, and don't be aggressive or defensive yourself. And be honest. If you can't or don't want to answer, say so, or offer to get back to the questioner afterwards. Next, irrelevant questions. Double-check quickly that they are irrelevant, comment tactfully and move on. Then there are unnecessary questions, which you've already covered. Point this out, summarize briefly and move on. And finally, 'no questions'. Maybe your presentation was perfect and your audience is speechless! Unfortunately, in most cases two other scenarios are more common: either, they need a bit of encouragement or you've put them to sleep! In either case, if you don't want to finish on a low, you need to start them off. Tell them a question you're often asked and then answer it! The chances are the questions will begin to flow. OK. Let's look in a bit more detail at …

6.6 Case study: Angels or demons?

🔘 2:30

Luis: Kate, if I didn't know you better, I'd say you brought me here to boost my morale. The food's OK, and the decor isn't bad, but if this is the best Montreal can offer, then I think we can do better with Kaluma.
Kate: Shh, Luis. The waitress! Yeah, but you're right, I'm sure we can.
L: Did you bring the executive summary headings? Sorry, I forgot to print them out.
K: Yes! Here you go. Shall we just take it as it comes?
L: Yeah, go for it. Hm, *outline* … Kaluma …
K: Well, we need to say a bit about what Kaluma is. You know, a medium-sized restaurant selling organic food, and so on. We also need to say we have an emphasis on fair trade. I think people think that's more and more important. Now, *target customers*?
L: Well, I suggest we need to think a bit more about that one before we define a precise target market. After all, Montreal's a big city and I'm sure if the product is good, the customers will come.
K: OK, let's leave that for later. So, *core products*? We have to say that we are selling healthy, organic cuisine. But to me it's not just a question of that. We have to also mention the cool atmosphere. So it's not just the food but the whole concept that we're offering, that sort of thing.
L: Yeah, I'll go for that. OK … *management team*. Mm …Well, that's easy really. We can mention that I'm the general manager. That's probably all they need to know about me. And you're the financial manager.
K: Don't forget about Mario, though. He's one of the most experienced chefs in town. Let's mention that he's the head chef.
L: OK. Now, what's next? Oh, *keys to success*. Well, we have to mention the location. We've talked about that a lot, haven't we?
K: Mm. We should definitely emphasize our location, which is excellent. The other thing we should mention is the training we're giving our staff. Good service is everything. So, location and training.
L: Yeah. You know, I think we're gonna be better than the competition. The whole experience is gonna be, well, just so much nicer than a place like this!
K: Shh! The waitress!
L: Sorry, I'm just getting overexcited again!
K: Yeah, well the *financials* should calm you down. After all, that's why we're here in the first place! I think we should just stick to some basic figures. Let's just give our predicted turnover. I think we said $380,000 in Year 1. That was right wasn't it? And then $550,000 by the end of Year 2.
L: Yeah. $380,000 and $550,000. And lastly, our *mission*. I think we should keep it really simple.
K: I agree. I had two main things in mind. To be a great place to eat, with an engaging atmosphere.
L: That's obvious enough.
K: And to provide great healthy food.
L: Fantastic. Mario really is a devil in the kitchen. We're gonna be unbeatable.
K: Well, let's hope that general manager Luis Hernández, with his fifteen years of management experience, and our devil in the kitchen, Mario, can persuade an angel to give us that $50,000 next week!

🔘 2:31

Darren: So, to summarize. First, you have to grab your audience with your opening sentence. You may have a fantastic product and a dynamite team, but if you don't get investors' attention, you won't get funded. So make sure you have a great hook.

Then, cut out all the hype or exaggeration. Don't use superlatives like 'cheapest', 'fastest' and so on. Be specific: say 15% cheaper, 10% faster than the competition, and be relevant, because you just don't have the time in 60 seconds to go into detail. And, of course, make sure your pitch can be delivered in 60 seconds without rushing. That means a maximum of 150 words and probably something nearer 100.

Finally, questions. The angels may have only three minutes to ask them, but those three minutes will seem like an eternity to you if you aren't prepared. So, think about the sort of questions they might ask – the tough ones – and decide how you're gonna respond. Now, I know …

Unit 7 Financial control

7.1 About business: Accountants

🔘 2:32

Interviewer: Welcome to Next Steps, the graduate career podcast. I'm joined today by Pedro Avalleneda, a Manchester-based careers consultant who's been researching changing attitudes to the financial services industry, in particular, accountancy. Pedro, why do you think accountancy has had an image problem?
Pedro: Well, it's a stereotype, and in that sense it's unfair. But there's often an element of truth to a stereotype, and the image may have had some basis in fact in the past. There are several reasons why I think the image developed. Firstly, accountancy is seen as based on numbers. Most people aren't that keen on maths, and it's a subject that a lot of people give up as soon as they can. It's a shame people make this association, because these days much of the maths is taken care of by computers and the accountants can focus on analysis and strategy. Another reason is that accountancy is seen as predictable: I guess what people have in mind is that the tasks you have to do are often similar – relating to balance sheets, profit and loss accounts, and so on. This isn't really true anymore, since accountants do a lot else besides. Finally, accountancy is seen as a steady job. You might ask what's the problem with that, but for some people it implies that accountants are not risk-takers.
I: And what's changing now? I mean, how would you say the accountancy profession is breaking out of the stereotype?
P: Well, the best way to answer that is to look at the facts. A recent survey into job satisfaction showed that people who entered so-called creative professions like advertising and the media were often the least satisfied with their jobs. Accountancy, however, reported excellent job satisfaction. 67% said they wanted to stay in their jobs. So it seems people who pursue accountancy don't find it predictable. Another reason for its changing image is that it's friendly to women. In the USA, 60% of public accountants are women, and in the UK levels are also high. So, it's a female-friendly profession, and this has changed some of the negative perception – the stereotypical accountant was often a man. Finally, accountants really are key decision makers. Accountants today are important figures in the boardroom, and it's often accountants who have the best understanding to make big management decisions. In that sense, it's a very responsible position. As a consequence, I think graduates are recognizing that accountancy is a profession in which they can expect to have real influence on a business.
I: OK, thanks Pedro. Now, I have got some questions for you. We've had some emails …

7.4 Speaking: Communicating in meetings

🔘 2:33

Alice: OK, guys. Your financial reporting system looks to be in good shape, but it needs some tweaking on the reporting period side.
Serge: Eh, sorry, Alice. Could you repeat?
A: Sure, Serge. We need to do a bit of tweaking on the reporting period side. And we need to iron out some IT issues, too, David. But I reckon we'll need a separate meeting to take stock of things.
David: What, Alice? I, erm...
A: Yeah, Dave, a meeting with your team. What about tomorrow morning at eight-thirty?
D: Um, what? Oh, OK, eight-thirty.
A: So that's all clear, then. Great, now, what about lunch? I didn't have time to grab breakfast. I'm starving! Shall we meet back at two?
S: Eh, two?
D: Yes, OK, two.
A: Great, well, bon appétit, as you guys say.
S: David, what is 'tweaking'?
D: I don't know, Serge. I just know I've agreed to a meeting tomorrow morning to discuss 'stacks' or 'stocks'!

🔘 2:34

Alice: OK, guys. Your financial reporting system looks to be in good shape, but it needs some tweaking on the reporting period side.
Serge: Eh, sorry, Alice. I'm not sure I follow you. Could you be more specific?
A: Sure, Serge. What I mean is that we need to standardize the procedures … make them the same as our US ones.

S: So, what you're saying is that we're going to have to produce financial statements more often, is that right?
A: Yeah. To be precise, every month.
S: I see.
A: Now, we need to iron out some issues on the IT side, too, David. But, I reckon we're gonna have to set up a separate meeting to take stock of things, 'cause we don't really have time today, OK?
David: Sorry, Alice. You've lost me. We need to do what?
A: Well, in other words, we need to deal with some IT problems. And to do that, first we need to take stock … erm … see where we are at the moment. Do you see what I mean?
D: Yes, that's clear now. I could set up a meeting tomorrow morning at half past eight.
A: OK. That's great. So, can we go over what we've decided? We're going to standardize the financial reporting, and David and I will meet tomorrow to discuss the IT problems. Does everyone agree with that?
S: Yes, that's fine.
A: OK. Now, I don't know about you guys, but I didn't have time to grab breakfast this morning and I'm starving – very hungry – so what do you say if we go eat?
S: Good idea, Alice. Just thinking about monthly reporting has made me hungry.
D: Let's go!

7.5 Writing: Minutes

🔊 2:35

Part 1
Enzo: OK, François. Thanks for those statistics on late payers. I can see why management want us to cut late payment time by at least fifteen working days. Any ideas on how to do it? Alice?
Alice: Well, it's pretty clear to me, Enzo. We have to put more pressure on the slow payers much sooner than we do at present – I think François will back me on that?
François: Absolutely, Alice. In my opinion, we need to do two things. We need to reword our standard chasing emails to make them sound more threatening and …
E: Threatening, François? I don't really want chasing emails sounding like that!
F: OK, let's say more assertive or persuasive. Anyway, they've got to show the customer that we require prompt payment. And the second thing is, we need to send the first reminder out earlier.
E: Right, so let's make the chasing email more assertive and send the first reminder out more quickly. Erm, François, could you look after redrafting the standard email? And Alice, perhaps you could review the current schedule of when we send each chasing email and see how we can reduce the whole timescale. Can you both report back at our next meeting in two weeks?
A: Fine, yeah, erm, OK.

🔊 2:36

Part 2
Dylan: So, to put it briefly, covering for absent colleagues instead of just leaving their work until they get back is not just a question of efficiency. It will also improve the department's image both inside the company and with our customers and suppliers. Of course, it will mean slightly more work at certain times, but I'm convinced the effort will be worth it.
Alice: I see your point Dylan, but I'm not sure that the end of the year is the best time to run a major project like this. Staff will need training to be able to do their colleagues' work and you know that the end of the year is always our busiest time.
Enzo: Alice is right, Dylan. Why don't we give ourselves more time on this point.
D: Oh, I'm quite happy to have more time. If you like, I'll draw up a training schedule for February next year and show it to you at our first meeting in January. How's that?
E: Sounds great, Dylan. We'll look forward to hearing your conclusions in the New Year.

🔊 2:37

Part 3
François: Let me see. What else? … Electricity saving measures, toner and ink cartridge recycling, reductions in the use of paper, proper sorting of waste into plastics and paper, and … I think that's about it.
Enzo: Hm, well I think this brainstorming session has been very useful. It's certainly thrown up a whole lot of good ideas. But I get the feeling that we need some outside help on this if we really want a lasting reduction in waste.
Alice: You're right, Enzo. We should get in touch with an environmental consultant or something for some basic advice.
E: Fine, well, I'll deal with that, if you like. I don't think I'll be ready in two weeks so I'll come back to you on it in October, OK?

7.6 Case study: Car-Glazer

🔊 2:38

Nina: Hello. Accounts.
Emily: Oh, hello. Is that Nina Kovar?
N: Speaking.
E: Good morning, Nina. This is Emily Wyatt from Car-Glazer in Prague. Robert Smid asked me to call you. It's about an outstanding bill from July.
N: Ah, yes, well, in fact, can I put you through to Mr Miler? I think he'd like to talk to you about this himself.
E: Well, yes, of course.
Jakob: Miler speaking.
E: Good morning, Mr Miler. Emily Wyatt from Car-Glazer. I was calling about the outst …
J: Yes, yes, I know why you're calling, Ms Wyatt. Look, I'm sorry to sound so rude, but this whole matter has made me rather angry. It's that Sales Manager of yours, Filip Novak!
E: Filip Novak, our Sales Manager for the East? I'm sorry, Mr Miler, I'm not sure I follow you.
J: Yes, well, let me explain. He brought his BMW in to the garage to be …
E: Sorry to interrupt, Mr Miler. You said his BMW?
J: That's right.
E: But our Sales Managers drive company Volkswagens!
J: Well, that explains a lot. Anyway, he brought the car in to be repaired at the beginning of July. He'd had an accident and we had to do a lot of work on it. He told us you knew all about it and that Car-Glazer would pay the bill. Here in Brno we trust people. We simply sent you the bill with our normal July claim – for about 81,000 koruna, I believe – and thought no more of it. But we still haven't been paid the 378,000 koruna for the work we did on his car. And that's why we haven't paid you. It seemed like the only way of being paid what your Mr Novak owes us! I've been trying to call him for the last three weeks but had no luck.
E: Well, I see what you mean, Mr Miler, and I can understand why you're annoyed. I'll need to talk to my boss, Artur Nemec, about this, but I'll get back to you as soon as I can. I think Filip Novak owes everybody an explanation!

🔊 2:39

Artur: Well, that was our friend, Filip Novak! He's just landed us the biggest deal we've ever made. We're going to be the preferred glass replacement company for the number one insurance company in the Czech Republic! So, where do we go from here?

Unit 8 Fair trade

8.1 About business: Fair trade or free trade?

🔊 2:40

Oh, yes, hello. This is Margaret, from Cheltenham. I'm phoning to comment on the article 'Why fair trade is a bad deal' which appeared on your website. I just wanted to say that fair trade supporters are not as misguided as the article suggests. It's rather surprising that the writer himself has forgotten to mention that free trade and globalization are all about the survival of the fittest. Free trade is a jungle! It may be true that big producers who sell to Starbucks™ and Caffè Nero can improve their productivity and command higher prices, but what happens to the small farmers? They're forced out of business altogether. Fair trade may never make small coffee farmers rich, but at least it lets small farmers make a living! And on a larger scale, free trade is dangerous because it encourages unbalanced economies. Take Mr Singleton's example of Mexico. With free trade, Mexico might decide to stop growing coffee, corn, or rice. All their farmers would only grow chilli peppers because it's more profitable, and they would make enough profit to be able to import everything else. But what would happen if the world market for chilli suddenly collapsed? With fair trade, you spread the risk and you give everybody a chance to make a decent living.

8.2 Vocabulary: Contracts and corporate ethics

🔊 2:41–2:48

Speaker 1: Well, talking about unethical behaviour, do you remember the name Victor Lustig? He was the man who sold the Eiffel Tower – twice!
Speaker 2: You must know the story about the American CEO who sold her company shares only days before the share price crashed? She said it was 'an unfortunate coincidence'! I wonder how many people believe that!
Speaker 3: Paying government officials to avoid red tape is well-known, but did you know that music companies have been paying radio DJs to play their music since the nineteen fifties? That might explain why some number one records are so bad!
Speaker 4: Did you hear about the mayor of that small town in Italy? He used his position and influence to get local contractors to build him this enormous castle in the mountains – for nothing! Incredible!
Speaker 5: And there was this Korean scientist, a top researcher, a really famous guy. Anyway, it turned out that he'd been using government research funds to pay for luxury hotels, restaurants and even a round-the-world cruise for his wife!

Speaker 6: A couple of years ago there was an HR Director who managed to hire and promote several of her brothers and sisters to important positions in the same multinational. That's what you call keeping it in the family!

Speaker 7: I heard about these marketing executives who were so desperate to succeed that they planted bombs in their competitors' factories. Fortunately, they were caught before they went off.

Speaker 8: Of course, everybody's heard about the offshore banks which process large cash transactions for drug dealers. I just don't understand why governments seem to wash their hands of the matter!

8.3 Grammar: Obligation and permission, inversion

2:49

Oksana: Right, Eddie, if you go through the main issues in this outsourcing agreement, then I'll get Jan to draft the guidelines tomorrow morning, OK?

Eddie: Sounds good to me, Oksana. It's a question of giving ourselves the right image. Basically, we can't afford the sort of bad publicity we had last year, when the media suggested our suppliers were treating staff badly. We need to look at everything to do with working conditions, minimum age, working hours, safety, that sort of stuff.

O: Yes, well let's start with minimum age. I guess that'll be the usual over sixteen the day they join the company.

E: Yeah, nobody under sixteen. And I mean nobody!

O: OK, agreed.

E: Regarding working hours, our suppliers need some flexibility, but we need to stick to a maximum of twelve hours in any one shift. And at least a half-hour break every four hours.

O: OK, so that's no more than twelve hours at a stretch and a half-hour break every four hours. Now, what about safety?

E: Well, in fact I'm gonna have to get back to you on that, because I don't have details of all the machines they use. But basically, it's a question of ensuring that all the machines have the necessary guards and that the operators use them. The other thing is that they must give all employees protective gloves, of course. Still, you can ask Jan to draft the basic clause and I'll get back to you with the details.

O: Great! Now, let's see ... accommodation? Company dormitories and so on ...

E: Well, things are generally improving. But I think we should insist on a minimum personal space of six square metres and ...

8.4 Speaking: Negotiating a compromise

2:50

Leah: I'm sorry, Alfredo, but we can't go as high as $160. Our normal fair trade premium for top grade cocoa beans is world market price plus $140 per ton. I can't go higher than $150.

Alfredo: ... We need $160.

L: Yes, I know that, Alfredo, but ... What about prefinancing?

A: We need advance payments of 60 per cent.

L: 60 per cent?... Only if at least half of the crop is grown under shade trees.

A: No. Shade trees mean extra cost. And if you won't let children help on the farms, that means even more cost.

L: Alfredo, you know our customers won't accept child labour!

A: It's not labour, they just help out. Anyway, it's traditional, and I don't think your customers have any right to criticise our culture.

L: Look, Alfredo, they're not criti ... Oh, forget it!

2:51

Leah: I'm sorry, Alfredo, but we can't go as high as $160. Our normal fair trade premium for top grade cocoa beans is world market price plus $140 per ton. But look, I know how important this is to your cooperative: assuming we can reach a compromise on the question of prefinancing, I'm prepared to meet you half way – $150. Is that acceptable?

Alfredo: All right; that seems fair.

L: Good. So what about prefinancing?

A: We would like to be able to ask for advance payments of up to 60% of the value of the contract.

L: Well, OK, we are willing to agree to 60%, provided that at least half of the crop is grown under shade trees.

A: Leah, as you know, shade trees mean extra cost. I'd be reluctant to make that sort of commitment unless you can review your position on children under fifteen. You see, it's a tradition in our country that children help their parents on the farms.

L: Alfredo, I think we'll have to agree to disagree on that. Child labour is something that fair trade customers feel very strongly about.

A: Hm. All right, I understand that. So, at least half the crop under shade trees and up to 60% of payment in advance.

L: OK. And no more children working on the farms?

A: All right. I can live with that.

8.6 Case study: Green Hills Coffee

2:52

Magda: Fabio, stop talking about Gordon Hills as if he was some kind of saint! *Gordon always said this, Gordon always did that!*

Fabio: Listen, Magda. Gordon was my father's best friend. He was a good and generous man and, if it wasn't for him, Granos Cabrera wouldn't be where it is today.

M: A good and generous man? No, he was just a clever businessman. He knew your father grew good coffee and he knew he could make a good profit on it. And unlike his daughter, he wasn't worried about details like pesticides or children working on the farms.

F: Fiona is very fair. She has strong ideas about ecology and human rights, and she wants a fair deal for everyone.

M: Fabio, Fiona doesn't really care about pesticides or child labour. For her, it's just a good excuse to negotiate even lower prices! She's only interested in the bottom line. Why do you think Green Hills is so profitable?

F: That's not fair! Green Hills is profitable because Fiona is a good manager.

M: Well, she's certainly a good negotiator. She always gets the lowest possible prices. She's the reason for all our problems – Green Hills pay us less every year! It's no wonder we're not making any money!

F: Magda, it's not Fiona's fault. Granos Cabrera's problems are due to world market prices – they keep going down. It's very technical.

M: Well, I know I'm only from Germany and we Germans know nothing about the 'very technical' international coffee market; but I do know that if Green Hills paid a fair price – the organic price – the farmers would be able to send their kids to school instead of sending them out to work!

F: Well, sure, fair trade is the future. That and going organic probably would be the solution to our problems. But Magda, we can't afford fair trade certification. It's just too expensive.

M: Well, then, the solution is very simple. Green Hills should pay for fair trade certification and lend us some money to invest in new equipment to go organic! It's in everybody's interests.

F: I don't know. It's very difficult. If Dad was still alive, he'd just have a friendly chat with Gordon and everything would be OK.

M: Yes, but he's not, is he, Fabio? Now that your dad and Gordon Hills are no longer with us, you'd better start getting tough with Fiona. Otherwise, we're beaten.

Glossary

The definitions for the words in this glossary are from the *Macmillan Dictionary*. The red words are high-frequency words, that is to say that they are among the 7,500 which native speakers use for 90% of what they speak or write. See http://www.macmillandictionary.com for more information.

Business fundamentals

page 6 Business organization

beverage /ˈbev(ə)rɪdʒ/ noun [count] FORMAL a drink
debt /det/ noun [count] an amount of money that you owe
dividend /ˈdɪvɪdend/ noun [count] a share of the profits of a company, paid once or twice a year to the people who own the company's shares
equities /ˈekwətiz/ noun [uncount/plural] company shares that can be bought and sold on a stock market
limited company /ˌlɪmɪtɪd ˈkʌmp(ə)ni/ noun [count] BUSINESS a company whose owners are legally responsible for only a limited amount of its debts
mining /ˈmaɪnɪŋ/ noun [uncount] the process of getting coal or metal from under the ground
proprietorship /prəˈpraɪətə(r)ʃɪp/ noun [uncount] a business structure in which an individual and his/her company are considered a single entity for tax and liability purposes
public limited company /ˌpʌblɪk ˈlɪmɪtɪd ˌkʌmp(ə)ni/ noun [count] BRITISH a company in which people can invest their money. It has 'plc' at the end of its name.
real estate /ˈrɪəl ɪˌsteɪt/ noun [uncount] MAINLY AMERICAN the business of buying and selling land and property
retail /ˈriːteɪl/ noun [uncount] the sale of goods directly to the public for their own use
share /ʃeə(r)/ noun [count] BUSINESS one of the equal parts of a company that you can buy as a way of investing money
sole trader /ˌsəʊl ˈtreɪdə(r)/ noun [count] a business structure in which an individual and his/her company are considered a single entity for tax and liability purposes
third-party /ˌθɜː(r)d ˈpɑː(r)ti/ adjective relating to a person or organization that is not one of the two main people or organizations involved in a legal agreement or case
utility /juːˈtɪləti/ noun [count usually plural] a public service such as gas, water or electricity
vendor /ˈvendə(r)/ noun [count] FORMAL a company or person that sells a particular product or service

page 7 Economic cycles

bear market /ˈbeə(r) ˌmɑː(r)kɪt/ noun [count] a situation in the stock market in which the prices of shares are falling
bond /bɒnd/ noun [count] a document given to someone who invests money in a government or company, promising to pay back the money with interest
bottom /ˈbɒtəm/ verb [intransitive] to reach the lowest point
breakeven /ˌbreɪkˈiːv(ə)n/ noun [uncount] the point at which a business operation no longer loses money and can begin to make a profit
bull market /ˈbʊl ˌmɑː(r)kɪt/ noun [count] a situation in the stock market in which the prices of shares are rising
euphoric /juːˈfɒrɪk/ adjective feeling extremely happy, usually for a short time only
greater fool investor /ˌgreɪt(r) ˈfuːl ɪnˌvestə(r)/ noun [count] an investor who buys at a high price believing there will always be someone they can sell to at an even higher price
innovator /ˈɪnəveɪtə(r)/ noun [count] someone who invents or begins using new ideas, methods, equipment, etc.
peak /piːk/ noun [count] the time when something is at its highest or greatest level
plunge /plʌndʒ/ verb [intransitive] to fall quickly from a high position
recession /rɪˈseʃ(ə)n/ noun [count/uncount] ECONOMICS a period when trade and industry are not successful and there is a lot of unemployment
staple /ˈsteɪp(ə)l/ noun [count] an important product, especially a food, that people eat or use regularly
trough /trɒf/ noun [count] a period when something that rises and falls regularly is at a low level, especially economic activity
value investor /ˈvælju: ɪnˌvestə(r)/ noun [count] an investor who buys stocks they believe the market has undervalued

page 8 Breakeven analysis

cost of goods sold /ˌkɒst əv ˌgʊdz ˈsəʊld/ noun an income statement figure which reflects the cost of obtaining the raw materials and of producing the finished goods that are sold to consumers
fixed cost /ˌfɪkst ˈkɒst/ noun [usually plural] costs such as rent that a company has to pay that does not depend on how much it produces
operating profit /ˈɒpəreɪtɪŋ ˌprɒfɪt/ noun [count] the profit that a company makes from its normal activities of selling goods or services
plot /plɒt/ verb [transitive] to mark points on a graph
recommended retail price (RRP) /ˌrekəˌmendɪd ˈriːteɪl praɪs/ noun [count] the price at which a manufacturer of a product suggests it should be sold on the retail market
record label /ˈrekɔː(r)d ˌleɪb(ə)l/ noun [count] a company that produces records
royalty /ˈrɔɪəlti/ noun [count usually plural] a payment that someone such as a writer or musician gets each time their work is sold or performed
sales revenue /ˈseɪls ˌrevənju:/ noun [count/uncount] income earned from selling products or services
turnover /ˈtɜː(r)nˌəʊvə(r)/ noun [count/uncount] the value of the goods and services that a company sells in a particular period of time
variable cost /ˌveəriəb(ə)l ˈkɒst/ noun [count] a cost that changes according to how much of a product is made
wholesaler /ˈhəʊlˌseɪlə(r)/ noun [count] someone whose job is to sell large quantities of goods to shops or small businesses

page 9 CVs and recruitment

achieve /əˈtʃiːv/ verb [transitive] to succeed in doing or having what you planned or intended, usually after a lot of effort
budget /ˈbʌdʒɪt/ noun [count] the amount of money a person or organization has to spend on something

Glossary

deal with /ˈdiːl ˌwɪθ/ phrasal verb [transitive] to take action to do something, especially to solve a problem OR to buy goods or services from someone, or to sell them to someone

handle /ˈhænd(ə)l/ verb [transitive] to take action in order to deal with a difficult situation

liaise /liˈeɪz/ verb [intransitive] if one person liaises with another, or if people liaise, they talk to each other and tell each other what they are doing, so that they can work together effectively

manage /ˈmænɪdʒ/ verb [transitive] to organize and control the work of a company, organization, or group of people

objective /əbˈdʒektɪv/ noun [count] something that you plan to achieve, especially in business or work

reference /ˈref(ə)rəns/ noun [count] a statement from someone who knows you or has worked with you that gives information about you. You often need to provide a reference when you apply for a new job.

set up /ˌset ˈʌp/ phrasal verb [intransitive/transitive] to start something such as a business, organization, or institution

1 Building a career

1.1 About business
The education business

cap /kæp/ verb [transitive] to set a limit on the amount of money that someone can spend or charge

earnings /ˈɜː(r)nɪŋz/ noun [plural] BUSINESS the amount of money that you earn

exacerbate /ɪgˈzæsə(r)beɪt/ verb [transitive] FORMAL to make a problem become worse

extracurricular /ˌekstrəkəˈrɪkjʊlə(r)/ adjective extracurricular activities are things that you do at school or college that are not part of your course

faculty /ˈfæk(ə)lti/ noun [uncount] AMERICAN all the teachers in a school, college or university: *a meeting for students, faculty and administrators*

fee /fiː/ noun [count usually plural] money that you pay to a professional person or institution for their work: *Tuition fees at Stanford have now reached £9,000 a year.*

hike /haɪk/ noun [count] INFORMAL a sudden large increase in the amount or level of something

placement /ˈpleɪsmənt/ noun [count/uncount] a temporary job that is part of a course of study and that gives you experience of the work you hope to do at the end of the course

resources /rɪˈzɔː(r)sɪz/ noun [usually plural] something such as money, workers or equipment that can be used to help an institution or a business

spark or **spark off** /spɑː(r)k/ verb [transitive] MAINLY JOURNALISM to make something happen, especially something involving violence or angry feelings

spiralling /ˈspaɪrəlɪŋ/ adjective a situation that is continuously becoming worse, more, or less

subsidy /ˈsʌbsədi/ noun [count] ECONOMICS an amount of money that the government or another organization pays to help to reduce the cost of a product or service

trend /trend/ noun [count] a gradual change or development that produces a particular result

willing /ˈwɪlɪŋ/ adjective if you are willing to do something, you do it when someone asks you, sometimes when you do not want to

1.2 Vocabulary
Education and career

bind /baɪnd/ (past participle **bound** /baʊnd/) verb [transitive often passive] to limit what someone is allowed to do by making them obey a rule or agreement

boost /buːst/ verb [transitive] to help something to increase, improve or become more successful

deep pockets /ˌdiːp ˈpɒkɪts/ a lot of available money

drop out /drɒp ˈaʊt/ phrasal verb [intransitive] to leave something such as an activity, school or competition before you have finished what you intended to do

enhance /ɪnˈhɑːns/ verb [transitive] to improve something, or to make it more attractive or more valuable

lay off /leɪ ˈɒf/ phrasal verb [transitive] to end someone's employment, especially temporarily, because there is not enough work for them

miss out /mɪs ˈaʊt/ phrasal verb [intransitive] to lose an opportunity to do or to have something

redundant /rɪˈdʌndənt/ adjective if someone is redundant, they have been told they must leave their job because they are no longer needed

start over /ˌstɑː(r)t ˈəʊvə(r)/ phrasal verb [intransitive] AMERICAN to begin doing something again from the beginning

thoroughly /ˈθʌrəli/ adverb very carefully, so that nothing is missed: *The case will be studied thoroughly before any decision is made.*

working party /ˈwɜː(r)kɪŋ ˈpɑː(r)ti/ noun [count] BRITISH a group of people who examine a problem or situation and suggest a way of dealing with it

1.3 Grammar
Tense review

come along /ˌkʌm əˈlɒŋ/ phrasal verb [intransitive] to arrive or become available

downsize /ˈdaʊnˌsaɪz/ verb [intransitive] to make a company or organization smaller by reducing the number of workers

fancy /ˈfænsi/ expression SPOKEN used when you are very surprised about something: *Fancy you knowing my sister!*

put on weight /ˌpʊt ɒn ˈweɪt/ phrasal verb [transitive] to become fatter

sabbatical /səˈbætɪk(ə)l/ noun [count/uncount] a period away from work when people such as college or university teachers can study, rest or travel

streamline /ˈstriːmˌlaɪn/ verb [transitive] to improve a business, organization, process, etc. by making it more modern or simple

tutoring /ˈtjuːtə(r)ɪŋ/ noun [uncount] the act of teaching someone in a particular subject

1.4 Speaking
Interviewing: giving reasons

benchmark /ˈbentʃˌmɑː(r)k/ noun [count] an amount, level, standard, etc. that you can use for judging how good or bad other things are

feedback /ˈfiːdbæk/ noun [uncount] comments about how well or how badly someone is doing something, which are intended to help them do it better

personality clash /ˌpɜː(r)səˈnæləti ˈklæʃ/ noun [count] a situation in which two people are very different from each other so that they cannot work together

1.5 Writing
Cover letters

accomplishment /əˈkʌmplɪʃmənt/ noun [count/uncount] something difficult that you succeed in doing, especially after working hard over a period of time
bartending /ˈbɑː(r)ˌtendɪŋ/ noun [uncount] work serving drinks in a bar
brokering /ˈbrəʊkə(r)ɪŋ/ noun [uncount] AMERICAN (UK **brokerage**) the activity of organizing business deals for other people
debating society /dɪˈbeɪtɪŋ səˌsaɪəti/ noun [count] a group of people who debate a subject by discussing it formally before making a decision, usually by voting
embark on /ɪmˈbɑː(r)k ɒn/ phrasal verb [transitive] to start a new project or activity, usually one that will be difficult and will take time
lead /liːd/ noun [count] a piece of information or a contact that may bring new business
outgoing /ˌaʊtˈɡəʊɪŋ/ adjective someone who is outgoing is friendly and enjoys meeting and talking to people
tender /ˈtendə(r)/ noun [count/uncount] a formal written offer to provide goods or services for a particular price
venue /ˈvenjuː/ noun [count] the place where an activity or event happens: *a popular venue for corporate events*

1.6 Case study
Mangalia Business School

campus /ˈkæmpəs/ noun [count/uncount] an area of land containing all the main buildings of a school or university: *We have rooms for 2,000 students on campus.*
draw up /ˌdrɔː ˈʌp/ phrasal verb [transitive] to prepare and write something such as a document or a plan
heritage /ˈherɪtɪdʒ/ noun [count/uncount usually singular] the art, buildings, traditions and beliefs that a society considers important to its history and culture: *Ireland's rich musical heritage*
metropolis /məˈtrɒpəlɪs/ noun [count] a big, exciting city
pour millions into (**research**) /ˌpɔː(r) ˈmɪljəns ɪntuː/ phrase spend or invest a lot of money in something
procurement /prəˈkjʊə(r)mənt/ noun [uncount] the process of buying supplies or equipment for a government department or company
sit back /ˌsɪt ˈbæk/ phrasal verb [intransitive] to relax and stop making the effort to do something
tailor /ˈteɪlə(r)/ verb [transitive] **tailor something to/for:** to make or change something especially for a particular person or purpose

2 Information
2.1 About business
IT solutions

better off /ˌbetə(r) ˈɒf/ adjective in a better situation or having more money
bury /ˈberi/ verb [transitive often passive] to cover or hide something
cope (**with**) /ˈkəʊp wɪð/ verb [transitive] to deal successfully with a difficult situation or job
cram /kræm/ verb [transitive] to put too much into a space that is too small
errand /ˈerənd/ noun [count] a small job that involves going to collect or deliver something
fierce /fɪə(r)s/ adjective involving a lot of force or energy
headcount /ˈhedˌkaʊnt/ noun [count] a count of all the people in a company
hesitate /ˈhezɪteɪt/ verb [intransitive] to pause before doing something, or to do something very slowly, usually because you are nervous, embarrassed or worried
mad dash /ˌmæd ˈdæʃ/ noun [singular] an act of going somewhere very quickly in an extremely uncontrolled way: *At the end of the nineties there was a mad dash to buy shares in high-tech companies.*
mess up /ˌmes ˈʌp/ phrasal verb [intransitive/transitive] to do something wrong or spoil something, especially by making mistakes
oddly /ˈɒdli/ adverb or **oddly enough**: used for saying that something is not what you would expect in a particular situation
overhaul /ˌəʊvə(r)ˈhɔːl/ verb [transitive] to completely change a system to make it work more effectively
polish up /ˌpɒlɪʃ ˈʌp/ phrasal verb [transitive] to improve a skill by practising
pressure cooker /ˈpreʃə(r) ˌkʊkə(r)/ noun [count] INFORMAL a difficult situation in which people have to work very hard or experience a lot of strong emotions
quest /kwest/ noun [count] a long difficult search
slick /slɪk/ adjective done in a very impressive way that seems to need very little effort
take a breather /ˌteɪk ə ˈbriːðə(r)/ phrase INFORMAL to have a rest
untold /ʌnˈtəʊld/ adjective existing or present in an amount that is too large to be measured

2.2 Vocabulary
Information systems and communication

asap /ˌeɪ es eɪ ˈpiː/ or /ˈeɪsæp/ adverb **as soon as possible**: used especially for asking someone to do something quickly
biscuit /ˈbɪskɪt/ noun [count] BRITISH a type of small flat dry cake that is usually sweet and round. The usual American word is cookie.
crash /kræʃ/ noun [count] COMPUTING an occasion when a computer or a computer program suddenly stops working
give someone a hand /ˌɡɪv sʌmwʌn ə ˈhænd/ verb to help someone
hassle /ˈhæs(ə)l/ verb [transitive] to annoy someone, or to cause problems for them
in the know /ɪn ðə ˈnəʊ/ phrase people in the know have more information about something than other people
in the loop /ɪn ðə ˈluːp/ phrase INFORMAL belonging or not belonging to a group that has information and makes decisions about something
patch /pætʃ/ noun [count] COMPUTING a piece of software that you add to a computer program in order to improve it or remove a fault
plug-in /ˈplʌɡ ɪn/ noun [count] a piece of software or hardware that you add to a computer to increase the range of things it can do
snail mail /ˈsneɪl ˌmeɪl/ noun [uncount] COMPUTING letters that are sent by post
stretched /stretʃt/ adjective having difficulty doing everything that you should because you lack the necessary time, money, people or equipment

2.3 Grammar
Comparing solutions and getting help

bulky /ˈbʌlki/ adjective too big to be carried or stored easily

carbon footprint /ˌkɑː(r)bən ˈfʊtprɪnt/ noun [count] the amount of carbon dioxide released into the atmosphere as a result of the activities of an individual, organization or community

2.4 Speaking
Telephoning

acquaintance /əˈkweɪntəns/ noun [count] someone you know a little, who is not a close friend

IP address /ˌaɪ ˈpiː əˌdres/ noun [count] COMPUTING **Internet Protocol address:** a code that represents a particular computer and is used to send messages to it on a network or the Internet

mustn't grumble /ˈmʌs(ə)nt ˌɡrʌmb(ə)l/ phrase SPOKEN used as a reply to someone who asks you whether you are well, for saying that you feel all right

small talk /ˈsmɔːl tɔːk/ noun [uncount] INFORMAL conversation about things that are not important

trivial /ˈtrɪviəl/ adjective not very interesting, serious or valuable

2.5 Writing
Memos

alleviate /əˈliːvieɪt/ verb [transitive] to make something less painful, severe or serious

fine /faɪn/ noun [count] an amount of money that you have to pay because you have broken the law: *Firms could face fines of up to £5,000.*

forethought /ˈfɔː(r)ˌθɔːt/ noun [uncount] careful thought and planning that prepares you well for a future event

forthwith /fɔː(r)θˈwɪθ/ adverb FORMAL LEGAL immediately

imperative /ɪmˈperətɪv/ adjective FORMAL extremely important and urgent

officialese /əˌfɪʃəˈliːz/ noun [uncount] the way of speaking or writing used by people who work in government offices, especially when ordinary people cannot understand it

solicit /səˈlɪsɪt/ verb [transitive] FORMAL to ask someone for something such as money or support

time frame /ˈtaɪm ˌfreɪm/ noun [count] the period of time during which something happens or must happen

unambiguous /ˌʌnæmˈbɪɡjuəs/ adjective clear and with only one possible meaning

2.6 Case study
Meteor Bank

down time /ˈdaʊn taɪm/ noun [uncount] time when a computer or other machine is not working

drag someone kicking and screaming /ˈdræɡ sʌmwʌn ˌkɪkɪŋ ænd ˈskriːmɪŋ/ phrase to make someone do something that they do not want to do

malicious /məˈlɪʃəs/ adjective deliberately wanting to hurt someone or cause damage

morale /məˈrɑːl/ noun [count] the amount of enthusiasm that a person or group of people feel about their situation at a particular time

outsource /ˌaʊtsˈɔː(r)s/ verb [intransitive/transitive] to arrange for work to be done by people from outside your company, usually by a company that is expert in that type of work

recruit /rɪˈkruːt/ verb [intransitive/transitive] to get someone to work in a company or join an organization

subsidiary /səbˈsɪdiəri/ noun [count] a company that is owned by a larger company

turnover /ˈtɜː(r)nˌəʊvə(r)/ noun [count/uncount] the value of the goods and services that a company sells in a particular period of time

3 Quality
3.1 About business
What quality means

commitment /kəˈmɪtmənt/ noun [singular uncount] a strong belief that something is good and that you should support it: *The government has failed to honour its commitment to the railways.*

craze /kreɪz/ noun [count] something that suddenly becomes very popular, but only for a short time

elusive /ɪˈluːsɪv/ adjective an elusive person or animal is difficult or impossible to find or catch

enchanting /ɪnˈtʃɑːntɪŋ/ adjective very interesting and attractive

end /end/ noun [count] the reason for a particular action or the result you want to achieve

fad /fæd/ noun [count] something that is popular or fashionable for only a short time

fake /feɪk/ verb [transitive] to pretend to have a feeling that you do not have

intrinsically /ɪnˈtrɪnsɪkli/ adverb relating to the essential qualities or features of something or someone

planned/built-in obsolescence /ˈplænd/ˈbɪlt ɪn ˌɒbsəˈles(ə)ns/ noun [uncount] the practice of making products that will quickly become old-fashioned, or will not last long, so that people will need to replace them

rattle /ˈræt(ə)l/ verb [intransitive] if something rattles, it makes short sharp knocking sounds as it moves or shakes

roughly /ˈrʌfli/ adverb approximately: *The meeting lasted roughly 50 minutes.*

rumble /ˈrʌmb(ə)l/ verb [intransitive] to make a continuous deep sound

sake /seɪk/ noun [count usually singular] the purpose of doing, getting or achieving something: *For clarity's sake, let me explain that again.*

sour /ˈsaʊə(r)/ verb [intransitive/transitive] if a situation sours, it stops being successful or satisfactory

stream /striːm/ noun [count] a continuous flow of people or things

struggle /ˈstrʌɡ(ə)l/ verb [intransitive] to try hard to do something that you find very difficult: *He struggled to open the bottle with a knife.*

take for granted /ˌteɪk fə(r) ˈɡrɑːntɪd/ phrase to expect something always to exist or happen in a particular way: *People take it for granted that the weather in Spain will be sunny.*

trap /træp/ noun [count] a mistake or problem that you should try to avoid

white goods /ˈwaɪt ɡʊdz/ noun [count] large pieces of electrical equipment used in people's homes

3.2 Vocabulary
Quality and standards

cost-effective /kɒst ɪˈfektɪv/ adjective giving the most profit or advantage in exchange for the amount of money that is spent

exacting /ɪɡˈzæktɪŋ/ adjective needing a lot of skill and care

fit for purpose /ˌfɪt fə(r) ˈpɜː(r)pəs/ adjective of a good enough standard for a particular use

flawed /flɔːd/ adjective spoiled by something such as a fault or mark, or lacking something

flimsy /ˈflɪmzi/ adjective badly built or made, and so likely to break easily

heavy-duty /ˌhevi ˈdjuːti/ adjective strong and not easily damaged

in the eye of the beholder /ɪn ði ˌaɪ əv ðə bɪˈhəʊld(r)/ phrase used for saying that different people perceive things differently: *Beauty is in the eye of the beholder.*

lean /liːn/ adjective a lean business spends as little money and employs as few workers as possible so that it will make a good profit

machine /məˈʃiːn/ verb [transitive] to give metal, wood or plastic a particular shape by cutting it on a machine

shoddy /ˈʃɒdi/ adjective shoddy work, services or products are of a very low standard

stakeholder /ˈsteɪkˌhəʊldə(r)/ noun [count] somebody who is affected by or who has an interest in the success or activities of a company

tolerance /ˈtɒlərəns/ noun [count/uncount] the amount by which the size of a part of a machine can be different from the standard size before it prevents the machine from operating correctly

3.3 Grammar
Passive structures and *have something done*

admit /ədˈmɪt/ verb [intransitive/transitive] to agree that something is true, especially when you are unhappy, sorry, or surprised about it

faded /ˈfeɪdɪd/ adjective if something fades, it gradually becomes less clear or noticeable until it finally disappears

fitting /ˈfɪtɪŋ/ noun [count often plural] a small part that you connect to something

forklift /ˈfɔː(r)klɪft/ noun [count] a vehicle that uses two long metal bars at the front for lifting and moving heavy objects

heap /hiːp/ noun [count] a large pile of something, especially an untidy pile

loading bay /ˈləʊdɪŋ beɪ/ noun [count] an area from which goods can be loaded on and off trucks, trains, etc.

logistics /ləˈdʒɪstɪks/ noun [plural] the activity of transporting goods to customers or to places where they are bought or sold

mislay /mɪsˈleɪ/ verb [transitive] to lose something for a time, especially because you cannot remember where you put it

night shift /ˈnaɪt ʃɪft/ noun [count] a period when some people work during the night in a workplace

overflow /ˌəʊvə(r)ˈfləʊ/ verb [intransitive] to flow over the top of a container because it is too full

rack /ræk/ noun [count] an object used for storing things that consists of a row of small shelves, spaces or hooks

round-the-clock /ˌraʊnd ðə ˈklɒk/ adjective happening or done all day or all night

skip /skɪp/ noun [count] BRITISH a very large metal container used in the building industry for waste. It is carried away by a truck when it is full.

spot /spɒt/ verb [transitive] to notice someone or something

stack /stæk/ verb [transitive] to arrange things so that they are placed one on top of another

tactful /ˈtæk(t)f(ə)l/ adjective someone who is tactful is very careful in the way that they speak and behave so that they do not upset other people

take the blame /ˌteɪk ðə ˈbleɪm/ verb [intransitive] to accept that you are responsible for an accident, problem or bad situation

underlying /ˌʌndə(r)ˈlaɪɪŋ/ adjective underlying causes, facts, ideas, etc. are the real or basic ones, although they are not obvious or directly stated

3.4 Speaking
Delivering presentations

acronym /ˈækrənɪm/ noun [count] LINGUISTICS an abbreviation consisting of letters that form a word

digress /daɪˈɡres/ verb [intransitive] if you digress from a subject, you start to talk or write about something else

jargon /ˈdʒɑː(r)ɡən/ noun [uncount] SHOWING DISAPPROVAL special words and phrases that are only understood by people who do the same kind of work

make or break /ˌmeɪk ɔː(r) ˈbreɪk/ phrase to help someone or something to be very successful or to cause them to fail completely

signposting /ˈsaɪnˌpəʊstɪŋ/ noun [uncount] clear or noticeable indicators that give structure to speech of writing

3.5 Writing
Emailing: quality problems

batch /bætʃ/ noun [count] a number of things or people that arrive or are dealt with at the same time

bin liner /ˈbɪn ˌlaɪnə(r)/ noun [count] BRITISH a plastic bag that you put in a bin to hold the rubbish

dashboard /ˈdæʃˌbɔː(r)d/ noun [count] a visual display with business information presented on a single screen

ERP /ˌiː ɑː(r) ˈpiː/ abbreviation **enterprise resource planning**: the management of a company's information and resources by means of an integrated computer system

flaw /flɔː/ noun [count] a mistake or fault in something that makes it useless or less effective

lab-ware /ˈlæb weə(r)/ noun [uncount] objects that are used in a laboratory

leak /liːk/ verb [intransitive] if a container leaks, liquid or gas comes out of it through a hole or crack

pallet /ˈpælət/ noun [count] a flat wooden or metal surface used for moving or storing heavy goods

scratch /skrætʃ/ noun [count] a thin mark on a surface

stain /steɪn/ verb [intransitive/transitive] to leave a mark on something accidentally

teething problems /ˈtiːðɪŋ ˌprɒbləmz/ noun [plural] minor problems that a new company, project, product, etc. may have in the beginning

vial /ˈvaɪəl/ noun [count] a small bottle used especially for storing liquid medicines

3.6 Case study
Zaluski Strawberries

bruise /bruːz/ verb [transitive] to damage a piece of fruit and cause a soft brown area to appear on its surface
bulk /bʌlk/ noun [count usually singular] the bulk of something is the majority or largest part of something
decay /dɪˈkeɪ/ verb [intransitive] to be gradually destroyed as a result of a natural process of change
harvest /ˈhɑː(r)vɪst/ noun [count] the activity of collecting a crop: *the corn harvest*
outlet /ˈaʊtˌlet/ noun [count] a shop or place where a particular product is sold: *Most of the sales are through traditional retail outlets.*
punnet /ˈpʌnɪt/ noun [count] BRITISH a small container like a basket, in which fruit such as strawberries are sold
ripe /raɪp/ adjective ripe fruit or crops have grown to their full size and are ready to eat or use
shallow /ˈʃæləʊ/ adjective with only a short distance from the top or surface to the bottom; the opposite of **deep**
shed /ʃed/ noun [count] a building, usually made of wood, in which you store things
shelf life /ˈʃelf ˌlaɪf/ noun [singular] the amount of time that a food, medicine or similar product can be kept in a shop before it is too old to sell
shrivelled /ˈʃrɪv(ə)ld/ adjective if something such as a plant shrivels or shrivels up, it becomes smaller and thinner than usual and it does not look fresh and healthy
sound /saʊnd/ adjective healthy or in good condition
squash /skwɒʃ/ verb [transitive] to damage something by pressing or crushing it and making it lose its normal shape
stack /stæk/ verb [transitive] to arrange things so they stand one on top of another: *She began stacking plates on the trolley.*
straw /strɔː/ noun [uncount] the yellow stems of dried crops such as wheat: *a straw hat*
tray /treɪ/ noun [count] a flat open container with raised edges used for holding or carrying things
wastage /ˈweɪstɪdʒ/ noun [uncount] the amount of something that is wasted

4 Feedback
4.1 About business
The project team

accomplish /əˈkʌmplɪʃ/ verb [transitive] to succeed in doing something: *We accomplished a lot at work this week.*
allied (with) /ˈælaɪd (wɪð)/ adjective if something is allied to or with something else, it is connected with it or working together with it
apathy /ˈæpəθi/ noun [uncount] a feeling of having no interest in or enthusiasm about anything, or not being willing to make any effort to change things
aspiring /əˈspaɪərɪŋ/ adjective hoping and trying to be successful at something, especially in your career
bang on /ˌbæŋ ˈɒn/ phrase exactly right
better off /ˌbetə(r) ˈɒf/ adjective in a better situation
blindfold /ˈblaɪn(d)ˌfəʊld/ noun [count] something that is tied over someone's eyes so that they cannot see
bunch /bʌntʃ/ noun [singular] INFORMAL a group of people
buy into /ˌbaɪ ˈɪntuː/ phrasal verb [transitive] INFORMAL to believe something that a lot of other people believe

dam /dæm/ noun [count] a wall built across a river to stop the water from flowing, especially in order to create a lake or to help to produce electric power
feasibility /ˌfiːzəˈbɪləti/ noun [uncount] a feasibility study investigates the chances that something has of happening or being successful
foundations /faʊnˈdeɪʃ(ə)nz/ noun [count often plural] the part of a structure of a building that is below the ground and supports the rest of it
milestone /ˈmaɪlˌstəʊn/ noun [count] an event or achievement that marks an important stage in a process
offend /əˈfend/ verb [transitive] to make someone upset and angry by doing or saying something
prevail /prɪˈveɪl/ verb [intransitive] FORMAL to exist at a particular time or in a particular situation
resettlement /ˌriːˈset(ə)lmənt/ noun [uncount] the process of people being moved by a government or other authority, and going to live in a different region or country
scope /skəʊp/ noun [uncount] the things that a particular activity, organization, subject, etc. deals with: *These issues are beyond the scope of this book.*
silly /ˈsɪli/ adjective not intelligent, serious, important or practical
start from scratch /ˌstɑː(r)t frɒm ˈskrætʃ/ phrase to start from the beginning again, not using all the work that you have done before
touchy-feely /ˌtʌtʃi ˈfiːli/ adjective tending to express feelings in an honest and physical way. This word often shows that you dislike people like this.

4.2 Vocabulary
Managing people and projects

appraisal interview /əˈpreɪz(ə)l ˌɪntə(r)vjuː/ noun [count] BRITISH an interview between a manager and an employee designed to evaluate how well the employee is doing their job
bully /ˈbʊli/ noun [count] someone who uses their influence or status to threaten or frighten someone else in order to get what they want
hectic /ˈhektɪk/ adjective full of busy activity
loner /ˈləʊnə(r)/ noun [count] someone who likes to be alone and has few friends
maverick /ˈmæv(ə)rɪk/ noun [count] an independent person who has ideas and behaviour that are very different from other people's
milestone /ˈmaɪlˌstəʊn/ noun [count] an event or achievement that marks an important stage in a process
pass the buck /ˌpɑːs ðə ˈbʌk/ phrase to make someone else deal with something that you should take responsibility for
pull your weight /ˌpʊl jə(r) ˈweɪt/ phrase to do your share of work

4.3 Grammar
Regrets, speculation and habits

downshift /ˈdaʊnˌʃɪft/ verb [intransitive] to change to a different job or way of life, so that you have less money and responsibility but more satisfaction and happiness
evacuate /ɪˈvækjueɪt/ verb [transitive] to make people leave a building or area because it is not safe
generator /ˈdʒenəˌreɪtə(r)/ noun [count] a machine that produces electricity

impact /ˈɪmpækt/ noun [count] an effect, or an influence

reactor /riˈæktə(r)/ noun [count] a machine used for producing nuclear energy, usually in the form of electricity

seismic /ˈsaɪzmɪk/ adjective SCIENCE relating to earthquakes

turn (something) down /tɜː(r)n ˈdaʊn/ phrasal verb [transitive] to not accept an offer or request

4.4 Speaking
Coaching

elicit /ɪˈlɪsɪt/ verb [transitive] FORMAL to obtain information by encouraging someone to talk

mess up /mes ˈʌp/ phrasal verb [intransitive/transitive] to make a mistake, or to do something badly: *You messed up. Don't let it happen again.*

overdo /ˌəʊvə(r)ˈduː/ verb [transitive] to do more of something than you should; **overdo it**: to work too hard, making yourself tired or ill

praise /preɪz/ noun [uncount] an expression of strong approval or admiration: *Give your child plenty of praise and encouragement.*

4.5 Writing
Reports

engage /ɪnˈɡeɪdʒ/ verb [transitive] to start to employ someone or use their services

foster /ˈfɒstə(r)/ verb [transitive] to help something to develop over a period of time: *This approach will foster an understanding of environmental issues.*

team spirit /ˌtiːm ˈspɪrɪt/ noun [uncount] an enthusiastic attitude towards working or playing together with other people as a team

touch on /ˈtʌtʃ ɒn/ phrasal verb [transitive] to mention something when you are talking or writing

4.6 Case study
Trident Overseas

could do with (something) /kʊd ˈduː wɪð/ phrase SPOKEN used for saying that you want or need something

dealer /ˈdiːlə(r)/ noun [count] a person or company that buys and sells a particular product: *a car dealer*

forecourt /ˈfɔː(r)ˌkɔː(r)t/ noun [count] an open area in front of a large building or service station

handle someone with kid gloves /ˈhænd(ə)l sʌmwʌn wɪð ˌkɪd ˈɡlʌvz/ phrase to treat someone in a very careful or gentle way

mess /mes/ noun [singular] a difficult situation with lots of problems, especially because people have made mistakes

put up with /pʊt ˈʌp wɪð/ phrasal verb [transitive] to accept something or someone unpleasant in a patient way

sort out /ˈsɔː(r)t ˈaʊt/ phrasal verb [transitive] to solve a problem or deal with a difficult situation successfully

top up /tɒp ˈʌp/ phrasal verb [transitive] to completely fill a container that is already partly full

windscreen /ˈwɪn(d)ˌskriːn/ noun [count] BRITISH the large glass window at the front of a vehicle

work your fingers to the bone /ˌwɜː(r)k jə(r) ˈfɪŋɡə(r)z tə ði ˈbəʊn/ phrase to work very hard, especially doing something that involves a lot of physical effort

5 Selling more
5.1 About business
Social media marketing

bundle /ˈbʌnd(ə)l/ noun [count] a group of things that are sold or offered as a set

dodgy /ˈdɒdʒi/ adjective INFORMAL dishonest, criminal or not reliable

double-edged sword /ˈdʌb(ə)l edʒd ˌsɔː(r)d/ noun [singular] a situation or decision that has both positive and negative aspects

endorse /ɪnˈdɔː(r)s/ verb [transitive] if someone famous endorses a product, they say in advertisements that they like it

gripe /ɡraɪp/ noun [count] INFORMAL a complaint about something that is annoying but not very important

inclined to believe /ɪnˈklaɪnd tə bɪˌliːv/ phrase having an opinion but not completely sure about it

lobby /ˈlɒbi/ verb [intransitive/transitive] to try to influence people in authority on a particular subject

on the house /ɒn ðə ˈhaʊs/ phrase given to you free in a restaurant, hotel, pub or club

stack up /stæk ˈʌp/ phrasal verb [intransitive] INFORMAL to appear good, bad, etc. when compared with someone or something else: *Teachers will know how they stack up against national standards.*

suck /sʌk/ verb [intransitive] MAINLY AMERICAN VERY INFORMAL to be very bad, very annoying, etc. This is used only in the present tense. *If your job really sucks, leave it.*

thrive /θraɪv/ verb [intransitive] to become very successful, happy or healthy

vertical market /ˌvɜː(r)tɪk(ə)l ˈmɑː(r)kɪt/ noun [count] a business market focused on a particular industry sector or niche

5.2 Vocabulary
The marketing mix

blend /blend/ verb [transitive] to mix different foods, styles or qualities together in a way that is attractive or effective

coupon /ˈkuːpɒn/ noun [count] a piece of paper that allows you to buy something at a reduced price: *This coupon gives £2 off the price of a meal.*

marmalade /ˈmɑː(r)məleɪd/ noun [uncount] a sweet food made from cooked fruit such as oranges or lemons that is usually spread onto bread and eaten at breakfast

razor /ˈreɪzə(r)/ noun [count] a small tool used for shaving

SMS /ˌes em ˈes/ noun [uncount] **short message service:** a method of sending a text message to a mobile phone

spare /speə(r)/ adjective [only before noun] a spare object is one that you keep in addition to other similar objects in case you need it: *a spare key/battery/pair of glasses*

stealth /stelθ/ noun [uncount] a quiet and secret way of behaving so that no one sees you or hears you

subliminal /sʌbˈlɪmɪn(ə)l/ adjective a subliminal influence is one that may affect you even though you do not notice or think about it

timeshare /ˈtaɪmˌʃeə(r)/ noun [count] a flat or house that you buy with other people so that you can each use it for a particular amount of time every year

5.3 Grammar
Questions for persuading

cold calling /ˌkəʊld ˈkɔːlɪŋ/ noun [uncount] unexpected telephone calls or visits by someone trying to sell something

luncheon voucher /ˈlʌntʃ(ə)n ˌvaʊtʃə(r)/ noun [count] a piece of paper given by an employer that can be used for buying lunch in some restaurants and shops

on the clock /ˌɒn ðə ˈklɒk/ phrase INFORMAL used for saying how many miles a vehicle's speedometer shows

tax-deductible /ˌtæks dɪˈdʌktəb(ə)l/ adjective able to be taken away from the total amount of money on which you pay tax

5.4 Speaking
Dealing with objections

compromise /ˈkɒmprəmaɪz/ noun [count/uncount] a way of solving a problem or ending an argument in which both people or groups accept that they cannot have everything they want

5.5 Writing
Mailshots and sales letters

briefing /ˈbriːfɪŋ/ noun [count] a meeting or document in which people receive information or instructions

credentials /krɪˈdenʃ(ə)lz/ noun [plural] personal qualities, achievements or experiences that make someone suitable for something

CRM /ˌsiː ɑː(r) ˈəm/ abbreviation BUSINESS **customer relationship management:** a system used by a business to organize and manage interaction with its customers, particularly sales, marketing, customer support, etc.

grab someone's attention /ˈgræb sʌmwʌnz əˌtenʃ(ə)n/ phrase to succeed in getting someone to listen or be interested: *It's often the bad characters in a story who grab our attention.*

handling /ˈhændlɪŋ/ noun [uncount] the handling of a vehicle is how easy it is to control

PPS /ˌpiː piː ˈes/ abbreviation written before a note at the end of a letter, after the ps note

PS /ˌpiː ˈes/ abbreviation **postscript:** used for introducing some additional information at the end of a letter after you have signed your name

trawl through /ˈtrɔːl ˌθruː/ verb [intransitive/transitive] to look for someone or something, for example by searching through a large amount of information

USP /ˌjuː es ˈpiː/ noun [count] BUSINESS **unique selling point/proposition:** the thing that makes a product or service different from others

5.6 Case study
Backchat Communications

Bluetooth™ /ˈbluːˌtuːθ/ TRADEMARK radio technology which allows electronic devices to communicate with each other

courier /ˈkʊriə(r)/ noun [count] someone whose job is to deliver documents or parcels

flat /flæt/ adjective a flat battery does not have enough power left in it

fleet /fliːt/ noun [count] a group of vehicles or machines, especially when they are owned by one organization or person: *the company's fleet of vehicles*

GPS /ˌdʒiː piː ˈes/ noun [uncount] **global positioning system:** a system for finding exactly where you are anywhere in the world using satellites

handset /ˈhæn(d)ˌset/ noun [count] the part of a telephone which you hold next to your ear

keep up with /ˌkiːp ˈʌp wɪð/ phrasal verb [intransitive] to continue to find out about what's happening

won /wʌn/ noun [count] ECONOMICS the currency of South Korea: 1 US$ = approx. 1,100 won

6 New business

6.1 About business
Developing a business

bandwagon /ˈbændˌwæɡən/ noun [count usually singular] an idea or activity, especially in politics or business, that suddenly becomes very popular or fashionable, so that a lot of people want to be involved in it

batch /bætʃ/ noun [count] a quantity of a substance needed or produced at one time: *Mix up another batch of cement.*

emulate /ˈemjʊleɪt/ verb [transitive] to try to be like someone or something else, usually because you admire them

found /faʊnd/ verb [transitive often passive] to start an organization, company, political party, etc.

knack /næk/ noun [singular] INFORMAL a skill or ability: *She had a knack of making people feel really special.*

nurture /ˈnɜː(r)tʃə(r)/ verb [transitive] to help someone or something to develop: *The magazine had a reputation for nurturing young writers.*

outlet /ˈaʊtˌlet/ noun [count] a shop or place where a particular product is sold

ring up /ˌrɪŋ ˈʌp/ verb [transitive] to make or lose a particular amount of money in sales, profits or losses in a period of time: *The bank rang up about £600 million in trading losses.*

rub shoulders with /ˌrʌb ˈʃəʊldə(r)z wɪð/ phrase INFORMAL to meet and talk to important or famous people: *She's rubbed shoulders with millionaires.*

sing somebody's praises /ˌsɪŋ sʌmbədiz ˈpreɪzɪz/ phrase to talk about how good someone or something is: *Mary likes you. She's always singing your praises.*

stake /steɪk/ noun [count] the part of a business that you own because you have invested money in it: *They took a 40% stake in the company last year.*

yearn /jɜː(r)n/ verb [intransitive] MAINLY LITERARY to want something a lot, especially something that you know you may not be able to have: *They were yearning to have a baby.*

6.2 Vocabulary
Funding a start-up

asset /ˈæset/ noun [count] something such as money or property that a person or company owns: *The business has assets totalling £5.1 million.*

household /ˈhaʊsˌhəʊld/ adjective [only before nouns] relating to homes

outstanding /aʊtˈstændɪŋ/ adjective a job or action that is outstanding has not yet been completed or dealt with

pitch /pɪtʃ/ noun [count] the things that you say to persuade someone to buy something or to support you

raw materials /rɔː məˈtɪəriəlz/ noun [plural] substances such as coal or iron that are in their natural state before being processed or made into something: *The raw materials are stored in silos.*

strain (on) /streɪn/ noun [count/uncount] pressure caused by a difficult situation

temping agency /ˈtempɪŋ ˌeɪdʒ(ə)nsi/ noun [count] a business that provides a service for people or companies by supplying temporary staff

track record /træk ˈrekɔː(r)d/ noun [count] your reputation, based on things you have done or not done

weed out /wiːd ˈaʊt/ phrasal verb [transitive] to remove a person or thing that is not suitable or good enough, especially from a group or collection

6.3 Grammar
Future continuous and future perfect

black tie /ˌblæk ˈtaɪ/ noun [uncount] very formal men's clothes worn for a social event, usually including a black bow tie

fancy dress /ˌfænsi ˈdres/ noun [uncount] BRITISH clothes that you wear for fun to make you look like a particular famous person or a particular type of person, at a fancy-dress party

plant /plɑːnt/ noun [count] a factory that produces power, or processes chemicals, etc.

sustainable /səˈsteɪnəb(ə)l/ adjective using methods that do not harm the environment

6.4 Speaking
Presentations: taking questions

awkward /ˈɔːkwə(r)d/ adjective difficult to deal with and embarrassing: *After he spoke there was an awkward silence.*

bluff /blʌf/ verb [intransitive/transitive] to deliberately give a false idea to someone about what you intend to do or about the facts of a situation, especially in order to gain an advantage

do your homework /duː jə(r) ˈhəʊmˌwɜː(r)k/ phrase to prepare for something by learning as much as you can about it

field /fiːld/ verb [transitive] to deal with something such as a question or a telephone call, especially a difficult one

nod /nɒd/ verb [intransitive/transitive] to move your head up and down to answer 'Yes' to a question or to show that you agree, approve or understand: *The manager nodded in agreement.*

recap /ˌriːˈkæp/ verb [intransitive/transitive] to describe what has already been done or decided, without repeating the details

threat /θret/ noun [count/uncount] a situation or an activity that could cause harm or danger

6.5 Writing
A company profile

elevator pitch /ˈeləveɪtə(r) pɪtʃ/ noun [count] BUSINESS a very brief summary of what a business does and why it is special, usually lasting 30–60 seconds

faux pas /fəʊ ˈpɑː/ noun [count] FORMAL something embarrassing that you say or do in a social situation

high-end /haɪ ˈend/ adjective high-end goods and services are more expensive and more advanced than other similar goods and services

quibble /ˈkwɪb(ə)l/ verb [intransitive] to argue or complain about something that is not important

showcase /ˈʃəʊˌkeɪs/ verb [transitive] to show someone or something in a way that attracts attention and emphasizes their good qualities

snappy /ˈsnæpi/ adjective a snappy title or advertisement is clever and does not use many words

turnaround /ˈtɜː(r)nəˌraʊnd/ noun [count/uncount] the time that it takes a company or an institution to complete a process

6.6 Case study
Angels or demons?

be up for /biː ˈʌp fɔː(r)/ phrase MAINLY SPOKEN willing to do a particular activity

boost morale /ˌbuːst məˈrɑːl/ verb to make someone feel more positive or more confident

cunning /ˈkʌnɪŋ/ adjective used to describe behaviour in which people use their intelligence to get what they want, especially by tricking or cheating people

drop someone a line /ˌdrɒp sʌmwʌn ə ˈlaɪn/ phrase to contact somebody by writing to them

grab /græb/ verb [transitive] to interest someone and make them feel enthusiastic

hype /haɪp/ noun [uncount] INFORMAL the use of a lot of advertisements and other publicity to influence or interest people

resilient /rɪˈzɪliənt/ adjective able to quickly become healthy, happy or strong again after an illness, disappointment or other problem

think laterally /θɪŋk ˈlæt(ə)rəli/ phrase to solve a problem by using your imagination to try to think about it in a different or unusual way

upbeat /ˈʌpbiːt/ adjective INFORMAL happy and positive

7 Financial control
7.1 About business
Accountants

bribery /ˈbraɪb(ə)ri/ noun [uncount] the crime of giving money or presents to someone so that they will help you by doing something dishonest or illegal.

(the) forefront /ˈfɔː(r)ˌfrʌnt/ noun a leading or important position

fraudster /ˈfrɔːdstə(r)/ noun [count] someone who commits the crime of **fraud** (= obtaining money from someone by tricking them)

litigation /ˌlɪtɪˈɡeɪʃ(ə)n/ noun [uncount] use of the legal system to settle a disagreement

makeover /ˈmeɪkˌəʊvə(r)/ noun [count] a set of changes that make a person or thing look better

net worth /ˌnet ˈwɜː(r)θ/ phrase the value of all your property, possessions and money after you remove what you owe

notorious /nəʊˈtɔːriəs/ adjective famous for something bad

pivotal /ˈpɪvət(ə)l/ adjective extremely important and affecting how something develops

policy-maker /ˈpɒləsi ˌmeɪkə(r)/ noun [count] a person responsible for deciding on a set of plans or actions for a government, political party, business or other group

protection racket /prəˈtekʃ(ə)n ˌrækɪt/ noun [count] an illegal system in which criminals threaten to harm you or your property if you do not give them money

scam /skæm/ noun [count] INFORMAL a dishonest plan, especially for getting money

tax evasion /ˈtæks ɪˌveɪʒ(ə)n/ noun [uncount] the use of illegal methods to pay less tax or no tax at all

undercover /ˌʌndə(r)ˈkʌvə(r)/ adjective working or done secretly in order to catch criminals, get secret information, etc.

white-collar crime /ˌwaɪt kɒlə(r) ˈkraɪm/ noun [uncount] crimes in which people who work in offices steal money from the company they work for

7.2 Vocabulary
Financial documents and regulation

depreciation /dɪˌpriːʃiˈeɪʃ(ə)n/ noun [uncount] the process of becoming less valuable

pellet /ˈpelɪt/ noun [count] a small round piece of a substance

snapshot /ˈsnæpˌʃɒt/ noun a short explanation or description that tells you what a particular situation or place is like

7.3 Grammar
Cause and effect, ability, articles

admin /ˈædmɪn/ noun [uncount] INFORMAL the administration of a company, organization, etc.

knock-on /ˈnɒkɒn/ adjective BRITISH a knock-on effect is the indirect result of something

misery /ˈmɪzəri/ noun [uncount] the state of being extremely unhappy or uncomfortable

notably /ˈnəʊtəbli/ adverb FORMAL especially: used for introducing a good example of something

raw materials /ˌrɔː məˈtɪəriəlz/ noun [plural] substances such as coal or iron that are in their natural state before being changed by chemical processes

spiralling /ˈspaɪrəlɪŋ/ adjective continuously becoming worse, more or less

stem from /ˈstem ˌfrəm/ phrasal verb [transitive] to be caused by something

7.4 Speaking
Communicating in meetings

in good shape /ɪn ˌɡʊd ˈʃeɪp/ phrase in good condition

iron out /ˌaɪə(r)n ˈaʊt/ phrasal verb [transitive] to deal successfully with a disagreement or problem, especially by removing the last remaining difficulties

starving /ˈstɑː(r)vɪŋ/ adjective INFORMAL very hungry

take stock /teɪk ˈstɒk/ verb [intransitive] to review your position

tweak /twiːk/ verb [transitive] INFORMAL to make small changes to improve something

7.5 Writing
Minutes

chair /tʃeə(r)/ noun [count] the person who is in charge of a meeting, committee or company

open-plan office /ˈəʊpən plæn ˈɒfɪs/ noun [count] an office with few walls and a lot of space

partition /pɑː(r)ˈtɪʃ(ə)n/ noun [count] a wall, screen or piece of glass used to separate one from another in a room or vehicle

venue /ˈvenjuː/ noun [count] the place where an activity or event happens

7.6 Case study
Car-Glazer

bodyshop /ˈbɒdiʃɒp/ noun [count] a place where cars are repaired, especially after an accident

chasing letter /ˈtʃeɪsɪŋ ˌletə(r)/ noun [count] a reminder to pay an outstanding invoice

dent /dent/ noun [count] a place where a surface has been pushed or knocked inwards

embezzle /ɪmˈbez(ə)l/ verb [intransitive/transitive] to steal money that people trust you to look after as part of your work

evasive /ɪˈveɪsɪv/ adjective not talking or answering questions in an honest way

petty cash /ˌpeti ˈkæʃ/ noun [uncount] a small amount of money in coins or notes that an organization or company keeps available to pay for small things

reprimand /ˈreprɪˌmɑːnd/ verb [transitive] to tell someone officially and in a serious way that something they have done is wrong

scratch /skrætʃ/ noun [count] a thin mark on a surface: *There were some nasty scratches on the paintwork.*

sickie /ˈsɪki/ noun [count] BRITISH VERY INFORMAL a day when you say you are ill because you do not want to go to work

suspension /səˈspenʃ(ə)n/ noun [count/uncount] a punishment in which someone is removed from a team, job or school, for a short time

8 Fair trade
8.1 About business
Fair trade or free trade?

affluent /ˈæfluːənt/ adjective rich enough to buy things for pleasure

altruism /ˈæltruˌɪz(ə)m/ noun [uncount] a way of thinking and behaving that shows you care more about other people and their interests than about yourself

command /kəˈmɑːnd/ verb [transitive] FORMAL to have a particular price or value, especially a high one

crop /krɒp/ noun [count] a plant grown for food, usually on a farm: *They're all out planting the crops today.*

deprive /dɪˈpraɪv/ verb [transitive] if you deprive someone of something, you take it away from them or prevent them from having it

distort /dɪˈstɔː(r)t/ verb [transitive] to change something such as information so that it is no longer true or accurate

ignore /ɪɡˈnɔː(r)/ verb [transitive] to not consider something or not let it influence you: *This ignores the complexity of modern business.*

illiteracy /ɪˈlɪtərəsi/ noun [uncount] the state of not being able to read or write

magic wand /ˌmædʒɪk ˈwɒnd/ noun [count] a short thin stick used for performing magic or magic tricks; **wave a magic wand:** find an easy and immediate solution to a problem

misguided /mɪsˈɡaɪdɪd/ adjective a misguided idea or action is based on judgments or opinions that are wrong

naive /naɪˈiːv/ adjective a naive person lacks experience of life and tends to believe things too easily

pursue /pə(r)ˈsjuː/ verb [transitive] to follow a course of activity: *They have continued to pursue a policy or repression.*

relieve /rɪˈliːv/ verb [transitive] to make pain or another feeling less unpleasant

threaten /ˈθret(ə)n/ verb [transitive] to be likely to harm or destroy something: *Their actions threaten the stability and security of the region.*

toil /tɔɪl/ verb [intransitive] LITERARY to work very hard doing something difficult and tiring, especially physical work

8.2 Vocabulary
Contracts and corporate ethics

advocate /ˈædvəkeɪt/ verb [transitive] to publicly support a particular policy or way of doing things

amend /əˈmend/ verb [transitive] to make changes to a document, law, agreement, etc, especially in order to improve it: *A law amending the Chilean constitution was approved on 22nd January.*

bend the rules (for someone) /bend ðə ˈruːlz/ phrase to do something or allow someone to do something that is not usually allowed, especially in order to make things easier on one occasion

beyond reproach /bɪˈjɒnd rɪˈprəʊtʃ/ phrase impossible to criticise because of being so good

bribery /ˈbraɪb(ə)ri/ noun [uncount] the crime of giving money or presents to someone so that they will help you by doing something dishonest or illegal

conspiracy /kənˈspɪrəsi/ noun [uncount] LEGAL the legal offence of planning a serious crime

corruption /kəˈrʌpʃ(ə)n/ noun [uncount] dishonest or illegal behaviour by officials or people in positions of power, especially when they accept money in exchange for doing things for someone

deem /diːm/ verb [transitive never progressive] FORMAL to consider that someone or something has a particular quality

embezzlement /ɪmˈbez(ə)lmənt/ noun [uncount] the theft of money that people trust you to look after as part of your work

fraud /frɔːd/ noun [uncount] the crime of obtaining money from someone by tricking them

insider trading /ɪnˌsaɪdə(r) ˈtreɪdɪŋ/ noun [uncount] the crime of buying or selling shares in a company using information that is available only to people working within that company

irrevocable /ɪˈrevəkəb(ə)l/ adjective FORMAL impossible to change or stop

lapse /læps/ verb [intransitive] if an official document, decision or right lapses it is no longer effective

litigation /ˌlɪtɪˈɡeɪʃ(ə)n/ noun [uncount] use of the legal system to settle a disagreement

money-laundering /ˈmʌni ˌlɔːndə(r)ɪŋ/ noun [uncount] to hide the origin of money obtained from illegal activities by putting it into legal businesses

nepotism /ˈnepəˌtɪz(ə)m/ noun [uncount] the practice of using your power and influence to give jobs to people in your family instead of to people who deserve to have them

offshore /ˌɒfˈʃɔː(r)/ adjective [only before noun] an offshore bank or company is not in your own country but in a country where the law is different

part and parcel /ˌpɑːt ænd ˈpɑː(r)s(ə)l/ phrase an aspect of something that has to be accepted

renege /rɪˈneɪɡ/ verb [intransitive] FORMAL **renege on:** to decide not to do something that you promised to do

warranty /ˈwɒrənti/ noun [count] a company's written promise to repair or replace a product if it does not work, usually for a specific period of time

wash your hands of /ˌwɒʃ jɔː(r) ˈhændz əv/ phrase to say or show that you do not want to be involved with someone or something and that you are not responsible for them

8.3 Grammar
Obligation and permission, inversion

at a stretch /ət ə ˈstretʃ/ phrase continuously during a period of time

disclose /dɪsˈkləʊz/ verb [transitive] to give information to people, especially information that was secret

landlord /ˈlæn(d)ˌlɔː(r)d/ noun [count] a man who owns a house, flat or room that people can rent

notice /ˈnəʊtɪs/ noun [uncount] the period between the time that you tell someone you are going to do something and the time you do it

occupancy /ˈɒkjʊpənsi/ noun [uncount] the use, or the period of use, of a place

outsourcing /ˈaʊtˌsɔː(r)sɪŋ/ noun [uncount] BUSINESS an arrangement in which work is done by people from outside your company, usually by a company that is expert in that type of work

premises /ˈpremɪsɪz/ noun [plural] the buildings and land that a business or organization uses

refurbished /riːˈfɜː(r)bɪʃt/ adjective a refurbished room or a building has been improved by cleaning and painting it, adding new furniture or equipment, etc.

sewer /ˈsuːə(r)/ noun [count] an underground pipe or passage that carries waste substances, especially waste removed from houses and other buildings

tenant /ˈtenənt/ noun [count] someone who rents a flat, house, office, piece of land, etc. from the person who owns it

thriving /ˈθraɪvɪŋ/ adjective very successful

wear and tear /ˌweər ən ˈteə(r)/ noun [uncount] the changes or damage that normally happen to something that has been used, causing it to be less useful or less valuable

worn /wɔː(r)n/ adjective something that is worn looks old and damaged because it has been used a lot

8.4 Speaking
Negotiating a compromise

compromise /ˈkɒmprəmaɪz/ noun [count/uncount] a way of solving a problem or ending an argument in which both people or groups accept that they cannot have everything they want

premium /ˈpriːmiəm/ noun [count] an amount of money paid in addition to the normal amount: *Customers are prepared to pay a premium for fair-trade goods.*

shade tree /ˈʃeɪd ˌtriː/ noun [count] a tree which grows above other plants, protecting them from the sun and providing a natural habitat for birds and animals

8.5 Writing
Assertive writing

annoying /əˈnɔɪɪŋ/ adjective making you feel slightly angry or impatient

assertive /əˈsɜː(r)tɪv/ adjective behaving in a confident way in which you are quick to express your opinions and feelings

evasive /ɪˈveɪsɪv/ adjective not talking or answering questions in an honest way

submissive /səbˈmɪsɪv/ adjective willing to do what other people tell you to do without arguing

sue /suː/ verb [intransitive/transitive] to make a legal claim against someone: *Burnett sued the newspaper for libel and won.*

8.6 Case study
Green Hills Coffee

binding /ˈbaɪndɪŋ/ adjective if an agreement, contract, decision, etc. is binding you must do what it says: *Remember that this is a legally binding document.*

breach /briːtʃ/ noun [count] a failure to follow a law or a rule; **be in breach of something:** *The company was found to be in breach of environmental regulations.*

gentleman's agreement /ˈdʒent(ə)lmənz əˈɡriːmənt/ noun [count] a business agreement in which people trust each other without a written contract

jeopardize /ˈdʒepə(r)daɪz/ verb [transitive] to risk damaging or destroying something important

practice /ˈpræktɪs/ noun [count/uncount] a way of doing something, especially as a result of habit, custom or tradition

turn a blind eye (to something) /ˈtɜː(r)n ə ˌblaɪnd ˈaɪ/ phrase to pretend you do not notice something, because you should do something about it but you do not want to

Macmillan Education Limited
4 Crinan Street
London N1 9XW

Companies and representatives throughout the world

ISBN 978-0-230-43796-8

Text © John Allison, Jeremy Townend and Paul Emmerson 2013
Design and illustration © Macmillan Education Limited 2013
The authors have asserted their rights to be identified as the authors of this work in accordance with the Copyright, Design and Patents Act 1988.

This edition published 2013
First edition published 2008

All rights reserved; no part of this publication may be reproduced, stored in a retrieval system, transmitted in any form, or by any means, electronic, mechanical, photocopying, recording, or otherwise, without the prior written permission of the publishers.

Original design by Keith Shaw, Threefold Design Ltd
Page make-up by eMC Design Ltd
Cover design by Keith Shaw, Threefold Design Ltd
Cover photography by Corbis/Ken Seet
Picture research by Susannah Jayes

Authors' acknowledgements
We would like to thank everybody at Macmillan Oxford; Lidia Zielińska and the English teachers at Cracow University of Economics; our colleagues at Infolangues; and, last but not least, Brigitte, Pascale and our families.

The publishers would like to thank the following people for piloting and commenting on material for this coursebook:
Paul Bellchambers, Business and Technical Languages, Paris, France; Bunmi Rolland, Pôle Universitaire Léonard de Vinci, Paris, France; Prof. Vanessa Leonardi, Faculty of Economics, University of Ferrara, Italy; Prof. Paola De La Pierre, Faculty of Economics, University of Turin, Italy; Elżbieta Typek, Cracow University of Economics, Poland; Marlena Nowak, Cracow University of Economics, Poland; Lucyna Wilinkiewicz-Górniak, Cracow University of Economics, Poland; Jolanta Regucka-Pawlina, Cracow University of Economics, Poland; Sebastian Florek-Paszkowski, Cracow University of Economics, Poland; Bożena Bielak, Cracow University of Economics, Poland; Małgorzata Held, Cracow University of Economics, Poland; Anna Wróblewska-Marzec, Cracow University of Economics, Poland; Lidia Zielińska, Cracow University of Economics, Poland; Olga Druszkiewicz, Cracow University of Economics, Poland; Maciej Krzanowski, Cracow University of Economics, Poland; Lubov Kulik, Moscow Lomonosov State University, Russia; Irina Ekareva, The Russian Plekhanov University of Economics, Russia; Larisa Tarkhova, The Russian Plekhanov University of Economics, Russia; Irina Schemeleva, Higher School of Economics, Russia; Irina Matveeva, The Academy of Social and Labour Relations, Russia; Galina Makarova, Denis' School, Russia, Liam James Tyler, IPT, Russia; Tatiana Efremtseva, The Russian International Academy of Tourism, Russia; Tatiana Sedova, The University of Finance, Russia; Tony Watson and Kim Draper, MLS Bournemouth, Bournemouth, UK; Louise Raven, Marcus Evans Linguarama, Stratford-upon-Avon, UK.

The publishers would like to thank the following people for piloting and commenting on material for the original edition of this coursebook: Annette Nolan, Folkuniversitetet, Sweden; Elena Ivanova Angelova, Pharos School of Languages and Computing, Bulgaria; Sabine Schumann, Berufsakademie (University of Co-operative Education), Germany; Vladimir Krasnopolsky, East Ukrainian National University, Ukraine.

The authors and publishers would like to thank the following for permission to reproduce their images: **Alamy**/Rancz Andrei p62, Alamy/annete p75, Alamy/Mile Atanasov p43(cr), Alamy/Steve Atkins Photography p26(tl), Alamy/Adam Burton p100(tl), Alamy/Corbis Flirt p13(bl), Alamy/Corbis RF p59(bcr), Alamy/dbimages p58, Alamy/Danita Delimont Creative p67, Alamy/Inspirestock Inc. p26(tcr), Alamy/ITAR-TASS Photo Agency p41(cl), Alamy/Juice Images pp28(br), 31(bl), Alamy/Mikhail Lavrenov p91(bl), Alamy/Marshall Ikonography p46, Alamy/Neil McAllister p14(c), Alamy/Derek Mitchell p106, Alamy/ONOKY Photononstop p68(tl), Alamy/Chuck Pefley pp10, 98, Alamy/Ted Pink p84, Alamy/Prisma Bildagentur AG p69, Alamy/Pxel p36, Alamy/Edwin Remsberg p15(tr), Alamy/Alex Segre p45, Alamy/Stockbroker p93, Alamy/Lana Sundman p71, Alamy/Homer Sykes Archive p72, Alamy/Hugh Threlfall p43(bcr), Alamy/Rachel Torres p19(cr), Alamy/Travel Pictures p26(tr), Alamy/vario images GmbH & Co.KG p43(br), Alamy/View Pictures Ltd p22(tr), Alamy/Westend61 GmbH p79(tl); **Corbis**/Jose Luis Pelaez, Inc./Blend Images pp33(tcr), 66(tr), Corbis/Ariel Skelley/Blend Images p99, Corbis/Bloominage p37(br), Corbis/Jorge Cruz p91(cl), Corbis/Owen Franken p110(b), Corbis/HBSS p85(c), Corbis/Nice One Productions p68(cl), Corbis/Ocean pp15(cr), 19(cl), 103, Corbis/Tim Pannell p40, Corbis/JLP/Jose Luis Pelaez p14(cl), Corbis/Simon Potter p53(tr), Corbis/Didier Robcis p63, Corbis/Bill Varie/Somos Images p16, Corbis/Magomed Magomedagaev/Spaces Images p41(tr), Corbis/JLP/Sylvia Torres p23, Corbis/Julian Winslow p8, Corbis/Olix Wirtinger p32(tcl), Corbis/Lo Ping Fai/Xinhua Press p49, Corbis/Bo Zaunders p47; **Getty Images**/AFP pp17(br), 52, 109, Getty Images/Jochen Arndt p101, Getty Images/ArtBox Images RM p100(tr), Getty Images/Marco Baass p83, Getty Images/Jon Feingersh/Blend Images p33(tl), Getty Images/Jetta Productions/Blend Images p117, Getty Images/Jose Luis Pelaez Inc/Blend Images p33(tcr), Getty Images/Bloomberg pp37(tl), 38(c), 73, Getty Images/J.A. Bracchi p95, Getty Images/Kaz Chiba p13(bc), Getty Images/Comstock Images pp14(br), 25, Getty Images/Gary Conner p6(bcl), Getty Images/Jeffrey Coolidge p44(tl), Getty Images/Gregory Costanzo p85(cl), Getty Images/Digital Vision pp53(tcl), 94, Getty Images/George Doyle p9, Getty Images/Melanie Acevedo/FoodPix p6(tcl), Getty Images/Monashee Frantz p55(bl), Getty Images/Fuse p24, Getty Images/Gamma-Rapho p26(cl), Getty Images/Adam Gault p104(bcl), Getty Images/Glow Images pp59(cr),76, Getty Images/Colin Gray p104(bl), Getty Images/Chris Hackett pp114,116, Getty Images/Michael Hitoshi p14(cr), Getty Images/Jeff Hunter p26(tcl), Getty Images/Hybrid Images p29(cr), Getty Images/Image Source pp33(tcl), 85(cr), 97, Getty Images/Emportes Jm p31(br), Getty Images/Jupiterimages p59(tcr), Getty Images/Sean Justice p48, Getty Images/Rob Lewine p29(tr), Getty Images/Ghislain & Marie David de Lossy p66(bl), Getty Images/Dick Luria p91(bcl), Getty Images/LWA pp78–79(b), Getty Images/McClatchy-Tribune p74, Getty Images/Ryan McVay p55(cl), Getty Images/Klaus Mellenthin p39, Getty Images/John Miller Photographer p6(bcl), Getty Images/Hans Neleman p107, Getty Images/Nicholas Pitt pp20–21, Getty Images/PM Images p51, Getty Images/Mike Powell p50, Getty Images/Purestock p13(br), Getty Images/David Redfern p102, Getty Images/Andersen Ross p54, Getty Images/SelectStock p56, Getty Images/Pankaj & Insy Shah p28(bcr), Getty Images/Stockbyte p33(tr), Getty Images/Stok-Yard Studio p110(tl), Getty Images/Superstock p22(tl), Getty Images/Travelpix Ltd p89, Getty Images/Diverse Images/UIG p17(bl), Getty Images/UpperCut Images p80, Getty Images/Abel Mitja Varela p42, Getty Images/Dougal Waters p65, Getty Images/Kaori Yoshida p44(tcl); **INSEAD** p11; **Mary Evans Picture Library** p108; **Panos**/George Osodi p32(b); **Science Photo Library**/Tex Image p6(tl).

The authors and publishers are grateful for permission to reprint the following copyright material: Extracts from *'Are you capable of minding your own business?'* by Barbara Oaff, copyright © Barbara Oaff 2004, first published in The Observer 27.06.04, reprinted by permission of the author; Extract from *'Turn It Off'* by Gil Gordon, copyright © Gil Gordon, reprinted by permission of Nicholas Brealey Publishers, London; Extracts from *'Smells Like Team Spirit' & 'Delivering Two Kinds of Quality'* by Keith McFarland both copyright © Keith McFarland, first published in BusinessWeek online 17.05.06 & 15.02.06 respectively, reprinted by permission of the publisher; Material from *'For Entrepreneurs'* copyright © New York Angels 2005; Extract from *'Why 'fair' trade is a bad deal for poorest farmers'* by Alex Singleton, copyright © Alex Singleton, first published in The Business 12.03.06; Material from *'Five simple Rules for Building a Blockbuster Brand'* copyright © 2012 Entrepreneur Media, Inc. 88153:412SH, reprinted with permission; Adapted material from *'Social Marketing doesn't Have To Suck'* by Eliot Van Buskirk. Copyright © 2008, Condé Nast Publications. All rights reserved. Originally published in Wired. Reprinted by permission; Material from *'Market Cycles: The Key to Maximum Returns'* first appeared on website www.investopedia.com 02.10.09.

These materials may contain links for third party websites. We have no control over, and are not responsible for, the contents of such third party websites. Please use care when accessing them.

Although we have tried to trace and contact copyright holders before publication, in some cases this has not been possible. If contacted, we will be pleased to rectify any errors or omissions at the earliest opportunity.

Printed and bound in Poland by CGS
2025 2024 2023 2022 2021
37 36 35 34 33 32 31 30 29